RISE AND FALL OF THE MUSTACHE.

THE

RISE AND FALL

OF

THE MUSTACHE

AND OTHER

"HAWK-EYETEMS."

BY ROBERT J. BURDETTE,

The Humorist of the Burlington "Hawk-Eye."

ILLUSTRATED BY R. W. WALLIS.

IOWA STATE UNIVERSITY PRESS / AMES

I·O·W·A
HERITAGE
COLLECTION

ROBERT J. BURDETTE was a humor columnist for the Burlington (Iowa) *Hawk-Eye.*

Foreword © 1988 by Chuck Offenburger
All rights reserved

This printing produced from the original edition published by Burlington Publishing Company
Text reprinted from the original without correction

Manufactured in the United States of America

No part of this book may be reproduced in any form or by any electronic or mechanical means, including information storage and retrieval systems, without written permission from the publisher, except for brief passages quoted in a review.

First edition, 1877
Iowa Heritage Collection edition, 1988

Library of Congress Cataloging-in-Publication Data
Burdette, Robert J. (Robert Jones), 1844–1914.
   The rise and fall of the mustache and other "hawk-eyetems."

  (Iowa heritage collection)
  Reprint. Originally published: Burlington, Iowa : Burlington Pub. Co., 1877.
    1. Iowa—Poetry. 2. Iowa—Humor. I. Title. II. Series.
PS1205.R5   1988   811'.4   88–23013
ISBN 0-8138-0138-9

TO

FRANK HATTON,
Editor-in-Chief,

AND

MY ASSOCIATES ON THE HAWKEYE,

IN HAPPY REMEMBRANCE

OF OUR PLEASANT FELLOWSHIP, THIS VOLUME

IS INSCRIBED.

PREFACE

The appearance of a new book is an indication that another man has found a mission, has entered upon the performance of a lofty duty, actuated only by the noblest impulses that can spur the soul of man to action. It is the proudest boast of the profession of literature, that no man ever published a book for selfish purposes or with ignoble aim. Books have been published for the consolation of the distressed; for the guidance of the wandering; for the relief of the destitute; for the hope of the penitent; for uplifting the burdened soul above its sorrows and fears; for the general amelioration of the condition of all mankind; for the right against the wrong; for the good against the bad; for the truth. This book is published for two dollars per volume.

R. J. B.

FOREWORD

Being a 1988 journalist and having read this work, I find myself green with envy at the liberty, license, and space the *Burlington Hawk-Eye* obviously granted to Robert J. Burdette back in 1877.

It's clear, however, why the paper did so. With his ability to slice life with such keen and genteel humor, he must have had *Hawk-Eye* subscribers rolling with laughter down those big hills of Burlington. Even when read a century later, the man's writing is still a hoot.

Who was Robert J. Burdette? I'd call him an 1877 Iowa blend of David Letterman, Garrison Keillor, and H. L. Mencken.

Chuck Offenburger, Iowa Boy
Des Moines Register

CONTENTS.

	PAGE.
A Boy's Day at Home,	273
A Burlington Adder,	94
A Burlington Novelette,	173
A Candid Confession,	171
A Modern Goblin,	210
A Rainy Day Idyl,	86
A Reminiscence of Exhibition Day,	177
A Safe Bet,	204
A Sunday Idyl,	262
A Taciturn Witness,	124
A Thrilling Encounter,	144
A Trying Situation,	193
An Autumnal Reverie,	286
Buying a Tin Cup,	119
Cornering the Boys,	128
Dangers of Bathing,	164
Driving the Cow,	64
Five Women,	146
Getting Ready for the Train,	59
Hawk-Eyetems	298-328
Infantile Scintillations,	293
Inspirations of Truth,	156
Life in the "Hawkeye" Sanctum,	109
Master Bilderback Returns to School,	74
Master Bilderback's Poultry-Yard,	258
Middlerib's Dog,	270
Middlerib's Picnic,	250
Mind Reading,	200
Misapplied Science,	96
Mr. Baringer's House Cleaning,	282
Mr. Bilderback Loses His Hat,	195
Mr. Gerolman Loses His Dog,	82
Mr. Olendorf's Complaint,	180

CONTENTS.

Ode to Autumn,	78
One of the Legion,	121
Rupertino's Panorama,	266
Rural Felicity,	185
Selling the Heirloom,	129
Settling Under Difficulties,	296
Singular Transformation,	87
Sodding as a Fine Art,	135
Special Providences,	279
Spirit Photography,	158
Spring Days in Burlington,	108
Spring Time in America,	115
Suburban Solitude,	90
The Amenities of Politics,	139
The Artless Prattle of Childhood,	102
The Automatic Clothes-Line Reel,	152
The Demand for Light Labor,	70
The Garden of the Gods,	189
The Goblin Gate,	148
The Language of Flowers,	113
The Lay of the Cow,	206
The Power of Dignity,	169
The Rise and Fall of the Mustache,	9
The Romance of the Carpet,	132
The Seedsman,	127
The Sorrows of the Poor,	79
Voices of the Night,	67
Why Mr. Bostwick Moved,	275
Wide Awake,	99
Woodland Music and Poetry,	116
Writing for the Press,	161
Young Mr. Coffinberry Buys a Dog,	207

The Rise and Fall

OF

The Mustache.

WE open our eyes in this living world around us, in a wonder land, peopled with dreams, and haunted with wonderful shapes; and every day dawns upon us in a medley of new marvels. We are awakened from these dreams by contact with hard, stubborn facts, not rudely and harshly, but gradually and tenderly. So much that is bright and beautiful, and full of romance and wonder, passes away with the earlier years of life, that by the time we are able to earn our first salary we hold in our hands only the crumpled, withered leaves of childhood's simple creeds and loving superstitions. Year after year, the inconoclastic hand of earnest, real life, tears from the lofty pedestals upon which our loving fancy had enshrined them, the gods of gold that crumble into worthless clay at our feet. We live to lose faith, at last, in "Puss in Boots;" we cease to weep over the sad tragedy of "Cock Robin;" there comes a time when we can read "Arabian Nights," and then go to bed without a tremor; with one heart-breaking pang at last we give up darling "Jack the Giant Killer," and acknowledge him to be the fraud he stands confessed; it is not long after that, we learn to look upon William Tell as a national myth, and then we come to know, in spite of all that orthodox theology has taught us to the contrary, that Adam was not the first man — that raised a mustache. Adam was too old — when he was born — to care very much about what our grander and more gradually developed civilization considers the crowning facial ornament. And after his natural human idleness got him into perfectly natural human trouble, he was kept too busy raising something to put under his lip, to think much about what grew above it. If Adam wore a mustache, he never raised it. It raised itself. It evolved itself out of its own inner consciousness, like a primordial germ. It grew, like the weeds on his farm, in spite of him, and to torment him. For Adam had hardly got his farm reduced to a kind of turbulent, weed producing, granger fighting, regular order of things — had scarcely settled down to the quiet, happy, care-free, independent life of a jocund farmer, with nothing under the canopy to molest or make him afraid, with every thing on the plantation going on smoothly and lovelily, with a little rust in the oats; army worm in the corn; Colorado beetles swarming up and down the potato patch; cutworms laying waste the cucumbers; curculio in the plums and borers in the apple trees; a new kind of bug that he didn't know the name of desolating the wheat fields; dry weather burning up the wheat, wet weather blighting the corn; too cold for the melons, too dreadfully hot for the strawberries; chickens dying with the pip; hogs being gathered to their fathers with the cholera; sheep fading away with a complication of things that no man could remember; horses getting along as well as could be expected, with a little spavin, ring bone, wolf teeth, distemper, heaves, blind staggers, collar chafes, saddle galls, colic now and then, founder occasionally, epizootic when there was nothing else; cattle going wild with the horn ail; moth in the bee hives; snakes in the milk house; moles in the kitchen garden — Adam had just about got through breaking wild land with a crooked stick, and settled down comfortably, when the sound of the boy was heard in the land.

Did it ever occur to you that Adam was probably the most troubled and worried man that ever lived? We have always pictured Adam as a care-worn looking man; a puzzled looking granger who would sigh fifty times a day, and sit down on a log and run his irresolute fingers through his hair while he wondered what under the canopy he was going to do with those boys, and whatever was going to become of them. We have thought too, that as often as our esteemed parent asked himself this conundrum, he gave it up. They must have been a source of constant trouble and mystification to him. For you see they were the first boys that humanity ever had any experience with. And there was no one else in the neighborhood who had any boy, with whom Adam, in his moments of perplexity, could consult. There wasn't a boy in the country with whom Adam's boys were on speaking terms, and with whom they could play and fight. Adam, you see, labored under the most distressing disadvantages that ever opposed a married man and the father of a family. He had never been a boy himself, and what could he know about boy nature or boy troubles and pleasure? His perplexity began at an early date. Imagine, if you can, the celerity with which he kicked off the leaves, and paced up and down in the moonlight the first time little Cain made the welkin ring when he had the colic. How did Adam know what ailed him? He couldn't tell Eve that she had been sticking the baby full of pins. He didn't even know enough to turn the vociferous infant over on his face and jolt him into serenity. If the fence corners on his farm had been overgrown with catnip, never an idea would Adam have had what to do with it. It is probable that after he got down on his knees and felt for thorns or snakes or rats in the bed, and thoroughly examined young Cain for bites or scratches, he passed him over to Eve with the usual remark, "There, take him and hush him up, for heaven's sake," and then went off and sat down under a distant tree with his fingers in his ears, and perplexity in his brain. And young Cain just split the night with the most hideous howls the little world had ever listened to. It must have stirred the animals up to a degree that no menagerie has ever since attained. There was no sleep in the vicinity of Eden that night for anybody, baby, beasts or Adam. And it is more than probable that the weeds got a long start of Adam the next day, while he lay around in shady places and slept in troubled dozes, disturbed, perhaps by awful visions of possible twins and more colic.

And when the other boy came along, and the boys got old enough to sleep in a bed by themselves, they had no pillows to fight with, and it is a moral impossibility for two brothers to go to bed without a fracas. And what comfort could two boys get out of pelting each other with fragments of moss or bundles of brush? What dismal views of future humanity Adam must have received from the glimpses of original sin which began to develop itself in his boys. How he must have wondered what put into their heads the thousand and one questions with which they plied their parents day after day. We wonder what he thought when they first began to string buckeyes on the cat's tail. And when night came, there was no hired girl to keep the boys quiet by telling them ghost stories, and Adam didn't even know so much as an anecdote.

Cain, when he made his appearance, was the first and only boy in the fair young world. And all his education depended on his inexperienced parents, who had never in their lives seen a boy until they saw Cain. And there wasn't an educational help in the market. There wasn't an alphabet block in the county; not even a Centennial illustrated handkerchief. There were no other boys in the republic, to teach young Cain to lie, and swear, and smoke, and drink, fight, and steal, and thus develop the boy's dormant statesmanship, and prepare him for the sterner political duties of his maturer years. There wasn't a pocket knife in the universe that he could borrow — and lose, and when he wanted to cut his finger, as all boys must do, now and then, he had to cut it with a clam shell. There were no country relations upon whom little Cain could be inflicted for two or three weeks at a time, when his wearied parents wanted a little rest. There was nothing for him to play with. Adam couldn't show him how to make a kite. He had a much better idea of angels' wings than he had of a kite. And if little Cain had even asked for such a simple bit of mechanism as a shinny club, Adam would have gone out into the depths of the primeval forest and wept in sheer mortification and helpless, confessed ignorance. I don't wonder that Cain turned out bad. I always said he would. For his entire education depended upon a most ignorant man, a man in the very palmiest days of his ignorance, who couldn't have known less if he had tried all his life on a high salary and had a man to help him. And the boy's education had to be conducted entirely upon the catechetical system; only, in this instance, the boy pupil asked the questions, and his parent teachers, heaven help them, tried to answer them. And they had to answer at them. For they could not take refuge from the steady stream of questions that poured in upon them day after day, by interpolating a fairy story, as you do when your boy asks you questions about something of which you never heard. For how could Adam begin, "Once upon a time," when with one quick, incisive question, Cain could pin him right back against the dead wall of creation, and make him either specify exactly what time, or acknowledge the fraud? How could Eve tell him about "Jack and the bean stalk," when Cain, fairly crazy for some one to play with, knew perfectly well there was not, and never had been, another boy on the plantation? And as day by day Cain brought home things in his hands about which to ask questions that no mortal could answer, how grateful his bewildered parents must have been that he had no pockets in which to transport his collections. For many generations came into the fair young world, got into no end of trouble, and died out of it, before a boy's pocket solved the problem how to make the thing contained seven times greater than the container. The only thing that saved Adam and Eve from interrogational insanity was the paucity of language. If little Cain had possessed the verbal abundance of the language in which men are to-day talked to death, his father's bald head would have gone down in shining flight to the ends of the earth to escape him, leaving Eve to look after the stock, save the crop, and raise her boy as best she could. Which would have been, 6,000 years ago, as to-day, just like a man.

Because, it was no off hand, absent-minded work answering questions about things in those spacious old days, when there was crowds of room, and everything grew by the acre. When a placid, but exceedingly unanimous looking animal went rolling by, producing the general effect of an eclipse, and Cain would shout, "Oh, lookee, lookee pa! what's that?" the patient Adam, trying to saw enough kitchen wood to last over Sunday, with a piece of flint, would have to pause and gather up words enough to say:

"That, my son? That is only a mastodon giganteus; he has a bad look, but a Christian temper."

And then, presently:

"Oh, pop! pop! What's that over yon?"

"Oh, bother," Adam would reply; "it's only a paleotherium, mammalia pachydermata."

"Oh, yes; theliocomeafterus. Oh! lookee, lookee at this 'un!"

"Where, Cainny? Oh, that in the mud? That's only an acephala lamelli branchiata. It won't bite you, but you mustn't eat it. It's poison as politics."

"Whee! See there! see, see, see! What's him?"

"Oh, that? Looks like a plesiosaurus; keep out of his way; he has a jaw like your mother."

"Oh yes; a plenosserus. And what's that fellow, poppy?"

"That's a silurus malapterus. Don't you go near him, for he has the disposition of a Georgia mule."

"Oh, yes; a slapterus. And what's this little one?"

"Oh, it's nothing but an aristolochioid. Where did you get it? There now, quit throwing stones at that acanthopterygian; do you want to be kicked? And keep away from the nothodenatrichomanoides. My stars, Eve! where *did* he get that anonaceo-hydrocharideo-nymphæoid? Do you never look after him at all? Here, you Cain, get right away down from there, and chase that megalosaurius out of the melon patch, or I'll set the monopleuro branchian on you."

Just think of it, Christian man with a family to support, with last year's stock on your shelves, and a draft as long as a clothes-line to pay to-morrow! Think of it, woman with all a woman's love and constancy, and a mother's sympathetic nature, with three meals a day 365 times a year to think of, and the flies to chase out of the sitting-room; think, if your cherub boy was the only boy in the wide wide world, and all his questions which now radiate in a thousand directions among other boys, who tell him lies and help him to cut his eye-teeth, were focused upon you! Adam had only one consolation that has been denied his more remote descendants. His boy never belonged to a base ball club, and never teased his father from the first of November till the last of March for a pair of skates.

Well, you have no time to pity Adam. You have your own boy to look after. Or, your neighbor has a boy, whom you can look after much more closely than his mother does, and much more to your own satisfaction than to the boy's comfort. Your boy is, as Adam's boy was, an animal that asks questions. If there were any truth in the old theory of the transmigration of souls, when a boy died he would pass into an interrogation point. And he'd stay there. He'd never get out of it; for he never gets through asking questions. The older he grows the more he asks, and the more perplexing his questions are, and the more unreasonable he is about wanting them answered to suit himself. Why, the oldest boy I ever knew — he was fifty-seven years old, and I went to school to him — could and did ask the longest, hardest, crookedest questions, that no fellow, who used to trade off all his books for a pair of skates and a knife with a corkscrew in it, could answer. And when his questions were not answered to suit him, it was his custom—a custom more honored in the breeches, we used to think, than in the observance — to take up a long, slender, but exceedingly tenacious rod, which lay ever near the big dictionary, and smite with it the boy whose naturally derived Adamic ignorance was made manifest. Ah me, if the boy could only do as he is done by, and ferule the man or the woman who fails to reply to his inquiries, as he is himself corrected for similar shortcomings, what a valley of tears, what a literally howling wilderness he could and would make of this world.

Your boy, asking to-day pretty much the same questions, with heaven knows how many additional ones, that Adam's boy did, is told, every time he asks one that you don't know any thing about, just as Adam told Cain fifty times a day, that he will know all about it when he is a man. And so from the days of Cain down to the present wickeder generation of boys, the boy ever looks forward to the time when he will be a man and know everything. That happy, far away, omniscient, unattainable manhood, which never comes to your boy; which would never come to him if he lived a thousand years; manhood, that like boyhood, ever looks forward from to-day to the morrow; still peering into the future for brighter light and broader knowledge; day after day, as its world opens before it, stumbling upon ever new and unsolved mysteries; manhood, whose wisdom is folly and whose light is often darkness, and whose knowledge is selfishness; manhood, that so often looks over its shoulder and glances back toward boyhood, when its knowledge was at least always equal to its day; manhood, that after groping for years through tangled labyrinths of failing human theories and tottering human wisdom, at last only rises to the sublimity of childhood, only reaches the grandeur of boyhood, and accepts the grandest, eternal truths of the universe, truths that it does not comprehend, truths that it can not, by searching, find out, accepting and believing them with the simple, unquestioning faith of childhood in Truth itself.

And now, your boy, not entirely ceasing to ask questions, begins to answer them, until you stand amazed at the breadth and depth of his knowledge. He asks questions and gets answers of teachers that you and the school board know not of. Day by day, great unprinted books, upon the broad pages of which the hand of nature has traced characters that only a boy can read, are spread out before him. He knows now where the first snowdrop lifts its tiny head, a pearl on the bosom of the barren earth, in the Spring; he knows where the last Indian pink lingers, a flame in the brown and rustling woods, in the autumn days. His pockets are cabinets, from which he drags curious fossils that he does not know the names of; monstrous and hideous beetles and bugs and things that you never saw before, and for which he has appropriate names of his own. He knows where there are three orioles' nests, and so far back as you can remember, you never saw an oriole's nest in your life. He can tell you how to distinguish the good mushrooms from the poisonous ones, and poison grapes from good ones, and how he ever found out, except by eating both kinds, is a mystery to his mother. Every root, bud, leaf, berry or bark, that will make any bitter, horrible, semi-poisonous tea, reputed to have marvelous medicinal virtues, he knows where to find, and in the season he does find, and brings home, and all but sends the entire family to the cemetery by making practical tests of his teas.

And as his knowledge broadens, his human superstition

develops itself. He has a formula, repeating which nine times a day, while pointing his finger fixedly toward the sun, will cause warts to disappear from the hand, or, to use his own expression, will "knock warts." If the eight day clock at home tells him it is two o'clock, and the flying leaves of the dandelion declare it is half-past five, he will stand or fall with the dandelion. He has a formula, by which any thing that has been lost may be found. He has, above all things, a natural, infallible instinct for the woods, and can no more be lost in them than a squirrel. If the cow does not come home—and if she is a town cow, like a town man, she does not come home, three nights in the week—you lose half a day of valuable time looking for her. Then you pay a man three dollars to look for her two days longer, or so long as the appropriation holds out. Finally, a quarter sends a boy to the woods; he comes back at milking time, whistling the tune that no man ever imitated, and the cow ambles contentedly along before him. He has one particular marble which he regards with about the same superstitious reverence that a pagan does his idol, and his Sunday-school teacher can't drive it out of him, either. Carnelian, crystal, bull's eye, china, pottery, boly, blood alley, or commie, whatever he may call it, there is "luck in it." When he loses this marble, he sees panic and bankruptcy ahead of him, and retires from business prudently, before the crash comes, failing, in true centennial style, with both pockets and a cigar box full of winnings, and a creditors' meeting in the back room. A boy's world is open to no one but a boy. You never really revisit the glimpses of your boyhood, much as you may dream of it. After you get into a tail coat, and tight boots, you never again set foot in boy world. You lose this marvelous instinct for the woods, you can't tell a pig-nut tree from a pecan; you can't make friends with strange dogs; you can't make the terrific noises with your mouth, you can't invent the inimitable signals or the characteristic catchwords of boyhood.

He is getting on, is your boy. He reaches the dime novel age. He wants to be a missionary. Or a pirate. So far as he expresses any preference, he would rather be a pirate, an occupation in which there are more chances for making money, and fewer opportunities for being devoured. He develops a yearning love for school and study about this time, also, and every time he dreams of being a pirate he dreams of hanging his dear teacher at the yard arm in the presence of the delighted scholars. His voice develops, even more rapidly and thoroughly than his morals. In the yard, on the house top, down the street, around the corner; wherever there is a patch of ice big enough for him to break his neck on, or a pond of water deep enough to drown in, the voice of your boy is heard. He whispers in a shout, and converses, in ordinary, confidential moments, in a shriek. He exchanges bits of back-fence gossip about his father's domestic matters with the boy living in the adjacent township, to which interesting revelations of home life the intermediate neighborhood listens with intense satisfaction, and the two home circles in helpless dismay. He has an unconquerable hatred for company, and an aversion for walking down stairs. For a year or two his feet never touch the stairway in his descent, and his habit of polishing the stair rail by using it as a passenger tramway, soon breaks the other members of the family of the careless habit of setting the hall lamp or the water pitcher on the baluster post. He wears the same size boot as his father; and on the dryest, dustiest days in the year, always manages to convey some mud on the carpets. He carefully steps over the door mat, and until he is about seventeen years old, he actually never knew there was a scraper at the front porch. About this time, bold but inartistic pencil sketches break out mysteriously on the alluring back ground of the wall paper. He asks, with great regularity, alarming frequency, and growing diffidence, for a new hat. You might as well buy him a new disposition. He wears his hat in the air and on the ground far more than he does on his head, and he never hangs it up that he doesn't pull the hook through the crown ; unless the hook breaks off or the hat rack pulls over. He is a perfect Robinson Crusoe in inventive genius. He can make a kite that will fly higher and pull harder than a balloon. He can, and, on occasion, will, take out a couple of the pantry shelves and make a sled that is amazement itself. The mousetrap he builds out of the water pitcher and the family bible is a marvel of mechanical ingenuity. So is the excuse he gives for such a selection of raw material. When suddenly, some Monday morning, the clothes line, without any just or apparent cause or provocation, shrinks sixteen feet, philosophy can not make you believe that Prof. Tice did it with his little barometer. Because, far down the dusty street, you can see Tom in the dim distance, driving a prancing team, six-in-hand, with the missing link. You send him on an errand. There are three ladies in the parlor. You have waited, as long as you can, in all courtesy, for them to go. They have developed alarming symptoms of staying to tea. And you know there aren't half enough strawberries to go around. It is only a three minutes' walk to the grocery, however, and Tom sets off like a rocket, and you are so pleased with his celerity and ready good nature that you want to run after him and kiss him. He is gone a long time, however. Ten minutes become fifteen, fifteen grow into twenty; the twenty swell into the half hour, and your guests exchange very significant glances as the half becomes three-quarters. Your boy returns at last. Apprehension in his downcast eyes, humility in his laggard step, penitence in the appealing slouch of his battered hat, and a pound and a half of shingle nails in his hands. "Mother," he says, "what else was it you told me to get besides the nails?" And while you are counting your scanty store of berries to make them go round without a fraction, you hear Tom out in the back yard whistling and hammering away, building a dog house with the nails you never told him to get.

Poor Tom, he loves at this age quite as ardently as he makes mistakes and mischief. And he is repulsed quite as ardently as he makes love. If he hugs his sister, he musses her ruffle, and gets cuffed for it. Two hours later, another boy, not more than twenty-two or twenty-three years older than Tom, some neighbor's Tom, will come in, and will just make the most hopeless, terrible, chaotic wreck of that ruffle that lace or footing can be distorted into. And the only reproof he gets is the reproachful murmur, "Must he go so soon?" when he doesn't make a movement to go until he hears the alarm clock go off upstairs and the old gentleman in the adjoining room banging around building the morning fires, and loudly wondering if young Mr. Bostwick is going to stay to breakfast?

Tom is at this age set in deadly enmity against company, which he soon learns to regard as his mortal foe. He regards company as a mysterious and eminently respectable delegation that always stays to dinner, invariably crowds him to the second table, never leaves him any of the pie, and generally makes him late for school. Naturally, he learns to love refined society, but in a conservative, non-committal sort of a way, dissembling his love so effectually that even his parents never dream of its existence until it is gone.

Poor Tom, his life is not all comedy at this period. Go up to your boy's room some night, and his sleeping face will preach you a sermon on the griefs and troubles that sometimes weigh his little heart down almost to breaking, more eloquently than the lips of a Spurgeon could picture them. The curtain has fallen on one day's act in the drama of his active little life. The restless feet that all day long have pattered so far — down dusty streets, over scorching pavements, through long stretches of quiet wooded lanes, along the winding cattle paths in the deep, silent woods; that have dabbled in the cool brook where it wrangles and scolds over the shining pebbles, that have filled your house with noise and dust and racket, are still. The stained hand outside the sheet is soiled and rough, and the cut finger with the rude bandage of the boy's own surgery, pleads with a mute, effective pathos of its own, for the mischievous hand that is never idle. On the brown cheek the trace of a tear marks the piteous close of the day's troubles, the closing scene in a troubled little drama; trouble at school with books that were too many for him; trouble with temptations to have unlawful fun that were too strong for him, as they are frequently too strong for his father; trouble in the street with boys that were too big for him; and at last, in his home, in his castle, his refuge, trouble has pursued him until, feeling utterly friendless and in everybody's way, he has crawled off to the dismantled den, dignified usually by the title of "the boy's room," and his overcharged heart has welled up into his eyes, and his last waking breath has broken into a sob, and just as he begins to think that after all, life is only one broad sea of troubles, whose restless billows, in never-ending succession, break and beat and double and dash upon the short shore line of a boy's life, he has drifted away into the wonderland of a boy's sleep, where fairy fingers picture his dreams. How soundly, deeply, peacefully he sleeps. No mother, who has never dragged a sleepy boy off the lounge at 9 o'clock, and hauled him off up stairs to bed, can know with what a herculean grip a square sleep takes hold of a boy's senses, nor how fearfully and wonderfully limp and nerveless it makes him; nor how, in direct antagonism to all established laws of anatomy, it develops joints that work both ways, all the way up and down that boy. And what pen can portray the wonderful enchantments of a boy's dreamland! No marvelous visions wrought by the weird, strange power of hasheesh, no dreams that come to the sleep of jaded woman or tired man, no ghastly specters that dance attendance upon cold mince pie, but shrink into tiresome, stale, and trifling commonplaces compared with the marvelous, the grotesque, the wonderful, the terrible, the beautiful and the enchanting scenes and people of a boy's dreamland. This may be owing, in a great measure, to the fact that the boy never relates his dream until all the other members of the family have related theirs; and then he comes in, like a back county, with the necessary majority; like the directory of a western city, following the census of a rival town.

 Tom is a miniature Ishmaelite at this period of his career. His hand is against every man, and about every man's hand, and nearly every woman's hand, is against him, off and on. Often, and then the iron enters his soul, the hand that is against him holds the slipper. He wears his mother's slipper on his jacket quite as often as as she wears it on her foot. And this is all wrong, unchristian and impolitic. It spreads the slipper and discourages the boy. When he reads in his Sunday-school lesson that the wicked stand in slippery places, he takes it as a direct personal reference, and he is affronted, and maybe the seeds of atheism are implanted in his breast. Moreover, this repeated application of the slipper not only sours his temper, and gives a bias to his moral ideas, but it sharpens his wits. How many a Christian mother, her soft eyes swimming in tears of real pain that plashed up from the depths of a loving heart, as she bent over her wayward boy until his heartrending wails and piteous shrieks drowned her own choking, sympathetic sobs, has been wasting her strength, and wearing out a good slipper, and pouring out all that priceless flood of mother love and duty and pity and tender sympathy upon a concealed atlas-back, or a Saginaw shingle.

It is a historical fact that no boy is ever whipped twice for precisely the same offense. He varies and improves a little on every repetition of the prank, until at last he reaches a point where detection is almost impossible. He is a big boy then, and glides almost imperceptibly from the discipline of his father, under the surveillance of the police.

By easy stages he passes into the uncomfortable period of boyhood. His jacket develops into a tail-coat. The boy of to-day, who is slipped into a hollow, abbreviated mockery of a tail-coat, when he is taken out of long dresses, has no idea—not the faintest conception of the grandeur, the momentous importance of the epoch in a boy's life that was marked by the transition from the old-fashioned cadet roundabout to the tail-coat. It is an experience that heaven, ever chary of its choicest blessings, and mindful of the decadence of the race of boys, has not vouchsafed to the untoward, forsaken boys of this wicked generation. When the roundabout went out of fashion, the heroic race of boys passed away from earth, and weeping nature sobbed and broke the moulds. The fashion that started a boy of six years on his pilgrimage of life in a miniature edition of his father's coat, marked a period of retrogression in the affairs of men, and stamped a decaying and degenerate race. There are no boys now, or very few at least, such as peopled the grand old earth when the men of our age were boys. And that it is so, society is to be congratulated. The step from the roundabout to the tail-coat was a leap in life. It was the boy Iulus, doffing the *prætexta* and flinging upon his shoulders the *toga virilis* of Julius; Patroclus, donning the armor of Achilles, in which to go forth and be Hectored to death.

Tom is slow to realize the grandeur of that tail-coat, however, on its trial trip. How differently it feels from his good, snug-fitting, comfortable old jacket. It fits him too much in every direction, he knows. Every now and then he stops, with a gasp of terror, feeling positive, from the awful sensation of nothingness about the neck, that the entire collar has fallen off in the street. The tails are prairies, the pockets are caverns, and the back is one vast, illimitable, stretching waste. How Tom sidles along as close to the fence as he can scrape, and what a wary eye he keeps in every direction for other boys. When he forgets the school, he is half tempted to feel proud of his toga; but when he thinks of the boys, and the reception that awaits him, his heart sinks, and he is tempted to go back home, sneak up stairs, and rescue his worn old jacket from the rag-bag. He glances in terror at his distorted shadow on the fence, and, confident that it is a faithful outline of his figure, he knows that he has worn his father's coat off by mistake. He tries various methods of buttoning his coat, to make it conform more harmoniously to his figure and his ideas of the eternal fitness of things. He buttons just the lower button, and immediately it flies all abroad at the shoulders, and he beholds himself an exaggerated mannikin of "Cap'n Cuttle." Then he fastens just the upper button, and the frantic tails flap and flutter like a clothes-line in a cyclone. Then he buttons it all up, *a la militaire,* and tries to look soldierly, but the effect is so theological-studently that it frightens him until his heart stops beating. As he reaches the last friendly corner that shields him from the pitiless gaze of the boys he can hear howling and shrieking not fifty yards away, he pauses to give the final adjustment to the manly and unmanageable raiment. It is bigger and looser, flappier and wrinklier than ever. New and startling folds, and unexpected wrinkles, and uncontemplated bulges develop themselves, like masked batteries, just when and where their effect will be most demoralizing. And a new horror discloses itself at this trying and awful juncture. He wants to lie down on the sidewalk and try to die. For the first time he notices the color of his coat. Hideous! He has been duped, swindled, betrayed—made a monstrous idiot by that silver-tongued salesman, who has palmed off upon him a coat 2,000 years old; a coat that the most sweetly enthusiastic and terribly misinformed women's missionary society would hesitate to offer a wild Hottentot; and which the most benighted, old-fashioned Hottentot that ever disdained clothes, would certainly blush to wear in the dark, and would probably decline with thanks. Oh madness! The color is no color. It is all colors. It is a brindle—a veritable, undeniable brindle. There must have been a fabulous amount of brindle cloth made up into boys' first coats, sixteen or eighteen or nineteen years ago; because, out of 894 —I like to be exact in the use of figures, because nothing else in the world lends such an air of profound truthfulness to a discourse—out of 894 boys I knew in their first tail-coat period, 893 came to school in brindle coats. And the other one—the 894th boy—made his wretched debut in a bottle-green toga, with dreadful glaring brass buttons. He left school very suddenly, and we always believed that the angels saw him in that coat, and ran away with him. But Tom, shivering with apprehension, and faint with mortification over the discovery of this new horror, gives one last despairing scrooch of his shoulders, to make the coat look shorter, and, with a final frantic tug at the tails, to make it appear longer, steps out from the protecting ægis of the corner, is stunned with a vocal hurricane of "Oh, what a coat!" and his cup of misery is as full as a rag-bag in three minutes.

Passing into the tail coat period, Tom awakens to a knowledge of the broad physical truth, that he has hands. He is not very positive in his own mind how many. At times he is ready to swear to an even two; one pair; good hand. Again, when cruel fate and the non-appearance of some one's else brother has compelled him to accompany his sister to a church sociable, he can see eleven; and as he sits bolt upright in the grimmest of straight-back chairs, plastered right up against the wall, as the "sociable" custom is, or used to be, trying to find enough unoccupied pockets in which to sequester all his hands, he is dimly conscious that hands should come in pairs, and vaguely wonders, if he has only five pair of regularly ordained hands, where this odd hand came from. And hitherto, Tom has been content to encase his feet in anything that would stay on them. Now, however, he has an eye for a glove-fitting boot, and learns to wreathe his face in smiles, hollow, heartless, deceitful smiles, while his boots are as full of agony as a broken heart, and his tortured feet cry out for vengeance upon the shoemaker, and make Tom feel that life is a hollow mockery and there is nothing real but soft corns and bunions.

And: His mother never cuts his hair again. Never. When Tom assumes the manly gown she has looked her last upon his head, with trimming ideas. His hair will be trimmed and clipped, barberously it may be, but she will not be acscissory before the fact. She may sometimes long to have her boy kneel down before her, while she gnaws around his terrified locks with a pair of scissors that were sharpened when they were made; and have since then cut acres of calico, and miles and miles of paper, and great stretches of cloth, and snarls and coils of string; and furlongs of lamp wick; and have snuffed candles; and dug refractory corks out of the family ink bottle; and punched holes in skate straps; and trimmed the family nails; and have even done their level best, at the annual struggle, to cut stove-pipe lengths in two; and have successfully opened oyster and fruit cans; and pried up carpet tacks; and have many a time and oft gone snarlingly and toilsomely around Tom's head, and made him an object of terror to the children in the street, and made him look so much like a yearling colt with the run of a bur pasture, that people have been afraid to approach him too suddenly, lest he should jump through his collar and run away.

He feels too, the dawning consciousness of another grand truth in the human economy. It dawns upon his deepening intelligence with the inherent strength and the unquestioned truth of a new revelation, that man's upper lip was designed by nature for a mustache pasture. How tenderly reserved he is when he is brooding over this momentous discovery. With what exquisite caution and delicacy are his primal investigations conducted. In his microscopical researches, it appears to him that the down on his upper lip is certainly more determined down; more positive, more pronounced, more individual fuzz than that which vegetates in neglected tenderness upon his cheeks. He makes cautious explorations along the land of promise with the tip of his tenderest finger, delicately backing up the grade the wrong way, going always against the grain, that he may the more readily detect the slightest symptom of an uprising by the first feeling of velvety resistance. And day by day he is more and more firmly convinced that there is in his lip, the primordial germs, the protoplasm of a glory that will, in its full development, eclipse even the majesty and grandeur of his first tail coat. And in the first dawning consciousness that the mustache is there, like the vote, and only needs to be brought out, how often Tom walks down to the barber shop, gazes longingly in at the window, and walks past. And how often, when he musters up sufficient courage to go in, and climbs into the chair, and is just on the point of huskily whispering to the barber that he would like a shave, the entrance of a man with a beard like Frederick Barbarossa, frightens away his resolution, and he has his hair cut again. The third time that week, and it is so short that the barber has to hold it with his teeth while he files it off, and parts it with a straight edge and a scratch awl. Naturally, driven from the barber chair, Tom casts longing eyes upon the ancestral shaving machinery at home. And who shall say by what means he at length obtains possession of the paternal razor? No one. Nobody knows. Nobody ever did know. Even the searching investigation that always follows the paternal demand for the immediate extradition of whoever opened a fruit can with that razor, which always follows Tom's first shave, is always, and ever will be, barren of results. All that we know about it is, that Tom holds the razor in his hand about a minute, wondering what to do with it, before the blade falls across his fingers and cuts every one of them. First blood claimed and allowed, for the razor. Then he straps the razor furiously. Or rather, he razors the strap. He slashes and cuts that passive implement in as many directions as he can make motions with the razor. He would cut it oftener if the strap lasted longer. Then he nicks the razor against the side of the mug. Then he drops it on the floor and steps on it and nicks it again. They are small nicks, not so large by half as a saw tooth, and he flatters himself his father will never see them. Then he soaks the razor in hot water, as he has seen his father do. Then he takes it out, at a temperature anywhere under 980° Fahrenheit, and lays it against his cheek, and raises a blister there the size of the razor, as he never saw his father do, but as his father most assuredly did, many, many years before Tom met him. Then he makes a variety of indescribable grimaces and labial contortions in a frenzied effort to get his upper lip into approachable shape, and at last, the first offer he makes at his embryo mustache, he slashes his nose with a vicious upper cut. He gashes the corners of his mouth; wherever those nicks touch his cheek they leave a scratch apiece, and he learns what a good nick in a razor is for, and at last when he lays the blood stained weapon down, his gory lip looks as though it had just come out of a long, stubborn, exciting contest with a straw cutter.

But he learns to shave, after a while—just before he cuts his lip clear off. He has to take quite a course of instruction, however, in that great school of experience about which the old philosopher had a remark to make. It is a grand old school; the only school at which men will study and learn, each for himself. One man's experience never does another man any good; never did and never will teach another man anything. If the philosopher had said that it was a hard school, but that some men would learn at no other than this grand old school of experience, we might have inferred that all women, and most boys, and a few men were exempt from its hard teachings. But he used the more comprehensive term, if you remember what that is, and took us all in. We have all been there. There is no other school, in fact. Poor little Cain; dear, lonesome, wicked little Cain—I know it isn't fashionable to pet him; I know it is popular to speak harshly and savagely about our eldest brother, when the fact is we resemble him more closely in disposition than any other member of the family— poor little Cain never knew the difference between his father's sunburned nose and a glowing coal, un il he had pulled the one and picked up the other. And Abel had to find out the difference in the same way, although he was told five hundred times, by his brother's experience, that the coal would burn him and the nose wouldn't. And Cain's boy wouldn't believe that fire was any hotter than an icicle, until he made a digital experiment, and understood why they called it fire. And so Enoch and Methusaleh, and Moses, and Daniel, and Solomon, and Cæsar, and Napoleon, and Washington, and the President, and the Governor, and the Mayor, and you and I have all of us, at one time or another, in one way or another, burned our fingers at the same old fires that have scorched human fingers in the same monotonous old ways, at the same reliable old stands, for the past 6,000 years; and all the verbal instruction between here and the silent grave couldn't teach us so much, or teach it so thoroughly, as one well directed singe. And a million of years from now—if this weary old world may endure so long—when human knowledge shall fall a little short of the infinite, and all the lore and erudition of this wonderful age will be but the primer of that day of light—the baby that is born into that world of knowledge and wisdom and progress, rich with all the years of human experience, will cry for the lamp, and, the very first time that opportunity favors it, will try to pull the flame up by the roots, and will know just as much as ignorant, untaught, stupid little Cain knew on the same subject. Year after year, century after unfolding century, how true it is that the lion on the fence is always bigger, fiercer, and more given to majestic attitudes and dramatic situations than the lion in the tent. And yet it costs us, often as the circus comes around, fifty cents to find that out.

But while we have been moralizing, Tom's mustache has taken a start. It has attained the physical density, though not the color, by any means, of the Egyptian darkness—it can be felt; and it is felt; very soft felt. The world begins to take notice of the new-comer; and Tom, as generations of Toms before him have done, patiently endures dark hints from other members of the family about his face being dirty. He loftily ignores his experienced father's suggestions that he should perform his tonsorial toilet with a spoonful of cream and the family cat. When his sisters, in meekly dissembled ignorance and innocence, inquire, "Tom, what *have* you on your lip?" he is austere, as becomes a man annoyed by the frivolous small talk of women. And when his younger brother takes advantage of the presence of a numerous company in the house, to shriek over the baluster up stairs, apparently to any boy anywhere this side of China, "Tom's a raisin' mustashers!" Tom smiles, a wan, neglected-orphan smile; a smile that looks as though it had come up on his face to weep over the barrenness of the land; a perfect ghost of a smile, as compared with the rugged 7×9 smiles that play like animated crescents over the countenances of the company. But the mustache grows. It comes on apace; very short in the middle, very no longer at the ends, and very blonde all round. Whenever you see such a mustache, do not laugh at it; do not point at it the slow, unmoving finger of scorn. Encourage it; speak kindly of it; affect admiration for it; coax it along. Pray for it—for it is a first. They always come that way. And when, in the fullness of time, it has developed so far that it can be pulled, there is all the agony of making it take color. It is worse, and more obstinate, and more deliberate than a meerschaum. The sun, that tans Tom's cheeks and blisters his nose, only bleaches his mustache. Nothing ever hastens its color; nothing does it any permanent good; nothing but patience, and faith, and persistent pulling.

With all the comedy there is about it, however, this is the grand period of a boy's life. You look at them, with their careless, easy, natural manners and movements in the streets and on the base ball ground, and their marvelous, systematic, indescribable, inimitable and complex awkwardness in your parlors, and do you never dream, looking at these young fellows, of the overshadowing destinies awaiting them, the mighty struggles mapped out in the earnest future of their lives, the thrilling conquests in the world of arms, the grander triumphs in the realm of philosophy, the fadeless laurels in the empire of letters, and the imperishable crowns that he who giveth them the victory binds about their brows, that wait for the courage and ambition of these boys? Why, the world is at a boy's feet; and power and conquest and leadership slumber in his rugged arms and care-free heart. A boy sets his ambition at whatever mark he will—lofty or groveling, as he may elect—and the boy who resolutely sets his heart on fame, on wealth, on power, on what he will; who consecrates himself to a life of noble endeavor, and lofty effort; who concentrates every faculty of his mind and body on the attainment of his one darling point; who brings to support his ambition courage and industry and patience, can trample on genius; for these are better and grander than genius; and he will begin to rise above his fellows as steadily and as surely as the sun climbs above the mountains. Hannibal, standing before the Punic altar fires and in the lisping accents of childhood swearing eternal hatred to Rome, was the Hannibal at twenty-four years commanding the army that swept down upon Italy like a mountain torrent, and shook the power of the mistress of the world, bid her defiance at her own gates, while affrighted Rome huddled and cowered under the protecting shadows of her walls. Napoleon, building snow forts at school and planning mimic battles with his playfellows, was the lieutenant of artillery at sixteen years, general of artillery and the victor of Toulon at twenty-four, and at last Emperor—not by the paltry accident of birth which might happen to any man, however unworthy, but by the manhood and grace of his own right arm, and his own brain, and his own courage and dauntless ambition—Emperor, with his foot on the throat of prostrate Europe. Alexander, daring more in his boyhood than his warlike father could teach him, and entering upon his all conquering career at twenty-four, was the boy whose vaulting ambition only paused in its dazzling flight when the world lay at his feet. And the fair-faced soldiers of the Empire, they who rode down upon the bayonets of the English squares at Waterloo, when the earth rocked beneath their feet and the incense smoke from the altars of the battle god shut out the sun and sky above their heads, who, with their young lives streaming from their gaping wounds, opened their pallid lips to cry, " Vive L'Empereur," as they died for honor and France, were boys—schoolboys—the boy conscripts of France, torn from their homes and their schools to stay the failing fortunes of the last grand army and the Empire that was tottering to its fall. You don't know how soon these happy-go-lucky young fellows, making summer hideous with base ball slang, or gliding around a skating rink on their backs, may hold the state and its destinies in their grasp; you don't know how soon these boys may make and write the history of the hour; how soon they alone may shape events and guide the current of public action; how soon one of them may run away with your daughter or borrow money of you.

Certain it is, there is one thing Tom will do, just about this period of his existence. He will fall in love with somebody before his mustache is long enough to wax.

Perhaps one of the earliest indications of this event, for it does not always break out in the same manner, is a sudden and alarming increase in the number and variety of Tom's neck-ties. In his boxes and on his dressing case, his mother is constantly startled by the changing and increasing assortment of the display. Monday he encircles his tender throat with a lilac knot, fearfully and wonderfully tied. A lavender tie succeeds the following day. Wednesday is graced with a sweet little tangle of pale, pale blue, that fades at a breath; Thursday is ushered in with a scarf of delicate pea green, of wonderful convolutions and sufficiently expansive, by the aid of a clean collar, to conceal any little irregularity in Tom's wash day; Friday smiles on a sailor's knot of dark blue, with a tangle of dainty forget-me-nots embroidered over it: Saturday tones itself down to a quiet, unobtrusive, neutral tint or shade, scarlet or yellow, and Sunday is deeply, darkly, piously black. It is difficult to tell whether Tom is trying to express the state of his distracted feelings by his neckties, or trying to find a color that will harmonize with his mustache, or match Laura's dress.

And during the variegated necktie period of man's existence how tenderly that mustache is coaxed and petted and caressed. How it is brushed to make it lie down and waxed to make it stand out, and how he notes its slow growth, and weeps and mourns and prays and swears over it day after weary day. And now, if ever, and generally now, he buys things to make it take color. But he never repeats this offense against nature. He buys a wonderful dye, warranted to " produce a beautiful glossy black or brown at one application, without stain or injury to the skin." Buys it at a little shabby, round the corner, obscure drug store, because he is not known there. And he tells the assassin who sells it him, that he is buying it for a sick sister. And the assassin knows that he lies. And in the guilty silence and solitude of his own room, with the curtains drawn and the door locked, Tom tries the virtues of that magic dye. It gets on his fingers and turns them black, to the elbow. It burns holes in his handkerchief when he tries to rub the malignant poison off his ebony fingers. He applies it to his silky mustache, real camel's hair, very cautiously and very tenderly, and with some misgivings. It turns his lip so black it makes the room dark. And out of all the clouds and the darkness and the sable splotches that pall every thing else in Plutonian gloom, that mustache smiles out, grinning like some ghastly hirsute specter, gleaming like the moon through a rifted storm cloud, unstained, untainted, unshaded; a natural, incorruptible blonde. That is the last time anybody fools Tom on hair dye.

The eye he has for immaculate linen and faultless collars. How it amazes his mother and sisters to learn that there isn't a shirt in the house fit for a pig to wear, and that he wouldn't wear the best collar in his room to be hanged in.

And the boots he crowds his feet into! A Sunday-school room, the Sunday before the pic-nic or the Christmas tree, with its sudden influx of new scholars, with irreproachable morals and ambitious appetites, doesn't compare with the overcrowded condition of those boots. Too tight in the instep; too narrow at the toes; too short at both ends; the only things about those boots that don't hurt him, that don't fill his very soul with agony, are the straps. When Tom is pulling them on, he feels that if somebody would kindly run over him three or four times, with a freight train, the sensation would be pleasant and reassuring and tranquilizing. The air turns black before his starting eyes, there is a roaring like the rush of many waters in his ears, he tugs at the straps that are cutting his fingers in two and pulling his arms out by the roots, and just before his blood-shot eyes shoot clear out of his head, the boot comes on— or the straps pull off. Then when he stands up, the earth rocks beneath his feet, and he thinks he can faintly hear the angels calling him home. And when he walks across the floor the first time his standing in the church and the Christian community is ruined forever. Or would be if any one could hear what he says. He never, never, never gets to be so old that he can not remember those boots, and if it is seventy years afterward his feet curl up in agony at the recollection. The first time he wears them, he is vaguely aware, as he leaves his room that there is a kind of "fixy" look about him, and his sisters' tittering is not needed to confirm this impression. He has a certain, half-defined impression that every thing he has on is a size too small for any other man of his size. That his boots are a trifle snug, like a house with four rooms for a family of thirty-seven. That the hat which sits so lightly on the crown of his head is jaunty but limited, like a junior clerk's salary; that his gloves are a neat fit, and can't be buttoned with a stump machine. Tom doesn't know all this: he has only a general, vague impression that it may be so. And he doesn't know that his sisters know every line of it. For he has lived many years longer, and got in ever so much more trouble, before he learns that one bright, good, sensible girl—and I believe they are all that—will see and notice more in a glance, remember it more accurately, and talk more about it, than twenty men can see in a week. Tom does not know, for his crying feet will not let him, how he gets from his room to the earthly paradise where Laura lives. Nor does he know, after he gets there, that Laura sees him trying to rest one foot by setting it up on the heel. And she sees him sneak it back under his chair and tilt it up on the toe for a change. She sees him ease the other foot a little by tugging the heel of the boot at the leg of the chair. A hazardous, reckless, presumptuous experiment. Tom tries it so far one night, and slides his heel so far up the leg of his boot, that his foot actually feels comfortable, and he thinks the angels must be rubbing it. He walks out of the parlor sideways that night, trying to hide the cause of the sudden elongation of one leg, and he hobbles all the way home in the same disjointed condition. But Laura sees that too. She sees all the little knobs and lumps on his foot, and sees him fidget and fuss, she sees the look of anguish flitting across his face under the heartless, deceitful, veneering of smiles, and she makes the mental remark that master Tom would feel much happier, and much more comfortable, and more like staying longer, if he had worn his father's boots.

But on his way to the house, despite the distraction of his crying feet, how many pleasant, really beautiful, romantic things Tom thinks up and recollects and compiles and composes to say to Laura, to impress her with his originality, and wisdom, and genius, and bright exuberant fancy and general superiority over all the rest of Tom kind. Real earnest things, you know; no hollow, conventional compliments, or nonsense, but such things, Tom flatters himself, as none of the other fellows can or will say. And he has them all in beautiful order when he gets at the foot of the hill. The remark about the weather, to begin with; not the stereotyped old phrase, but a quaint, droll, humorous conceit that no one in the world but Tom could think of. Then, after the opening overture about the weather, something about music and Beethoven's sonata in B flat, and Haydn's symphonies, and of course something about Beethoven's grand old Fifth symphony, somebody's else mass, in heaven knows how many flats; and then something about art, and a profound thought or two on science and philosophy, and so on to poetry and from poetry to "business."

But alas, when Tom reaches the gate, all these well ordered ideas display evident symptoms of breaking up; as he crosses the yard, he is dismayed to know that they are in the convulsions of a panic, and when he touches the bell knob, every, each, all and several of the ideas, original and compiled, that he has had on any subject during the past ten years, forsake him and return no more that evening. When Laura opened the door he had intended to say something real splendid about the imprisoned sunlight of something, beaming out a welcome upon the what you may call it of the night or something. Instead of which he says, or rather gasps: "Oh, yes, to be sure; to be sure; ho." And then, conscious that he has not said anything particularly brilliant or original, or that most any of the other fellows could not say with a little practice, he makes one more effort to redeem himself before he steps into the hall, and adds, "Oh, good morning; good morning." Feeling that even this is only a partial success, he collects his scattered faculties for one united effort and inquires: "How is your mother?" And then it strikes him that he has about exhausted the subject, and he goes into the parlor, and sits down, and just as soon as he has placed his reproachful feet in the least agonizing position, he proceeds to wholly, completely and successfully forget everything he ever knew in his life. He returns to consciousness to find himself, to his own amazement and equally to Laura's bewilderment, conducting a conversation about the crops, and a new method of funding the national debt, subjects upon which he is about as well informed as the town clock. He rallies, and makes a successful effort to turn the conversation into literary channels by asking her if she has read " Daniel Deronda," and wasn't it odd that George Washington Eliot should name her heroine " Grenadine," after a dress pattern? And in a burst of confidence he assures her that he would not be amazed if it should rain before morning, (and he hopes it will, and that it may be a flood, and that he may get caught in it, without an ark nearer than Cape Horn.) · And so, at last, the first evening passes away, and after mature deliberation and many unsuccessful efforts he rises to go. But he does not go. He wants to; but he doesn't know how. He says good evening. Then he repeats it in a marginal reference. Then he puts it in a foot note. Then he adds the remark in an appendix, and shakes hands. By this time he gets as far as the parlor door, and catches hold of the knob and holds on to it as tightly as though some one on the other side were trying to pull it through the door and run away with it. And he stands there a fidgetty statue of the door holder. He mentions, for not more than the twentieth time that evening that he is passionately fond of music but he can't sing. Which is a lie; he can. Did she go to the Centennial? " No." " Such a pity " — he begins, but stops in terror, lest she may consider his condolence a reflection upon her financial standing. Did he go? Oh, yes; yes; he says, absently, he went. Or, that is to say, no, not exactly. He did not exactly go to the Centennial; he staid at home. In fact, he had not been out of town this Summer. Then he looks at the tender little face; he looks at the brown eyes, sparkling with suppressed merriment; he looks at the white hands, dimpled and soft, twin daughters of the snow; and the fairy picture grows more lovely as he looks at it, until his heart outruns his fears; he must speak, he must say something impressive and ripe with meaning, for how can he go away with this suspense in his breast? His heart trembles as does his hand; his quivering lips part, and — Laura deftly hides a vagrom yawn behind her fan. Good night, and Tom is gone.

There is a dejected droop to the mustache that night, when in the solitude of his own room Tom releases his hands from the despotic gloves, and tenderly soothes two of the reddest, puffiest feet that ever crept out of boots not half their own size, and swore in mute, but eloquent anatomical profanity at the whole race of bootmakers. And his heart is nearly as full of sorrow and bitterness as his boots. It appears to him that he showed off to the worst possible advantage; he is dimly conscious that he acted very like a donkey, and he has the not entirely unnatural impression that she will never want to see him again. And so he philosophically and manfully makes up his mind never, never, never, to think of her again. And then he immediately proceeds, in the manliest and most natural way in the world, to think of nothing and nobody else under the sun for the next ten hours. How the tender little face does haunt him. He pitches himself into bed with an aimless recklessness that tumbles pillows, bolster, and sheets into one shapeless, wild, chaotic mass, and he goes through the motions of going to sleep, like a man who would go to sleep by steam. He stands his pillow up on end, and pounds it into a wad, and he props his head upon it as though it were the guillotine block. He lays it down and smooths it out level, and pats all the wrinkles out of it, and there is more sleeplessness in it to the square inch than there is in the hungriest mosquito that ever sampled a martyr's blood. He gets up and smokes like a patent stove, although not three hours ago he told Laura that he de - tes - ted tobacco.

This is the only time Tom will ever go through this, in exactly this way. It is the one rare golden experience, the one bright, rosy dream of his life. He may live to be as old as an army overcoat, and he may marry as many wives as Brigham Young, singly, or in a cluster, but this will come to him but once. Let him enjoy all the delightful misery, all the ecstatic wretchedness, all the heavenly forlornness of it as best he can. And he does take good, solid, edifying misery out of it. How he does torture himself and hate Smith, the empty headed donkey, who can talk faster than poor Tom can think, and whose mustache is black as Tom's boots, and so long that he can pull one end of it with both hands. And how he does detest that idiot Brown, who plays and sings, and goes up there every time Tom does, and claws over a few old forgotten five-finger exercises and calls it music; who comes up there, some night when Tom thinks he has the evening and Laura all to himself, and brings up an old, tuneless, voiceless, cracked guitar, and goes crawling around in the wet grass under the windows and makes night perfectly hideous with what he calls a serenade. And he speaks French, too, the beast. Poor Tom; when Brown's lingual accomplishments in the language of Charlemagne are confined to — "aw — aw — er ah — vooly voo?" and on state occasions to the additional grandeur of "avy voo mong shapo?" But poor Tom who once covered himself with confusion by telling Laura that his favorite in "Robert le Diable" was the beautiful aria, "Robert toy que jam," considers Brown a very prodigal in linguistic attainments; another Cardinal Mezzofanti; and hates him for it accordingly. And he hates Daubs, the artist, too, who was up there one evening and made an off hand crayon sketch of her in an album. The picture looked much more like Daubs' mother, and Tom knew it, but Laura said it was oh just delightfully, perfectly splendid, and Tom has hated Daubs most cordially ever since. In fact, Tom hates every man who has the temerity to speak to her, or whom she may treat with lady-like courtesy. Until there comes one night when the boots of the inquisition pattern sit more lightly on their suffering victims. When Providence has been on Tom's side and has kept Smith and Daubs and Brown away, and has frightened Tom nearly to death by showing him no one in the little parlor with its old-fashioned furniture but himself and Laura and the furniture. When, almost without knowing how or why, they talk about life and its realities instead of the last concert or the next lecture; when they talk of their plans, and their day dreams and aspirations, and their ideals of real men and women; when they talk about the heroes and heroines of days long gone by, grey and dim in the ages that are ever made young and new by the lives of noble men and noble women who lived, and did, and never died in those grand old days, but lived and live on, as imperishable and fadeless in their glory as the glittering stars that sang at creation's dawn. When the room seems strangely silent when their voices hush; when the flush of earnestness upon her face gives it a tinge of sadness that makes it more beautiful than ever; when the dream and picture of a home Eden, and home life, and home love, grows every moment more lovely, more entrancing to him until at last poor blundering, stupid Tom, speaks without knowing what he is going to say, speaks without preparation or rehearsal, speaks, and his honest, natural, manly heart touches his faltering lips with eloquence and tenderness and earnestness that all the rhetoric in the world never did and never will inspire, and ———. That is all we know about it. Nobody knows what is said or how it is done. Nobody. Only the silent stars or the whispering leaves, or the cat, or maybe Laura's younger brother, or the hired girl, who generally bulges in just as Tom reaches the climax. All the rest of us know about it is, that Tom doesn't come away so early that night, and that when he reaches the door he holds a pair of dimpled hands instead of the insensate door knob. He never clings to that door knob again; never. Unless ma, dear ma, has been so kind as to bring in her sewing and spend the evening with them. And Tom doesn't hate anybody, nor want to kill anybody in the wide, wide world, and he feels just as good as though he had just come out of a six months' revival; and is happy enough to borrow money of his worst enemy.

But, there is no rose without a thorn. Although, I suppose, on an inside computation, there is, in this weary old world as much as, say a peck, or a peck and a half possibly, of thorns without their attendant roses. Just the raw, bare thorns. In the highest heaven of his newly found bliss, Tom is suddenly recalled to earth and its miseries by a question from Laura which falls like a plummet into the unrippled sea of the young man's happiness, and fathoms its depths in the shallowest place. "Has her own Tom"—as distinguished from countless other Toms, nobody's Toms, unclaimed Toms, to all intents and purposes swamp lands on the public matrimonial domain—"Has her own Tom said anything to pa?" "Oh, yes! pa;" Tom says, "To be sure; yes." Grim, heavy browed, austere pa. The living embodiment of business. Wiry, shrewd, the life and mainspring of the house of Tare and Tret. "'M. Well. N' no," Tom had not exactly, as you might say, poured out his heart to pa. Somehow or other he had a rose-colored idea that the thing was going to go right along in this way forever. Tom had an idea that the programme was all arranged, printed and distributed, rose-colored, gilt-edged, and perfumed. He was going to sit and hold Laura's hands, pa was to stay down at the office, and ma was to make her visits to the parlor as much like angels', for their rarity and brevity, as possible. But he sees, now that the matter has been referred to, that it is a grim necessity. And Laura doesn't like to see such a spasm of terror pass over Tom's face; and her coral lips quiver a little as she hides her flushed face out of sight on Tom's shoulder, and tells him how kind and tender pa has always been with her, until Tom feels positively jealous of pa. And she tells him that he must not dread going to see him, for pa will be oh so glad to know how happy, happy, happy he can make his little girl. And as she talks of him, the hard working, old-fashioned, tender-hearted old man, who loves his girls as though he were yet only a big boy, her heart grows tenderer, and she speaks so earnestly and eloquently that Tom, at first savagely jealous of him, is persuaded to fall in love with the old gentleman—he calls him "Pa," too, now,—himself.

But by the following afternoon this feeling is very faint. And when he enters the counting room of Tare & Tret, and stands before pa—Oh, land of love, how could Laura ever talk so about such a man. Stubbly little pa; with a fringe of the most obstinate and wiry gray hair standing all around his bald, bald head; the wiriest, grizzliest mustache bristling under his nose; a tuft of tangled beard under the sharp chin, and a raspy undergrowth of a week's run on the thin jaws; business, business, business, in every line of the hard, seamed face, and profit and loss, barter and trade, dicker and bargain, in every movement of the nervous hands. Pa; old business! He puts down the newspaper a little way, and looks over the top of it as Tom announces himself, glancing at the young man with a pair of blue eyes that peer through old-fashioned iron-bowed spectacles, that look as though they had known these eyes and done business with them ever since they wept over their A B C's or peeped into the tall stone jar Sunday afternoon to look for the doughnuts.

Tom, who had felt all along there could be no inspiration on his part in this scene, has come prepared. At least he had his last true statement at his tongue's end when he entered the counting room. But now, it seems to him that if he had been brought up in a circus, and cradled inside of a sawdust ring, and all his life trained to twirl his hat, he couldn't do it better, nor faster, nor be more utterly incapable of doing anything else. At last he swallows a lump in his throat as big as a ballot box, and faintly gasps, "Good morning." Mr. Tret hastens to recognize him. "Eh? oh; yes; yes; yes; I see; young Bostwick, from Dope & Middlerib's. Oh yes. Well—?" "I have come, sir," gasps Tom, thinking all around the world from Cook's explorations to "Captain Riley's Narrative," for the first line of that speech that Tare & Tret have just scared out of him so completely that he doesn't believe he ever knew a word of it. "I have come—" and he thinks if his lips didn't get so dry and hot they make his teeth ache, that he could get along with it; "I have, sir,—come, Mr. Tret; Mr. Tret, sir—I have come—I am come—" "Yes, ye-es," says Mr. Tret, in the wildest bewilderment, but in no very encouraging tones, thinking the young man probably wants to borrow money; "Ye-es; I see you've come. Well; that's all right; glad to see you. Yes, you've come?" Tom's hat is now making about nine hundred and eighty revolutions per minute, and apparently not running up to half its full capacity. "Sir; Mr. Tret," he resumes, " I have come, sir; Mr. Tret — I am here to — to sue — to sue, Mr. Tret — I am here to sue — " "Sue, eh?" the old man echoes sharply, with a belligerent rustle of the newspaper; "sue Tare & Tret, eh? Well, that's right, young man; that's right. Sue, and get damages. We'll give you all the law you want." Tom's head is so hot, and his heart is so cold, that he thinks they must be about a thousand miles apart. "Sir," he explains, "that isn't it. It isn't that. I only want to ask — I have long known — Sir," he adds, as the opening lines of his speech come to him like a message from heaven, " Sir, you have a flower, a tender lovely blossom; chaste as the snow that crowns the mountain's brow; fresh as the breath of morn; lovelier than the rosy-fingered hours that fly before Aurora's car; pure as the lily kissed by dew. This precious blossom, watched by your paternal eyes, the object of your tender care and solicitude, I ask of you. I would wear it in my heart, and guard and cherish it—and in the—" "Oh-h, ye-es, yes, yes," the old man says soothingly, beginning to see that Tom is only drunk, "Oh yes, yes, I don't know much about them myself; my wife and the girls generally keep half the windows in the house littered up with them, Winter and Summer, every window so full of house plants the sun can't shine in. Come up to the house, they'll give you all you can carry away, give you a hat full of 'em." "No, no, no; you don't understand," says poor Tom, and old Mr. Tret now observes that Tom is very drunk indeed. " It isn't that, sir. Sir, that isn't it. I — I — I want to marry your daughter!" And there it is at last, as bluntly as though Tom had wadded it into a gun and shot it at the old man. Mr. Tret does not say any thing for twenty seconds. Tom tells Laura that evening that it was two hours and a half before her father opened his head. Then he says, "Oh, yes, yes, yes, yes; to be sure; to — be — sure." And then the long pause is dreadful. "Yes, yes. Well, I don't know. I don't know about that, young man. Said any thing to Jennie about it?" "It isn't Jennie," Tom gasps, seeing a new Rubicon to cross; "its——" "Oh, Julie, eh? well, I don't——" "No, sir," interjects the despairing Tom, "it isn't Julie, it's——" "Sophie, eh? Oh, well, Sophie——" "Sir," says Tom, "If you please, sir, it isn't Sophie, its——" "Not Minnie, surely? Why, Minnie is hardly—well, I don't know. Young folks get along faster than——" "Dear Mr. Tret," breaks in the distracted lover, "it's Laura."

As they sit and stand there, looking at each other, the dingy old counting-room, with the heavy shadows lurking in every corner, with its time-worn, heavy brown furnishings, with the scanty dash of sunlight breaking in through the dusty window, looks like an old Rubens painting; the beginning and the finishing of a race: the old man, nearly ready to lay his armor off, glad to be so nearly and so safely through with the race and the fight that Tom, in all his inexperience and with all the rash enthusiasm and conceit of a young man, is just getting ready to run and fight, or fight and run, you never can tell which until he is through with it. And the old man, looking at Tom, and through him, and past him, feels his old heart throb almost as quickly as does that of the young man before him. For looking down a long vista of happy, eventful years, bordered with roseate hopes and bright dreams and anticipations, he sees a tender face, radiant with smiles and kindled with blushes; he feels a soft hand drop into his own with its timid pressure; he sees the vision open, under the glittering summer stars, down mossy hillsides, where the restless breezes, sighing through the rustling leaves, whispered their tender secret to the noisy katydids; strolling along the winding paths, deep in the bending wild grass, down in the star-lit aisles of the dim old woods; loitering where the meadow brook sparkles over the white pebbles or murmurs around the great flat stepping-stones; lingering on the rustic foot-bridge, while he gazes into eyes eloquent and tender in their silent love-light; up through the long pathway of years, flecked and checkered with sunshine and cloud, with storm and calm, through years of struggle, trial, sorrow, disappointment, out at last into the grand, glorious, crowning beauty and benison of hard-won and well-deserved success, until he sees now this second Laura, re-imaging her mother as she was in the dear old days. And he rouses from his dream with a start, and he tells Tom he'll "Talk it over with Mrs. Tret, and see him again in the morning."

And so they are duly and formally engaged; and the very first thing they do, they make the very sensible, though very uncommon, resolution to so conduct themselves that no one will ever suspect it. And they succeed admirably. No one ever does suspect it. They come into church in time to hear the benediction—every time they come together. They shun all other people when church is dismissed, and are seen to go home alone the longest way. At pic-nics they are missed not more than fifty times a day, and are discovered sitting under a tree, holding each other's hands, gazing into each other's eyes and saying—nothing. When he throws her shawl over her shoulders, he never looks at what he is doing, but looks straight into her starry eyes, throws the shawl right over her natural curls, and drags them out by the hair-pins. If, at sociable or festival, they are left alone in a dressing-room a second and a half, Laura emerges with her ruffle standing around like a railroad accident; and Tom has enough complexion on his shoulder to go around a young ladies' seminary. When they drive out, they sit in a buggy with a seat eighteen inches wide, and there is two feet of unoccupied room at either end of it. Long years afterward, when they drive, a street car isn't too wide for them; and when they walk, you could drive four loads of hay between them.

And yet, as carefully as they guard their precious little secret, and as cautious and circumspect as they are in their walk and behavior, it gets talked around that they are engaged. People are so prying and suspicious.

And so the months of their engagement run on; never before, or since, time flies so swiftly—unless, it may be, some time when Tom has an acceptance in bank to meet in two days, that he can't lift one end of—and the wedding day dawns, fades, and the wedding is over. Over, with its little circle of delighted friends, with its ripples of pleasure and excitement, with its touches of home love and home life, that leave their lasting impress upon Laura's heart, although Tom, with man-like blindness, never sees one of them. Over, with ma, with the thousand and one anxieties attendant on the grand event in her daughter's life hidden away under her dear old smiling face, down, away down under the tender, glistening eyes, deep in the loving heart; ma, hurrying here and fluttering there, in the intense excitement of something strangely made up of happiness and grief, of apprehension and hope; ma, with her sudden disappearances and flushed reappearances, indicating struggles and triumphs in the turbulent world down stairs; ma, with the new-fangled belt, with the dinner-plate buckles, fastened on wrong side foremost, and the flowers dangling down the wrong side of her head, to Sophie's intense horror and pantomimic telegraphy; ma, flying here and there, seeing that every thing is going right, from kitchen to dressing-rooms; looking after everything and everybody, with her hands and heart just as full as they will hold, and more voices calling "ma," from every room in the house, than you would think one hundred mas could answer. But she answers them all, and she sees after everything, and just in the nick of time prevents Mr. Tret from going down stairs and attending the ceremony in a loud-figured dressing-gown and green slippers; ma, who, with the quivering lip and glistening eyes, has to be cheerful, and lively, and smiling; because, if, as she thinks of the dearest and best of her flock going away from her fold, to put her life and her happiness into another's keeping, she gives way for one moment, a dozen reproachful voices cry out, "Oh-h ma!" How it all comes back to Laura, like the tender shadows of a dream, long years after the dear, dear face, furrowed with marks of patient suffering and loving care, rests under the snow and the daisies; when the mother love that glistened in the tender eyes has closed in darkness on the dear old home; and the nerveless hands, crossed in dreamless sleep upon the pulseless breast, can never again touch the children's heads with caressing gesture; how the sweet vision comes to Laura, as it shone on her wedding morn, rising in tenderer beauty through the blinding tears her own excess of happiness calls up, as the rainbow spans the cloud only through the mingling of the golden sunshine and the falling rain.

And pa, dear old shabby pa, whose clothes will not fit him as they fit other men; who always dresses just a year and a half behind the style; pa, wandering up and down through the house, as though he were lost in his own home, pacing through the hall like a sentinel, blundering aimlessly and listlessly into rooms where he has no business, and being repelled therefrom by a chorus of piercing shrieks and hysterical giggling; pa, getting off his well worn jokes with an assumption of merriment that seems positively real; pa, who creeps away by himself once in a while, and leans his face against the window, and sighs, in direct violation of all strict household regulations, right against the glass, as he thinks of his little girl going away to-day from the home whose love and tenderness and patience she has known so well. Only yesterday, it seems to him, the little baby girl, bringing the first music of baby prattle into his home; then a little girl in short dresses, with school-girl troubles and school-girl pleasures; then an older little girl, out of school and into society, but a little girl to pa still. And then——. But, somehow, this is as far as pa can get; for he sees, in the flight of this, the first, the following flight of the other fledglings; and he thinks how silent and desolate the old nest will be when they have all mated and flown away. He thinks, when their flight shall have made other homes bright and cheery and sparkling, with music and prattle and laughter, how it will leave the old home hushed and quiet and still. How, in the long, lonesome afternoons, mother will sit by the empty cradle that rocked them all, murmuring the sweet old cradle songs that brooded over all their sleep, until the rising tears check the swaying cradle and choke the song—and back, over river and prairie and mountain, that roll and stretch and rise between the old home and the new ones, comes back the prattle of her little ones, the rippling music of their laughter, the tender cadences of their songs, until the hushed old home is haunted by memories of its children—gray and old they may be, with other children clustering about their knees; but to the dear old home they are "the children" still. And dreaming thus, when pa for a moment finds his little girl alone—his little girl who is going away out of the home whose love she knows, into a home whose tenderness and patience are all untried—he holds her in his arms and whispers the most fervent blessing that ever throbbed from a father's heart; and Laura's wedding day would be incomplete and unfeeling without her tears. So is the pattern of our life made up of smiles and tears, shadow and sunshine. Tom sees none of these background pictures of the wedding day. He sees none of its real, heartfelt earnestness. He sees only the bright, sunny tints and happy figures that the tearful, shaded background throws out in golden relief; but never stops to think that, without the shadows, the clouds, and the somber tints of the background, the picture would be flat, pale, and lusterless.

And then, the presents. The assortment of brackets, serviceable, ornamental and—cheap. The French clock, that never went, that does not go, that never will go. And the nine potato mashers. The eight mustard spoons. The three cigar stands. Eleven match safes; assorted patterns. A dozen tidies, charity fair styles, blue dog on a yellow background, barking at a green boy climbing over a red fence, after seal brown apples. The two churns, old pattern, straight handle and dasher, and they have as much thought of keeping a cow as they have of keeping a section of artillery. Five things they didn't know the names of, and never could find any body who could tell what they were for. And a nickel plated pocket corkscrew, that Tom, in a fine burst of indignation, throws out of the window, which Laura says is just like her own impulsive Tom. And not long after her own impulsive Tom catches his death of cold and ruins the knees of his best trowsers crawling around in the wet grass hunting for that same corkscrew. Which is also just like her own impulsive Tom.

And then, the young people go to work and buy e-v-e-r-y thing they need, the day they go to housekeeping. Every thing. Just as well, Tom says, to get every thing at once and have it delivered right up at the house, as to spend five or six or ten or twenty years in stocking up a house, as his father did. And Laura thinks so too, and she wonders that Tom should know so much more than his father. This worries Tom himself, when he thinks of it, and he never rightly understands how it is, until he is forty-five or fifty years old and has a Tom of his own to direct and advise him. So they make out a list, and revise it, and rewrite it, until they have every thing down, complete, and it isn't until supper is ready the first day, that they discover there isn't a knife, a fork, or a plate or a spoon in the new house. And the first day the washerwoman comes, and the water is hot, and the clothes are all ready, it is discovered that there isn't a wash-tub nearer than the grocery. And further along in the day the discovery is made that while Tom has bought a clothes line that will reach to the north pole and back, and then has to be coiled up a mile or two in the back yard, there isn't a clothes pin in the settlement. And in the course of a week or two, Tom slowly awakens to the realization of the fact that he has only begun to get. And if he should live two thousand years, which he rarely does, and possibly may not, he would think, just before he died, of something they had wanted the worst way for five centuries, and had either been too poor to get, or Tom had always forgotten to bring up. So long as he lives, Tom goes on bringing home things that they need — absolute, simple necessities, that were never so much as hinted at in that exhaustive list. And old Time comes along, and knowing that the man in that new house will never get through bringing things up to it, helps him out and comes around and brings things, too. Brings a gray hair now and then, to stick in Tom's mustache, which has grown too big to be ornamental, and too wayward and unmanageable to be comfortable. He brings little cares and little troubles, and little trials and little butcher bills, and little grocer's bills, and little tailor bills, and nice large millinery bills, that pluck at Tom's mustache and stroke it the wrong way and make it look more and more as pa's did the first time Tom saw it. He brings, by and by, the prints of baby fingers and pats them around on the dainty wall paper. Brings, some times, a voiceless messenger that lays its icy fingers on the baby lips, and hushes their dainty prattle, and in the baptism of its first sorrow, the darkened little home has its dearest and tenderest tie to the upper fold. Brings, by and by, the tracks of a boy's muddy boots, and scatters them all up and down the clean porch. Brings a messenger, one day, to take the younger Tom away to college. And the quiet the boy leaves behind him is so much harder to endure than his racket, that old Tom is tempted to keep a brass band in the house until the boy comes back. But old Time brings him home at last, and it does make life seem terribly real and earnest to Tom, and how the old laugh rings out and ripples all over Laura's face, when they see old Tom's first mustache budding and struggling into second life on young Tom's face.

And still old Time comes round, bringing each year

whiter frosts to scatter on the whitening mustache, and brighter gleams of silver to glint the brown of Laura's hair. Bringing the blessings of peaceful old age and a lovelocked home to crown these noble, earnest, real human lives, bristling with human faults, marred with human mistakes, scarred and seamed and rifted with human troubles, and crowned with the compassion that only perfection can send upon imperfection. Comes, with happy memories of the past, and quiet confidence for the future. Comes, with the changing scenes of day and night; with winter's storm and summer's calm; comes, with the sunny peace and the backward dreams of age; comes, until one day, the eye of the relentless old reaper rests upon old Tom, standing right in the swarth, amid the golden corn. The sweep of the noiseless scythe that never turns its edge, Time passes on, old Tom steps out of young Tom's way, and the cycle of a life is complete.

GETTING READY FOR THE TRAIN.

GETTING READY FOR THE TRAIN.

WHEN they reached the depot, Mr. Man and his wife gazed in unspeakable disappointment at the receding train, which was just pulling away from the bridge switch at the rate of a thousand miles a minute. Their first impulse was to run after it; but as the train was out of sight, and whistling for Sagetown before they could act upon the impulse, they remained in the carriage and disconsolately turned the horses' heads homeward.

"It all comes of having to wait for a woman to get ready," Mr. Man broke the silence with, very grimly.

"I was ready before you were," replied his wife.

"Great heavens!" cried Mr. Man, in irrepressible impatience, jerking the horses' jaws out of place, "just listen to that! And I sat out in the buggy ten minutes, yelling at you to come along, until the whole neighborhood heard me!"

"Yes," acquiesced Mrs. Man, with the provoking placidity which no one can assume but a woman, "and every time I started down stairs you sent me back for something you had forgotten."

Mr. Man groaned. "This is too much to bear," he said, "when everybody knows that if I was going to Europe, I would just rush into the house, put on a clean shirt, grab up my gripsack, and fly; while you would want at least six months for preliminary preparations, and then dawdle around the whole day of starting until every train had left town."

Well, the upshot of the matter was, that the Mans put off their visit to Peoria until the next week, and it was agreed that each one should get ready and go down to the train and go, and the one who failed to get ready should be left. The day of the match came around in due time. The train was to go at 10:30, and Mr. Man, after attending to his business, went home at 9:45.

"Now then," he shouted, "only three-quarters of an hour to train time. Fly around; a fair field and no favors, you know."

And away they flew. Mr. Man bulged into this room and rushed through that one, and dived into one closet after another with inconceivable rapidity, chuckling under his breath all the time, to think how cheap Mrs. Man would feel when he started off alone. He stopped on his way up stairs to pull off his heavy boots, to save time. For the same reason he pulled off his coat as he ran through the dining-room, and hung it on the corner of the silver closet. Then he jerked off his vest as he rushed through the hall, and tossed it on a hook in the hat-rack, and by the time he reached his own room he was ready to plunge into his clean clothes. He pulled out a bureau drawer and began to paw at the things, like a Scotch terrier after a rat.

"Eleanor!" he shrieked, "where are my shirts?"

"In your bureau drawer," quietly replied Mrs. Man, who was standing placidly before a glass, calmly and deliberately coaxing a refractory crimp into place.

"Well, by thunder, they ain't!" shouted Mr. Man, a little annoyed. "I've emptied every last thing out of the drawer, and there isn't a thing in it that I ever saw before."

Mrs. Man stepped back a few paces, held her head on one side, and after satisfying herself that the crimp would do, and would stay where she had put it, replied:

"These things scattered around on the floor are all mine. Probably you haven't been looking in your own drawer."

"I don't see," testily observed Mr. Man, "why you couldn't have put my things out for me, when you had nothing else to do all morning."

"Because," said Mrs. Man, settling herself into an additional article of raiment with awful deliberation, "nobody put mine out for me. 'A fair field and no favors,' my dear."

Mr. Man plunged into his shirt like a bull at a red flag.

"Foul!" he shouted, in malicious triumph. "No button on the neck!"

"Because," said Mrs. Man, sweetly, after a deliberate stare at the fidgeting, impatient man, during which she buttoned her dress and put eleven pins where they would do the most good, "because you have got the shirt on wrong side out."

When Mr. Man slid out of that shirt, he began to sweat. He dropped the shirt three times before he got it on, and while it was over his head he heard the clock strike ten. When his head came through he saw Mrs. Man coaxing the ends and bows of her neck-tie.

"Where's my shirt studs?" he cried.

Mrs. Man went out into another room and presently came back with gloves and hat, and saw Mr. Man emptying all the boxes he could find in and about the bureau. Then she said:

"In the shirt you just took off."

Mrs. Man put on her gloves while Mr. Man hunted up and down the room for his cuff buttons.

"Eleanor," he snarled, at last, "I believe you must know where those buttons are."

"I haven't seen them," said the lady, settling her hat,

"didn't you lay them down on the window-sill in the sitting room last night?"

Mr. Man remembered, and he went down stairs on the run. He stepped on one of his boots, and was immediately landed in the hall at the foot of the stairs with neatness and dispatch, attended in the transmission with more bumps than he could count with a Webb's adder, and landing with a bang like the Hellgate explosion.

"Are you nearly ready, Algernon?" asked the wife of his family, sweetly, leaning over the balusters.

The unhappy man groaned. "Can't you throw me down that other boot?" he asked.

Mrs. Man pityingly kicked it down to him.

"My valise?" he inquired, as he tugged away at the boot.

"Up in your dressing room," she answered.

"Packed?"

"I do not know; unless you packed it yourself, probably not," she replied, with her hand on the door knob; "I had barely time to pack my own."

She was passing out of the gate, when the door opened, and he shouted:

"Where in the name of goodness did you put my vest? It has all my money in it!"

"You threw it on the hat rack," she called back, "good-bye, dear."

Before she got to the corner of the street she was hailed again.

"Eleanor! Eleanor! Eleanor Man! Did you wear off my coat?"

She paused and turned, after signaling the street car to stop, and cried,

"You threw it on the silver closet."

And the street car engulfed her graceful figure and she

was seen no more. But the neighbors say that they heard Mr. Man charging up and down the house, rushing out at the front door every now and then, and shrieking up the deserted streets after the unconscious Mrs. Man, to know where his hat was, and where she put the valise key, and if she had any clean socks and undershirts, and that there wasn't a linen collar in the house. And when he went away at last, he left the kitchen door, side door and front door, all the down-stair windows and the front gate wide open. And the loungers around the depot were somewhat amused just as the train was pulling out of sight down in the yards, to see a flushed, perspiring man, with his hat on sideways, his vest buttoned two buttons too high, his cuffs unbuttoned and neck-tie flying and his grip-sack flapping open and shut like a demented shutter on a March night, and a door key in his hand, dash wildly across the platform and halt in the middle of the track, glaring in dejected, impotent, wrathful mortification at the departing train, and shaking his trembling fist at a pretty woman, who was throwing kisses at him from the rear platform of the last car.

DRIVING THE COW.

MR. FORBES is a nervous man, and it is not surprising that when Mrs. Forbes told him the cow had got out at the front gate, he was so startled and annoyed that he made some disjointed allusions to the scene of General Newton's dynamite explosions. When he went out the cow was standing very quietly in the street, just in front of the gate, chewing her cud, best navy, and looking as though she were trying to think of something mean to say. Mr. Forbes got around in front of her, raised both his hands above his head, and, extending his arms, waved them slowly up and down, at the same time ejaculating, "Shoo! shoo, there, I say! Shoo!" The cow turned her cud over to the other side, and gazed at the apparition in some astonishment, and then began to back away and maneuver to get around it. It is a remarkable fact, which we have never heard Prof. Huxley explain, that a cow is perfectly willing to go in any direction save the one in which you attempt to drive her. When the cow began to back, Mr. Forbes slowed up with his arms and assumed a more coaxing tone. When the cow started to make a flank movement off to the right, Mr. Forbes kept in front of her by sidling across in the same direction, at the same time raising his voice and accelerating the movement of his arms. When the cow made several cautious diversions and reconnoissances this way and that, Mr. Forbes was compelled to keep up a kind of Chinese cotillon, dancing to and fro across the road, keeping time with his shuffling feet and waving hands, and the children on their way to school gathered in little groups on the sidewalk and viewed the spectacle with great interest, alternately cheering the cow and encouraging Mr. Forbes, as one side or the other would gain a little advantage. When the cow would make a short, determined rush, causing Mr. Forbes to scuttle across the street, in a perfect whirlwind of dust and sticks and a rattling volley of "Hi! hoo-y! shoo, there! hoo-y!" the enthusiasm of the audience was unbounded. Once, Mr. Forbes got the cow fairly cornered and headed her right into the gate, but just as the gray light of victory fell upon his uplifted face, Mrs. Forbes and the hired girl came charging out in mad pursuit of a flock of geese that had taken advantage of the open gate to stroll in and have a nip at the house plants on the back porch. Squacking, whooping and screaming, the flying geese and the pursuing column came out like a runaway edition of chaos, and the cow gave a snort of terror and turned short upon Mr. Forbes, who tossed his hands more wildly and shouted more vociferously than ever, and got out of the way with neatness and dispatch, just as the cow went by with the swiftness of a golden opportunity or a vagrant thought. Mr. Forbes' blood was up, and he was bound to head off that cow if it was in the power of man. Spurred to intense energy, by the derisive shouts of the children, he bent his head and picked up his flying feet. They got a pretty fair send off, Mr. Forbes and the cow, and as they swept up the street, they could look into each other's eyes and glare defiance while they spurned the dust with flying feet. Mr. Forbes ran until his eyes seemed bursting out of his head and his very soul seemed to be in his legs; the perspiration started out of every pore; every time he struck the ground with his foot he thought he felt the earth shake, and yet, though he tugged and sweat and strained until all the landscape was yellow before his blood-shot eyes, he couldn't gain a hair's breadth on the shambling, awkward cow that went sprawling and kicking along by his side, filling the soft September air with such a wild, tumultuous, horrible jangling of bells that Forbes made up his mind to throw the bell away the moment he get the cow home. The people on the streets stopped and waved their hats and cheered enthusiastically as the procession swept past, ladies leaned out of the windows and smiled sweetly on the man and cow alike. Once Forbes stumbled over a crossing and had to take strides twenty-three feet long for the next half block to keep from falling, and he was sure he was split clear up to the chin and would have to button his trousers around his neck forever afterward, but he wouldn't give in to a cow if he died for it. At the next corner the cow turned off down a side street; Forbes shot across the sidewalk for a short cut, and the next instant he went crashing half way through a latticed tree box. A street car driver stopped his car and assisted Mr. Forbes to a sitting posture, leaned him up against a fence and went on with his train. And as Mr. Forbes sat in a dazed kind of way, mechanically rubbing the dust and dirt off his coat and pinning up long gashes and grimly grinning apertures in his clothes, there came to his ears the distant tinkle tankle of a far away cow bell, the mellowed sound rising and falling in tender cadences, with a dreamy, swaying melody, as though the bell was somewhere over in the adjoining county, and the cow that wore it was waltzing along over a country road a thousand miles a minute.

VOICES OF THE NIGHT.

MR. JOSKINS is not an old settler in Burlington. He came to the city of magnificent hills from Keokuk, and after looking around, selected a residence out on West Hill, because it was in such a quiet locality, and Mr. Joskins loves peace and seclusion. It is a rural kind of a neighborhood, and all of Mr. Joskins' neighbors keep cows. And every cow wears a bell. And with an instinct worthy of the Peak family, each neighbor had selected a cow bell of a different key and tone from any of the others, in order that he might know the cow of his heart from the other kine of the district. So that Mr. Joskins' nights are filled with music, of a rather wild, barbaric type; and the lone starry hours talk nothing but cow to him, and he has learned so exactly the tones of every bell and the habits of each corresponding cow, that the voices of the night are not an unintelligible jargon to him, but they are full of intelligence, and he understands them. It makes it much easier for Mr. Joskins, who is a very nervous man, than if he had to listen and conjecture and wonder until he was fairly wild, as the rest of us would have to do. As it is, when the first sweet moments of his slumber are broken by a solemn, ponderous, resonant

"Ka-lum, ka-lum, ka-lum!"

Mr. Joskins knows that the widow Barbery's old crumple horn is going down the street looking for an open front gate, and his knowledge is confirmed by a doleful "Ka-lum-pu-lum!" that occurs at regular intervals as old crumple pauses to try each gate as she passes it, for she knows that appearances are deceitful, and that a boy can shut a front gate in such a way as to thoroughly deceive his father and yet leave every catch unfastened. Then when Mr. Joskins is called up from his second doze by a lively serenade of

"To-link, to-lank, lank, lankle-inkle, lankle-inkle-tekinleinkletelink, kink, kink!"

He knows that Mr. Throop's young brindle is in Throstlewaite's garden and that Throstlewaite is sailing around after her in a pair of slippers and a few clothes. And by sitting up in bed Mr. Joskins can hear the things that Mr. Throstlewaite is throwing strike against the side of the house and the woodshed, thud, spat, bang, and the character of the noises tells him whether the missile was a clod, a piece of board, or a brick. And when the wind down the street is fair, it brings with it faint echoes of Mr. Throstlewaite's remarks, which bring into Mr. Joskins' bedroom the odor of bad grammatical construction and wicked wishes and very ill-applied epithets. Then when the final crash and tinkle announce that the cow has bulged through the front fence and got away, and Mr. Joskins turns over to try and get a little sleep, he is not surprised, although he is annoyed, to be aroused by a sepulchral

"Klank, klank, klank!"

Like the chains on the old-fashioned ghost of a murdered man, for he knows it is Throstlewaite's old duck-legged brown cow, going down to the vacant lot on the corner to fight anything that gives milk. And he waits and listens to the "klank, klank, klank," until it reaches the corner and a terrific din and medley of all the cow bells on the street tell him all the skirmishers have been driven in and the action has become general. And from that on till morning, Mr. Joskyns hears the "tinkle-tankle" of the little red cow going down the alley to prospect among the garbage heaps, and the "rankle-tankle, rankle-tankle" of the short-tailed black and white cow skirmishing down the street ahead of an escort of badly assorted dogs, and the "tringle-de-ding, tringle-de-ding, ding, ding," of the muley cow that goes along on the sidewalk, browsing on the lower limbs of the shade trees, and the "klank, klank, klank," of the fighting cow, whose bell is cracked in three places, and incessant "moo-o-*oo*-ah-ha" of the big black cow that has lost the clapper out of her bell and has ever since kept up an unintermittent bellowing to supply its loss. And Mr. Joskins knows all these cows by their bells, and he knows what they are doing and where they are going. And although it has murdered his dreams of a quiet home, yet it has given him an opportunity to cultivate habits of intelligent observation, and it has induced him to register a vow that if he is ever rich enough he will keep nine cows, trained to sleep all day so as to be ready for duty at night, and he will live in the heart of the city with them and make them wear four bells apiece just for the pleasure of his neighbors.

THE DEMAND FOR LIGHT LABOR.

ONE morning, just as the rush of house cleaning days was beginning to abate, a robust tramp called at a house on Barnes Street, and besought the inmates to give him something to eat, averring that he had not tasted food for nine days.

"Why don't you go to work?" asked the lady to whom he preferred his petition.

"Work!" he ejaculated. "Work! And what have I been doing ever since the middle of May but hunting work? Who will give me work? When did I ever refuse work?"

"Well," said the woman, "I guess I can give you some employment. What can you do?"

"Anything!" he shouted, in a kind of delirious joy. "Anything that any man can do. I'm sick for something to fly at. Why, only yesterday I worked all day, carrying water in an old sieve from Flint River and emptying it into the Mississippi, just because I was so tired of having nothing to do, that I had to work at something or I would have gone ravin' crazy. I'll do anything, from cleaning house to building a steamboat. Jest give me work, ma'am, an' you'll never hear me ask for bread agin."

The lady was pleased at the willingness and anxiety of this industrious man to do something, and she led him to the wood pile.

"Here," she said, "you can saw and split this wood, and if you are a good, industrious worker, I will find work for you to do, nearly all Winter."

"Well, now," said the tramp, while a look of disappointment stole over his face, "that's just my luck. Only three days ago I was pullin' a blind cow out of a well for a poor widow woman who had nothin' in the world but that cow to support her, an' I spraint my right wrist till I hain't been able to lift a pound with it sinst. You kin jest put your hand on it now and feel it throb, it's so painful and inflamed. I could jest cry of disappointment, but it's a Bible fact, ma'am, that I couldn't lift that ax above my head ef I died fur it, and I'd jest as lief let you pull my arm out by the roots as to try to pull that saw through a lath. Jest set me at something I kin do, though, if you want to see the dust fly."

"Very well," said the lady, "then you can take these flower beds, which have been very much neglected, and weed them very carefully for me. You can do that with your well hand, but I want you to be very particular with them, and get them very clean, and not injure any of the plants, for they are all very choice and I am very proud of them."

The look of disappointment that had been chased away from the industrious man's face when he saw a prospect of something else to do, came back deeper than ever as the lady described the new job, and when she concluded, he had to remain quiet for a moment before he could control his emotion sufficiently to speak.

"If I ain't the most onfortnit man in Ameriky," he sighed. "I'm jest dyin' for work, crazy to get somethin' to do, and I'm blocked out of work at every turn. I jest love to work among flowers and dig in the ground, but I never dassent do it fur I'm jest blue ruin among the posies. Nobody ever cared to teach me anythin' about flowers and its a Gospel truth, ma'am, I can't tell a violet from a sunflower nor a red rose from a dog fennel.

Last place I tried to git work at, woman of the house set me to work weedin' the garden, an' I worked about a couple of hours, monstrous glad to get work, now you bet, an' I pulled up every last livin' green thing in that yard. Hope I may die ef I didn't. Pulled up all the grass, every blade of it. Fact. Pulled up a vine wuth seventy-five dollars, that had roots reachin' cl'ar under the cellar and into the cistern, and I yanked 'em right up, every fiber of 'em. Woman was so heart broke when she come out and see the yard just as bare as the floor of a brick yard that they had to put her to bed. Bible's truth, they did, ma'am; and I had to work for that house three months for nothin' and find my board, to pay fur the damage I done. Hope to die ef I didn't. Jest gimme suthin' I kin do, I'll show you what work is, but I wouldn't dare to go foolin' around no flowers. You've got a kind heart ma'am, gimme some work; don't send a despairin' man away hungry for work."

"Well," the lady said, "you can beat my carpets for me. They have just been taken up, and you can beat them thoroughly, and by the time they are done, I will have something else ready for you."

The man made a gesture of despair and sat down on the ground, the picture of abject helplessness and disappointed aspirations.

"Look at me now," he exclaimed. "What is goin' to become o' me? Did you ever see a man so down on his luck like me? I tell you ma'am, you must give me somethin' I can do. I wouldn't no more dare for to tech them carpets than nothin' in the world. I'd tear 'em to pieces. I'm a awful hard hitter, an' the last time I beat any carpets was for a woman out at Creston, and I just welted them carpets into strings and carpet rags. I couldn't help it. I can't hold in my strength. I'm too glad to get to work, that's the trouble with me, ma'am, it's a Bible fact. I'll beat them carpets if you say so, but I won't be responsible fur 'em; no makin me work for nothin' fur five or six weeks to pay fur tearin 'em into slits yer know. I'll go at 'em if you'll say the word and take the responsibility, but the fact is, I'm too hard a worker to go foolin' around carpets, that's just what I am."

The lady excused the energetic worker from going at the carpets, but was puzzled what to set him at. Finally she asked him what there was he would like to do and could do, with safety to himself and the work.

"Well, now," he said, "that's considerit in ye. That's real considerit, and I'll take a hold and do something that'll give ye the wuth of your money, and won't give me no chance to destroy nothin' by workin' too hard at it. If ye'll jest kindly fetch me out a rockin' chair, I'll set down in the shade and keep the cows from liftin' the latch of the front gate and gettin' into the yard. An' I'll do it well and only charge you reasonable for it, fur the fact is I'm so dead crazy fur work that it isn't big pay I want so much as a steady job."

And when he was rejected and sent forth, jobless and breakfastless, to wander up and down the cold, unfeeling world in search of work, he cast stones at the house and said, in dejected tones,

"There, now, that's just the way. They call us a bad lot, and say we're lazy and thieves, and won't work, when a feller is just crazy to work and nobody won't give him nary job that he kin do. Won't work! Land alive, they won't give us work, an' when we want to an' try to, they won't let us work. There ain't a man in Ameriky that 'ud work as hard an' as stiddy as I would if they'd gimme a chance."

MASTER BILDERBACK RETURNS TO SCHOOL.

WE remember one day last Summer, during the long vacation, when the *Hawkeye* published a news item stating that a boy named Bilderback had fallen from the seat of a reaping machine, and got cut to pieces, a patient, weary looking, and rather handsome young lady called at the office, and appeared to be very anxious to have that item verified. And when we gave her all possible assurance that everything appearing in that great and good paper, the *Hawkeye*, was necessarily true, she drew a deep sigh of relief, and said she felt actually thankful she wouldn't have that boy to demoralize the school the next term. And then she smiled sweetly, and thanked us for our assuring words, and went away.

Imagine her dismay, then, about the third or fourth day of the fall term, when a terrific cheering in the yard, about ten minutes before school time, drew her to the window, whence looking down, she saw every last solitary lingering boy in that school district dancing and yelling about Master Bilderback, who was dancing higher and yelling louder than any other boy in the caucus. Her heart sank within her; but she braced up and went down stairs to quiet the bedlam, and in five minutes learned the dreadful truth. Master Bilderback had met with a reaping-machine accident, but the papers had reported it incorrectly. He had climbed into the seat the moment his uncle, on whose farm he was spending the vacation, got down. He prodded one of the horses with a pin in the end of a stick, and made the team run away. The terrified animals ran the machine over twenty stumps, and mashed it to pieces; one of the horses ran against a hedge-stake and was killed, and the other jumped off a bridge and broke a leg; Master Bilderback's uncle, chasing after the flying team, had dashed through a hornets' nest, and the sociable little insects came out and sat down on him to talk it over, until his head was swelled as big as a nail-keg, and he couldn't open his eyes for a week; a farm-hand who tried to stop the horses by rushing out in front of them, was hit by the tongue of the reaper and knocked into the middle of an Osage orange hedge, where he stuck for three hours, and lost his voice by screaming, and was scraped to the bone when they finally pulled him out with grappling hooks. And Master Bilderback, the author of all this calamity, was thrown from his seat at the first stump, and fell on a shock of grain, and wasn't jarred or bruised or scratched a particle. And that night, when his aunt handed his blinded uncle the halter-strap, and held Master Bilderback in front of him to receive merited castigation, that graceless young wretch seized his aunt around the neck after the first blow, and wheeling her into his place, held her there, drowning her piercing explanations and pleadings in his own tumultuous but deceitful howlings and roarings, until her back looked like a war map, and the exhausted uncle laid down the strap with the remark that he "guessed that would teach him something." And so the teacher, when she saw master Bilderback at school again, felt weary of life, and sighed to rest her deep in the silent grave—if she could find one that was for rent, and didn't cost more than a quarter's salary.

It being the young man's first day at school that term, he was feeling pretty well, thank you. He had a fight and a half before the bell rang; the half fight being an unsuccessful attempt on his part to pull enough hair out of the back of another boy's head to stuff a mattress, and a highly successful effort on the part of the other boy to claw enough hide off Master Bilderback's nose to make a pair of boots of, at which discouraging stage of the war Master B. drew off his forces, and in a conciliatory spirit informed the audience that he was only in fun. Then, before the opening exercises were half through, three boys in his neighborhood rose up in their seats and with bitter wails began feeling about in their persons for intrusive pins. When the first class filed out to its place, the circling grin told the anxious teacher that Master Bilderback had inked the end of his nose. Then he induced the boy next to him to lean his head back against the wall, just as master B. did; and when that complaisant boy was suddenly called on to rise and recite, he lifted up his voice and wept, for he had pulled a piece of shoemaker's wax and about two ounces of blackboard slating and plaster out of the wall with his back hair. Then he spread out the tail of another boy's coat on the seat, and piled a little pyramid of buckshot on it; and when the boy stood up to recite, he was waltzed out on the floor—bathed in innocent tears, and protesting his innocence—for throwing shot on the floor, and was told he was growing worse than that Bilderback boy. He tied the ends of a girl's sash around the back of her chair, and when she tried to stand up she was almost jerked out of existence. He was sent out with a boy who was taken with the nose-bleed, and found occasion to mix ink in the water he poured on the sufferer's hands; so that, on his return, the sufferer's appearance created such howls of derision that it started the nose-bleed afresh, and threw the teacher into hysterics. He enticed a gaunt hound into the girls' side of the yard, and clapping a patent clothes-pin on one of its pendant ears, raised the alarm of "mad dog!" and laughed till he choked to see the howling animal rushing around trying to paw the clothes-pin off; while the shrieking girls wrecked themselves in desperate and frequently successful attempts to climb over an eight foot fence. He put a pinching-bug as big as a postage-stamp down a boy's back. He got a long slate-pencil crossways in his mouth, and it nearly poked through his cheeks before they could break it and get it out. He tossed a big apple, hard as a rock, out of the third story window at random, and it struck an old lady in the eye as she was walking along admiring the building; and she came up and gave the poor tortured teacher a piece of her mind as long as the dog days. He dropped into the water-bucket a lot of oxalic acid, that had been brought to take some ink splotches out of the floor, and came within one of poisoning the whole school before they found it out; and, finally, he poked a bean so far up his nose that they thought it was coming out of his eye; and the happy teacher dismissed him, thoroughly frightened for the first time in his eventful life, and he ran like a race-horse all the way home, crying louder at every step, and never stopped to call a name or throw a stone.

ODE TO AUTUMN.

AFTER TENNYSON.

THE grasshopper creaks in the leafy gloom,
    And the bumble-bee bumbleth the live long day;
But the mathering nurks in the bran new broom,
    And hushed is the sound of the buzz saw's play.

Oh, it's little he thinks of the cold mince pie,
    And it's little he seeks of the raw ice cream;
For the dying old year with its tremulous sigh,
    Shall waken the lingering loon from his dream.

Oh, list! For the cricket, now far, now near,
    Full shrillfully singeth his roundelay;
While the negligent noodle his noisy cheer
    Screeps where the doodle bug eats the hay.

Oh, the buzz saw so buzzily buzzeth the stick
    And bumbling the bumble-bee bumbleth his tune
While the cricket cricks crickingly down at the creek
    And the noodle noods noodingly, "Ha! It is noon!"

The dog fennel sighs, "She is here! she is here!"
    And the smart weed says dreamily, "Give us a rest!"
The hop vine breathes tenderly, "Give us a beer!"
    While the jimson weed hollers, "Oh, pull down your vest!"

Oh, Anna Maria, why don't you come home?
    For the clock in the steeple strikes seven or eight;
Way down in the murky mazourka the gloam
    Is gloaming its gloamingest gloam on the gate.

THE SORROWS OF THE POOR.

IT was a poor, dejected looking tramp, who came limping wearily into town on the Fort Madison road, and, with the instinct of his class, made his way directly toward Main Street, where stimulants and company are most numerous. He had a very tired look, and his poorly shod feet seemed to weigh a ton a piece. The sun had burned his face to a deeper brown than even the knotty hands that swung listlessly at his side. He did not even carry the inevitable stick; and the little bundle, without which the tramp's outfit is never complete, although heaven only knows what is in it, was swung from his shoulders by a heavy twine string, like a rude knapsack. No man is alive now that wore clothes when the hat he wore was made. It was a fearful and wonderful hat, and attracted more attention than anything he had on or about him. He limped along Main Street from Locust, diving into private houses in occasional forays for bread, which were generally successful, for his poor, dejected, sorrowful looking face threw a great deal of silent eloquence into his pleading, and the women could not bear to send the low-voiced man away hungry. These forays were varied by occasional dives into places of refreshment, where he vainly pleaded for a small allowance of ardent spirits for a sick man; the general result being that he was courteously refused and gently but firmly kicked out by the urbane barkeeper, who saw too many of him every day to be much moved. The poor fellow limped along till he got a little above Division

Street, when he had to pass a knot of young men, and one of them, a smart looking young chap, in a very gamey costume, and carrying a broad pair of shoulders and a bullet head, surmounted with a silver-gray plug hat, hung on his right ear, sang out,

"Oh, shoot the hat!"

The poor tramp only looked more dejected than ever, if possible, and shook his head meekly and sorrowfully, and limped on. But the young sport shouted after him:

"Come back, young fellow, and see how you'll trade hats!"

The outcast paused and half turned, and said in mournful tones:

"Don't make game of a onfortnit man, young gents. I'm poor and I'm sick, but I've the feelin's of a man, an' I kin feel it when I'm made game of. If you could give me a job of work, now —"

A chorus of laughter greeted the suggestion, and the smartest young man repeated his challenge to trade hats, and finally induced the mendicant to limp back.

"Take off your hat," said the young man of Burlington, "and let's see whose make it is. If it isn't Stetson's, I won't trade."

"Oh, that's Stetson's," chorused the crowd. "He wouldn't wear anything but a first-class hat."

But the tramp replied, trying to limp away from the circle that was closing around him.

"Indeed, young gents, don't be hard on a onfortnit man. I don't believe I could git that hat off'n my head; I don't indeed. I haint had it off fur mor'n two months, indeed I haint. I don't believe I kin git it off at all. Please let me go on."

But the unfeeling young men crowded around him more closely and insisted that the hat should come off, and the smartest young man in company said he'd pull it off for him.

"Indeed, young gent," replied the tramp, apologetically, "I don't believe you could git it off. It's been on so long I don't believe you kin git it off; I don't really."

The young man advanced and made a motion to jerk off the hat, but the tramp limped back and threw up his hands with a clumsy frightened gesture.

"Come young gents," he whined, "don't play games on a poor fellow as is lookin' for the county hospital. I tell ye, young gents, I'm a sick man, I am. I'm on the tramp when I ought to be in bed. I can't hardly stand, and I haint got the strength to be fooled with. Be easy on a poor ——"

But the sporting young man cut him off with "Oh, give us a rest and take off that hat." And then he made a pass at the poor sick man's hat, but his hand met the poor, sick tramp's elbow instead. And then the poor man lifted one of his hands about as high as a derrick, and the next instant the silver-gray plug hat was crowded so far down on the young man's shoulders that the points of the dog's eared collar were sticking up through the crown of it. And then the poor sick man tried his other hand, and part of the crowd started off to help pick the young man out of a show window where he was standing on his head, while the rest of the congregation was trying its level best to get out of the way of the poor sick tramp, who was feeling about him in a vague, restless sort of way that made the street lamps rattle every time he found anybody. Long before any one could interfere the convention had adjourned *sine die*, and the poor tramp, limping on his way, the very personification of wretchedness, sighed as he remarked apologetically to the spectators:

"I tell you, gents, I'm a sick man; I'm too sick to feel like foolin'; I'm jest so sick that when I go gropin' around for somethin' to lean up agin I can't tell a man from a hitchin' post; I can't actually, and when I rub agin anybody, nobody hadn't ought to feel hard at me. I'm sick, that's wha. I am."

MR. GEROLMAN LOSES HIS DOG.

MR. GEROLMAN stood on the front porch of his comfortable home on West Hill, one morning looking out at the drizzling rain in any thing but a comfortable frame of mind. He looked up and down the yard, and then he raised his umbrella and went to the gate and looked up and down the street. Then he whistled in a very shrill manner three or four times, and listened as though he was expecting a response. If he was, he was disappointed, for there was no response save the pattering of the rain on his umbrella, and he frowned heavily as he returned to the porch, from which sheltered post of observation he gloomily surveyed the dispiriting weather.

"Dag gone the dag gone brute," he muttered savagely, "if ever I keep another dog again, I hope it will eat me up."

And then he whistled again. And again there was no response. It was evident that Mr. Gerolman had lost his dog, a beautiful ashes of roses hound with seal brown spots and soft satin-finish ears. He was a valuable dog, and this was the third time he had been lost, and Mr.

Gerolman was rapidly losing his temper as completely as he had lost his dog. He lifted his voice and called aloud:

"H'yuh-h-h Ponto! h'yuh Ponto! h'yuhp onto! h'yup onto, h'yup onto h'yuponto, h'yuponto! h'yup, h'yup, h'yup!"

As he ceased calling, and looked anxiously about for some indications of a dog, the front door opened and a woman's face, shaded with a tinge of womanly anxiety and fastened to Mrs. Gerolman's head, looked out.

"The children call him Hector," a low sweet voice said for the wistful, pretty face; but the bereaved master of the absent dog was in no humor to be charmed by a beautiful face and a flute-like voice.

"By George," he said, striding out into the rain and purposely leaving his umbrella on the porch to make his wife feel bad, "it's no wonder the dog gets lost, when he has so dod binged many names that he don't know himself. By Jacks, when I give eleven dollars for a dog, I want the privilege of naming him, and the next person about this house that tries to fasten an old pagan, Indian, blasphemous name on a dog of mine, will hear from me about it; now that's all."

And then he inflated his lungs and yelled like a scalp hunter.

"Here, Hector! here, Hector! here rector, hyur, rector, hyur rec, h'yurrec, k'yurrec, k'yurrec, k'yurrec! Godfrey's cordial, where's that dog gone to? H'yuponto, h'yupont! h'yuh, h'yuh, h'yuh! I hope he's poisoned—h'yurrector! By George, I do; h'yuh Ponto, good dog, Ponty, Ponty, Ponty, h'yuh Pont! I'd give fifty dollars if some one had strychnined the nasty, worthless, lop-eared cur; hyurrec, k'yurrec! By granny, I'll kill him when he comes home, if I don't I hope to die; h'yuh Ponto, h'yuh Ponto, *h'yuh* Hec!!

And as he turned back to the porch the door again opened and the tremulous voice sweetly asked :

"Can't you find him?"

"Naw!!!" roared the exasperated dog-hunter, and the door closed very precipitately and was opened no more during the session.

"Here, Ponto!" roared Mr. Gerolman, from his position on the porch, "Here, Hector!" And then he whistled until his head swam and his throat was so dry you could light a match in it. "Here, Ponto! Blast the dog. I suppose he's twenty-five miles from here. Hector! What are you lookin' at, you gimlet-eyed old Bedlamite?" he savagely growled, apostrophizing a sweet-faced old lady with silky white hair, who had just looked out of her window to see where the fire was, or who was being murdered. "Here, Ponto! here Ponto! Good doggie, nice old Pontie, nice old Heckie dog — Oh-h-h," he snarled, dancing up and down on the porch in an ecstasy of rage and impatience, "I'd like to tramp the ribs out of the long-legged worthless old garbage-eater ; *here, Ponto, here !*".

To his amazement he heard a canine yawn, a long-drawn, weary kind of a whine, as of a dog who was bored to death with the dismal weather ; then there was a scraping sound, and the dog, creeping out from under the porch, from under his very feet, looked vacantly around as though he wasn't quite sure but what he had heard some one calling him, and then catching sight of his master, sat down and thumped on the ground with his tail, smiled pleasantly, and asked as plainly as ever dog asked in the world,

"Were you wanting me?"

Mr. Gerolman, for one brief instant, gasped for breath. Then he pulled his hat down tight on his head, snatched up his umbrella with a convulsive grasp and yelled "Come 'ere!" in such a terrific roar that the white-haired old lady across the way fell back in a fit, and the dog, surmising that all was not well, briefly remarked that he had an engagement to meet somebody about fifty-eight feet under the house, and shot under the porch like a shooting dog-star. Mr. Gerolman made a dash to intercept him, but stumbled over a flower stand and plunged through a honey-suckle trellis, off the porch, and down into a raging volcano of moss-rose bush, straw, black dirt, shattered umbrella ribs, and a ubiquitous hat, while far under the house, deep in the cavernous darkness, came the mocking laugh of an ashes of roses dog with seal brown spots, accompanied by the taunting remark, as nearly as Mr. Gerolman could understand the dog,

"Who hit him? Which way did he go?"

A RAINY DAY IDYL.

HOW many times do I love you, dear?
    That is beyond my number's skill;
Dearer your smiles than aught else here,
    Unless it might be my amberill.

Sweet is the glance of your soft brown eyes,
    Veiled when the silken fringes fall;
Verse can not tell how much I prize
    Thee, and my constant umbersoll.

As the shadowy years speed on and by
    Over our lives like a magic spell;
Ever to thee I'll fondly fly,
    And shelter you under my amberell.

Time's wings are swifter than thought, my dear,
    When my heart is cheered by your sunny smile;
Never an hour is sad or drear,
    When I know where to look for my old umbrile.

Even when life its sands have run
    And my leaf has fallen sere and yellow,
Little I'll heed either storm or sun
    Safe 'neath the roof of my dear umbrellow.

Ha! But the world is wrapped in gloom—
    Storm, rain and tempest round me roll;
Show me the man! Oh, give me room!
    Some wretch has stolen my umbersole.

SINGULAR TRANSFORMATION.

IT appears that during vacation Master Bilderback, having fallen behind in his studies last term, was compelled by his ma to read his school books certain hours of the day, until he escaped that tyranny by going out to his uncle Keyser's farm. In order to make his study as light as possible, this ingenious boy had dissected, or rather skinned his books, and neatly inserted in their covers certain works of the most thrilling character known in modern literature. When he came back from the farm this transformation business had entirely escaped his memory, and it was not even recalled when he heard his mother tell the teacher, who called in the hopes of learning that that bean had sprouted and grown into his brain and would probably terminate fatally, that he was the best boy to study during vacation she ever saw, and would pore for hours over his books, and even seem anxious to get at them. Master Bilderback had forgotten all about it, and only thought it was some of his mother's foolishness, of which he believed her to possess great store. As for the bean, the amazed teacher learned that it never was discovered, it never came out and it never hurt him a particle, and had just naturally ceased to be. And the teacher went sadly away, moralizing over this case, and that of little Ezra Simpson, the best and most obedient, and most studious, and quietest, and most lovable boy in her school who, one day stumbled and ran the end of a slate pencil into his nose and died the next day. And long, long after she had got out of sight of Bilderback's house, she could hear the hopeful Master Bilderback shouting, "Shoot that hat!" and "Pull down your vest!" to gentlemen driving, with their families or sweethearts, past the mansion. Dreadful boy, she thought, he will surely come to some end, some day.

Well, it was only the next day when the reading class was called, Master Bilderback took his place for the first time. The boy next to him had no book, and as he was called first, he just took Master Bilderback's, who turned to look on with the boy on the other side. The class was reading the selection from "Old Curiosity Shop," and a girl had just finished reading the tender paragraphs, "She was dead. Dear, gentle, patient, noble Nell was dead. Her little bird — a poor slight thing the pressure of a finger would have crushed — was stirring nimbly in its cage, and the strong heart of its child-mistress was mute and motionless forever."

Imagine the feeling of the teacher when the boy who got up with Master Bilderback's reader went on:

"'Black fiend of the nethermost gloom, down to thy craven soul thou liest,' exclaimed Manfred, the Avenger, drawing his rapier, 'Draw, malignant hound, and die!'"

"'Down, perjured fool! Villain and double-dyed traitor, down with thy caitiff face in the dust. Dare'st thou defy me? Beast with a pig's head, thy doom is sealed!' exclaimed the Mystic Knight, throwing up his visor. 'Dost know me now? I am the Mad Muncher of the Bazzarooks!'"

"Manfred, the Avenger, dropped his blade at this terrible name, and — "

The teacher caught her breath and stopped the boy. In tones of forced calmness she asked what he was reading, and he told her it was Bilderback's reader, and looked in amazement at the innocent scholastic back

and the villainous interior, which was nothing less than
"The Blood on the Ceiling; or, the Death Track of the
Black Snoozer." After requesting Master Bilderback to
remain after school and explain, she called the next
class, one in Arithmetic.

"Fisher," she said, "you may read and analyze the
fourth problem."

And Fisher, who was Bilderback's next seat mate, and
had taken that young man's book by mistake, rose and
read,

>"The purtiest little baby, oh!
>   That ever I did see, oh!
>   They gave it paregoric, oh!
>   And sent it up to glory, oh!
>
>Fillacy, follacy, my black hen,
>She lays eggs for gentlemen;
>Sometimes ———"

"In mercy's name," shrieked the poor teacher, "what
have you got there?" And investigation revealed the
rather humiliating fact that when Mrs. Bilderback thought
her young son was poring over mathematical problems,
he was learning choice vocal selections out of "The Pull-
Back Songster and Ethiopian Glee Book."

When the grammar class was called, the teacher asked
some one to bring her a book. Master Bilderback was
the nearest, and he handed her his, innocently enough,
for he had been busy with more projects than we could
tell about in a week, since the arithmetic class had gone
down. The teacher was tired and listless with that
wearing worry and torture which is only found in the
school room, and she listlessly and mechanically opened
the book at the place, and said,

"Mamie, how would you analyze and parse this sentence," and casting her eyes on the page, she read:

"Ofer you dond vas got some glothes on, go on dark blaces, off you blease. Ain'd it?"

She laid down the book, and burst into hysterical tears, unable even to exert her authority to restrain the mirth that burst out all over the school room. She dismissed the school, and had not sufficient energy to punish even Master Bilderback, and that young gentleman only carried home a note to his father, requesting that citizen and tax payer to reorganize his son's school library before he sent him back to that palladium of our country's liberties, the public school.

SUBURBAN SOLITUDE.

MR. DRESSELDORF, who can't endure any noise since he sold his clarionet, has just moved into the sweetest little cottage out on South Hill, and here, he told Mrs. Dresseldorf, he would rest and spend his declining days under his own vine and fig tree, with no one to molest or make him afraid. "We have a few neighbors," he said, the afternoon they got comfortably and cozily settled; "Mr. Blodgers, next door, keeps a cow, and will supply us with an abundance of pure, fresh milk; Mr. Whackem, not far away, is an honest teamster, I understand, and will be convenient when we want a little hauling done from town; Mr. Sturvesant, just down the street, has a splendid dog that he says keeps an eye on the entire neighborhood, and I think we will live pleasantly and happily here." And Mr. Dresseldorf sat on the porch and solemnly contemplated the hammer

SUBURBAN SOLITUDE.

bruises and the tack holes and nail marks and abrasions of stove legs and the pinches of obstinate stove-pipe joints on his hands, and wondered if Providence would be merciful to him and strike the house with lightning before next moving day rolled round. And with this pleasant and soothing thought, Mr. Dresseldorf fell into a trance of ecstatic content, delighted with the holy quiet of the scene and the neighborhood, with Perkins' meadow in the serene distance, the sun sinking out of sight, throwing long bars of burnished gold through a clump of forest trees off to the west, and the summer air vibrating with the hushed hum of insect life that floated to the Dresseldorf porch. So quiet, so full of peace, so fraught with meditation and retrospective self-communings was the scene, that Mr. Dresseldorf wondered if he could endure so much happiness every evening. Just then,

"Whoa! Who-oh-oh-oh-h!!" Whack! whack! whack! "Whoa! ye son of a thief! Head him, Bill! Whoa!"

"What under the canopy—" began the startled and astonished Mr. Dresseldorf; but just then he saw a gray mule with a paint-brush tail flying down the road, head and tail up, and its heels making vicious offers at every animated object that came within range. It was plain that one of Mr. Whackem's mules had got away, as the honest teamster and his three sons were seen skirmishing down the street in hot pursuit. Mr. Dresseldorf groaned as the animal was cornered, and his picture of peaceful solitude fled.

"Whoa! Don't throw at him! Whoa now!" "Head him off, dad!" "Git down the road furder, Bill!" "Whoa, whoa, now!" "Hee haw! hee haw! hee haw!" "Hold on, Tom!" "Hurry up!" "Look out for his heels!" "Now ketch him!" Chorus, "Whoa! whoa!

whoa!" "Hee haw, hee haw, hee haw!" "Whoop!" "Hi!" "Whoop-pee!" "Dog gone the diddledy dog gone mule to thunder!"

Mr. Dresseldorf groaned as the cavalcade went storming and crashing and hallooing down the street. "Thank heaven they're gone," he said.

"Sook-kee! sook-kee! sook-kee!"

It sounded like a calliope, only it was too far from the river; but it brought the man of peace to his feet all the same.

"Sook-kee! sook-kee! Suke! suke! seuke!"

It was Mr. Blodgers calling his cow, and as he emphasized the summons by pounding on the bottom of a tin pail with the leg of a milking stool, Mr. Dresseldorf moaned and buried his nervous hands in his hair and tried to pull the top of his head off. While Mr. Blodgers was yelling and pounding, however, a hurricane came tearing up the road—a whirlwind of dust and whoops and paint-brush tails and horns and sticks—and from this awful confusion shot forth yells and brays and bawls and the discordant clangor of a cow bell. Mr. Blodgers ran out into the road, while Mr. Dresseldorf fell on his knees and crammed his fingers in his ears.

"What'n thunder's chasin' that keow, I'd like to know?" queried Mr. Blodgers; then, raising his voice, "Hey! Hi! I say! Whoop!" And he was tossed over Mr. Dresseldorf's fence into a garden urn, and the hurricane passed on up the street, leaving Mr. Blodgers howling like a dervish, and beseeching the demoralized Dresseldorf to bring him some arnica and whisky. The wretched man rose to minister to the sufferings of his neighbor, and got the two needful medicines; but just as he came out of the house the programme changed again. Mr. Sturvesant's dog, keeping an eye upon the entire neighborhood, had met the whirlwind above mentioned up at the next corner, and had promptly turned it back. This unexpected retrograde movement placed Mr. Whackem, the three Masters Whackem, and a small mob of juvenile volunteers who had been picked up at one point of the chase and another to help catch the mule, directly in the path of the charging mule and Mr. Blodgers' cow. An immediate adjournment was at once moved and carried, and the entire community lit out for the nearest place of refuge; but Mr. Sturvesant's dog kept up the chase with such vigor that the whole vociferous, yelling, braying, bawling, barking mass came bulging through Dresseldorf's front fence, upsetting the owner of the property and carrying him and Mr. Blodgers out into the alley, where the mass fell apart, the animals running to their respective stables, and the "human warious" seeking their homes as soon as they found each other. Mr. Dresseldorf advertised his place for sale the next morning. He is fond of the quiet life of a suburban residence, he says, but it is a little too far from business.

A BURLINGTON ADDER.

BURLINGTON rejoices in a mathematical prodigy. Indeed it is a perfect wonder, and our educational men and teachers used to find a great deal of instruction and some pleasure in interviewing the child, a bright boy of nine years. His name is Alfred J. Talbot, and his parents live at No. 1223 North Main Street. The boy's health is rather delicate, so that he has not been sent to school a great deal; but he can perform arithmetical feats that remind one of the stories told about Zerah Colburn. He was always bright, and possesses a remarkable memory. In company with two or three members of the school board, we went to the home of the prodigy for an interview. He was marvelously ready with answers to every question. Our easy starters, such as, "Add 6 and 3, and 7 and 8, and 2 and 9 and 5," were answered like a flash, and correctly every time. Then when we got the little fellow at his ease, one of the Directors took him in hand. He said:

"Three times 11, plus 9, minus 17, divided by 3, plus 1, multiplied by 3, less 3, add 7, is how many?"

"Nine," shouted the boy, almost before the last word was spoken; and the School Inspectors and the newspaper man looked at each other in blank amazement. Then the other Inspector tried it:

"Multiply 5 by 13, add 19, subtract 39, divide by 2, add 7, multiply by 9, add 15, divide by 7, add 8, multiply by 3, less 13, add 9, multiply by 7, divide by 9, add 13, divide by 11—how many?"

"Ninety-six!" fairly yelled the delighted boy, clap-

A BURLINGTON ADDER.

ping his hands with merriment at the amazement which crowned the countenances of his interviewers, and the Inspectors turned to the paper man and said, "Take him, Mr. *Hawkeye*."

Then we did our best to throw the boy. As fast as we could speak, and without punctuation, we rattled off this:

"Add 24 to 17½ multiply by 9½ divide by ½ add 33 per cent. multiply by 16 extract square root add 9 divide by 3-5 of 7-8 add 119 divide by 77½ times 44¾ square the quotient and multiply by 17⅔ add 77 and divide by 33 how ma——"

But before we could say the last syllable the boy fairly screamed,

"127⅞! Ask me a hard one!"

We had seen enough, and with feelings amounting almost to awe we left this wonderful boy. We talked about his marvelous powers all the way down. Finally it happened to occur to one of the Inspectors to ask the other Inspector,

"Did you follow my example through to notice whether the boy answered it correctly?"

The tone of amazement gradually passed away from the Inspector's face, as he faintly gasped,

"N-n-no, not exactly, did you?"

Then the first Inspector ceased to look mystified and began to look very much like Mr. Skinner did when he got the Nebraska fruit, and they both turned to the gentleman who represented the literary department of the expedition and said lugubriously,

"Did you?"

But he only said:

"The Burlington and Northwestern narrow-gauge railroad will be owned, not by eastern capitalists, but by the people through whose country it passes."

MISAPPLIED SCIENCE.

IT was only a few years ago the New York *Journal of Information* published the statement that a man in New Hampshire, who had been unable to speak for five years, went to sleep, one night, with a quid of tobacco in his mouth, and awoke the next morning with his voice perfectly strong and smooth and steady. Old Mr. Jarvis, who lives out on Vine Street, is sorely afflicted with an impediment in his speech, and often says he would give a hundred dollars if he could only " t - t - t - t - taw - taw-talk f - f - f - f -fast enough t - t - to t - t - tell a gug-gug - gug - grocer what he w - w - wants bub - bub - bub - before he gug - gug - gets it measured out." He takes the *Journal*, and had taken it for twenty - three years, and he firmly believed every thing he ever read in it; Sylvanus Cobb's stories, Mr. Parton's Lives of Eminent Americans, the answers to correspondents — Mr. Jarvis had taken them all in and believed every word. He thought that probably this quid-of-tobacco treatment might help his voice a little, and he resolved to give it a good trial any how. The first trouble was that he didn't chew, and Mrs. Jarvis would never allow a bit of tobacco about the house. But he begged a big " chaw " of navy, and when he went to bed he tucked it snugly away in his cheek, and prepared to sleep in hope. He had his misgivings, and they grew in number and strength as the quid began to assert itself, and be sociable, and assimilate itself with its surroundings. Mrs. Jarvis asked him if he fastened the front gate.

"Um," said Mr. Jarvis, meaning that he had.

"And are you sure you locked the front door?" queried his restless spouse.

"Um," replied Mr. Jarvis, meaning that he had not, for he was by this time in no condition to open his mouth.

"Hey?" she replied.

"Um," persisted Mr. Jarvis.

"What?" she demanded.

"Um-m-m!" protested Mr. Jarvis.

"Well," said she, "you can't make me believe you are that near asleep this soon."

"Um-m-m!" said Mr. Jarvis; meaning that he would get up and bounce her out of that front door if she didn't hold her clack.

Presently she sat up in bed. Sniff, sniff! "John Jarvis," she exclaimed, "if I don't smell tobacco in this house, I'm a sinful woman. Don't you smell it?"

"'M," replied Mr. Jarvis; which by interpretation is, that he didn't smell any thing and was going to sleep.

"It's in this very room," she persisted, excitedly.

"Um," said Mr. Jarvis, meaning that she must be crazy.

"It's under the bed!" she screamed. "There's a burglar under the bed! Oh, help! fire! police! John Jarvis!!!" And she smote Mr. Jarvis a furious pelt in the stomach to waken him up.

It was a terrific thump, and its first effect was to knock all the atmosphere out of Mr. Jarvis's lungs so far that he could only recover his breath by a violent gasp, which first carried the quid of tobacco and all the nicotine preparation that it had been steadily distilling down his throat, and was immediately succeeded by a tremendous cough, as he struggled to rise up in bed, which shot the quid squarely into the eye of the shrieking Mrs. Jarvis.

"Murder! murder!" she screamed, "I'm stabbed! I'm stabbed!"

And John Jarvis choked and coughed and spit and coughed and choked and clutched Mrs. Jarvis by the throat and tried to choke off her noise, but he grew so "ill" that he couldn't hold his grip, and Mrs. Jarvis, the moment her throat was released from his trembling pressure, rose from the half-strangled gurgles to the sublimity of double-edged screams, and made Rome howl with melody. And the neighbors broke into the house and found a bed-room that looked and smelled like a jury-room or a street car, with the sickest man they ever saw lying with his head over the side of the bed, groaning at the rate of a mile a minute, and the worst frightened woman since the flood sitting up beside him, screaming faster than he groaned, while one of her eyes was plastered up with a black quid of tobacco. And that is the way Mr. Jarvis came to stop his *Journal*. He denounces it as the most infamous, mendacious, pestilent sheet that ever disgraced American journalism.

WIDE AWAKE.

ONE day Mr. Bellamy, of Pond Street, read in a religious paper the following paragraph:

> Many very good people are annoyed by sleepiness in church. The following remedy is recommended: Lift the foot seven inches from the floor, and hold it in suspense without support for the limb, and repeat the remedy if the attack returns.

Now, Mr. Bellamy is a very good man, and he is subject to that very annoyance, which in his case amounts to a positive affliction. So he cut that paragraph out, in accordance with the appended instruction, and pasted it in his hat, and was rejoiced in his inmost soul to think that he had found a relief from his annoyance. He hoped that Deacon Ashbury, who had frowned at him so often and so dreadfully for nodding, hadn't seen the paragraph, for the deacon sometimes slept under the preached word, and Mr. Bellamy wanted to get even with him. And Mr. Driscoll, who used to sit in the choir, and cover his own sleepiness and divert attention from his own heavy eyes by laughing in a most irreverent and indecorous manner at Mr. Bellamy's sleepy visage and struggling eyes and head — how the good man did want to get it on Driscoll. So he chuckled and hugged his treasure, so to speak, in his mind. He was so confident that he had found the panacea for his trouble that he went to the minister and told him what a burden his drowsiness had been to him, but that he had made up his mind now to shake it off, and to continue to keep it off, and he was certain that he had sufficient strength of mind and force of will to overcome the habit. And the minister was so pleased, and commended Mr. Bellamy so warmly, and said so earnestly that he wished he had one hundred such men in his congregation, that Mr. Bellamy was so elated and happy and confident that he could hardly wait for Sunday to come to try his new method of averting drowsiness.

Sunday came, however, and soon enough too, for it was Saturday afternoon plumb, chick, chock full of men with bills, over-due notes, trifling accounts, little balances, pay-roll, rent, narrow-gauge subscription, political assessments and one little thing and another, almost before Mr. Bellamy knew it, although it hadn't been there half an hour before he had some suspicion of it, and was soon very confident of it. Sunday morning found the good man in his accustomed place, devout and drowsy as ever. The church was very comfortably filled with an attentive congregation, and Mr. Bellamy was soon cornered up in one end of the pew, and the strange young lady who sat next him was attended by a very small white dog, that looked like a roll of cotton batting with red eyes and a black nose. The opening exercises passed off without incident, but the minister hadn't got to secondly when Mr. Bellamy suddenly roused himself with a start from a doze into which he was dropping. His heart fairly stood still as he thought how nearly he had forgotten his recipe. He feared to attract any attention to himself lest his precious method should be discovered, and slowly lifted his left foot from the foot stool and held it about seven inches in the air. As he raised his foot the strange young lady shrunk away from him in evident alarm. This annoyed Mr. Bellamy and disconcerted him so that he was on the point of lowering his foot and whispering an explanation when the dog, which had been quietly sleeping by the footstool opened its eyes, and seeing the uplifted foot slowly descending in its direction, hastily scrambled to its feet and backed away, barking and yelping terrifically. The young lady, now thoroughly alarmed, jerked her feet from off the footstool, which immediately flew up under the weight of Mr. Bellamy's other foot, and the dog, excited by this additional catastrophe, fairly barked itself into convulsions. Deacon Ashbury, awakened by the racket, came tiptoeing and frowning down the aisle, bending his shaggy brows upon Mr. Bellamy, who actually believed that if he got much hotter he would break out in flames, that not even the beaded perspiration that was standing out on his scarlet face, could extinguish. The young lady rose to leave the pew, Mr. Bellamy rose to explain, and as he did so, she was quite convinced of what she had before been suspicious, that he was crazy. She backed out of the pew and sought Deacon Ashbury's protection. Mr. Bellamy attempted to whisper an explanation to the deacon, but that austere official motioned him back into his seat, and as the minister paused until the interruption should cease, said in a severe undertone that was heard all over the church.

"You've been dreaming again, Brother Bellamy."

Mr. Bellamy sank into his seat, quite covered with confusion as with a couple of garments and a bed quilt, and his distress was greatly aggravated when he looked up into the choir and saw Driscoll, convulsed with merriment, stuffing his handkerchief into his mouth, and shaking with suppressed laughter.

After service Mr. Bellamy, who was, all through the service, the center of attraction for the entire congregation, waited for his pastor, and made one more effort to explain his unfortunate escapade. But the minister, whose sermon had been quite spoiled by the affair, waved him to silence and said, quite coldly:

"Never mind, Brother Bellamy; don't apologize; you meant very well, I dare say, but if you make so much disturbance when you are awake, I believe I would prefer to have you sleep quietly through every sermon I preach."

Mr. Bellamy has since stopped his church paper, and transferred his subscription to the *Hawkeye*, saying that if he could just find the wretch who set stumbling blocks and snares in the columns of the religious press for the feet of weak believers, he could die happy.

THE ARTLESS PRATTLE OF CHILDHOOD.

WE always did pity a man who does not love children. There is something morally wrong with such a man. If his tenderest sympathies are not awakened by their innocent prattle, if his heart does not echo their merry laughter, if his whole nature does not reach out in ardent longings after their pure thoughts and unselfish impulses, he is a sour, crusty, crabbed old stick, and the world full of children has no use for him. In every age and clime, the best and noblest men loved children. Even wicked men have a tender spot left in their hardened hearts for little children. The great men of the earth love them. Dogs love them. Kamehamekemokimodahroah, the King of the Cannibal islands, loves them. Rare, and no gravy. Ah yes, we all love children.

And what a pleasure it is to talk with them. Who can chatter with a bright-eyed, rosy-cheeked, quick-witted little darling, anywhere from three to five years, and not appreciate the pride which swells a mother's breast, when she sees her little ones admired. Ah, yes, to be sure.

One day, ah can we ever cease to remember that dreamy, idle, Summer afternoon — a lady friend who was down in the city on a shopping excursion, came into the sanctum with her little son, a dear little tid-toddler of five bright Summers, and begged us to amuse him while she pursued the duties which called her down town. Such a bright boy; so delightful it was to talk to him. We can never forget the blissful half hour we spent booking that prodigy up in his centennial history.

"Now listen, Clary," we said — his name is Clarence Fitzherbert Alencon de Marchemont Caruthers — "and learn about George Washington."

"Who's he?" inquired Clarence, etc.

"Listen," we said, "he was the father of his country."

"Whose country?"

"Ours; yours and mine; the confederated union of the American people, cemented with the life blood of the men of '76, poured out upon the altars of our country as the dearest libation to liberty that her votaries can offer."

"Who did?" asked Clarence.

There is a peculiar tact in talking to children that very few people possess. Now most people would have grown impatient and lost their temper when little Clarence asked so many irrelevant questions, but we did not. We knew that, however careless he might appear at first, we could soon interest him in the story and he would be all eyes and ears. So we smiled sweetly, — that same sweet smile which you may have noticed on our photographs, just the faintest ripple of a smile breaking across the face like a ray of sunlight, and checked by lines of tender sadness, just before the two ends of it pass each other at the back of the neck.

And so, smiling, we went on,

"Well, one day George's father —— "

"George who?" asked Clarence.

"George Washington. He was a little boy then, just like you. One day his father —— "

"Whose father?" demanded Clarence, with an encouraging expression of interest.

"George Washington's, this great man we were telling you of. One day George Washington's father gave him a little hatchet for a —— "

"Gave who a little hatchet?" the dear child interrupted with a gleam of bewitching intelligence. Most men would have betrayed signs of impatience, but we didn't. We know how to talk to children. So we went on:

"George Washington. His —— "

"Who give him the little hatchet?"

"His father. And his father —— "

"Whose father?"

"George Washington's."

"Oh!"

"Yes, George Washington. And his father told him —— "

"Told who?"

"Told George."

"Oh, yes, George."

And we went on, just as patient and as pleasant as you could imagine. We took up the story right where the boy interrupted, for we could see that he was just crazy to hear the end of it. We said:

"And he told him that —— "

"Who told him what?" Clarence broke in.

"Why, George's father told George."

"What did he tell him?"

"Why, that's just what I am going to tell you. He told him —— "

"Who told him?"

"George's father. He —— "

"What for?"

"Why, so he wouldn't do what he told him not to do. He told him —— '

"George told him?" queried Clarence.

"No, his father told George —— "

"Oh!"

"Yes; told him that he must be careful with the hatchet —— "

"Who must be careful?"

"George must."

"Oh!"

"Yes; must be careful with the hatchet —— "

"What hatchet?"

"Why, George's."

"Oh!"

"Yes; with the hatchet, and not cut himself with it, or drop it in the cistern, or leave it out in the grass all night. So George went round cutting every thing he could reach with his hatchet. And at last he came to a splendid apple tree, his father's favorite, and cut it down, and —— "

"Who cut it down?"

"George did."

"Oh!"

" —— but his father came home and saw it the first thing, and —— "

"Saw the hatchet?"

"No; saw the apple tree. And he said, 'Who has cut down my favorite apple tree?'"

"What apple tree?"

"George's father's. And everybody said they didn't know any thing about it, and —— "

"Any thing about what?"

"The apple tree."

"Oh!"

"—— and George came up and heard them talking about it —— "

"Heard who talking about it?"

"Heard his father and the men."

"What was they talking about?"

"About this apple tree."

"What apple tree?"

"The favorite apple tree that George cut down."

"George who?"

"George Washington."

"Oh!"

"So George came up and heard them talking about it, and he —— "

"What did he cut it down for?"

"Just to try his little hatchet."

"Whose little hatchet?"

"Why, his own, the one his father gave him."

"Gave who?"

"Why, George Washington."

"Who gave it to him?"

"His father did."

"Oh!"

"So George came up and he said, 'Father, I can not tell a lie, I —— '"

"Who couldn't tell a lie?"

"Why, George Washington. He said, 'Father, I can not tell a lie. It was —— "

"His father couldn't?"

"Why no, George couldn't."

"Oh, George? oh, yes."

"—— It was I cut down your apple tree; I did——"

"His father did?"

"No, no; it was George said this."

"Said he cut his father?"

"No, no, no; said he cut down his apple tree."

"George's apple tree?"

"No, no; his father's."

"Oh!"

"He said——"

"His father said?"

"No, no, no; George said, 'Father, I can not tell a lie. I did it with my little hatchet.' And his father said, 'Noble boy, I would rather lose a thousand trees than have you tell a lie.'"

"George did?"

"No, his father said that."

"Said he'd rather have a thousand apple trees?"

"No, no, no; said he'd rather lose a thousand apple trees than——"

"Said he'd rather George would?"

"No, said he'd rather he would than have him lie."

"Oh! George would rather have his father lie?"

We are patient, and we love children, but if Mrs. Caruthers, of Arch Street, hadn't come and got her prodigy at that critical juncture, we don't believe all Burlington could have pulled us out of that snarl. And as Clarence Fitzherbert Alencon de Marchemont Caruthers pattered down the stairs, we heard him telling his ma about a boy who had a father named George, and he told him to cut down an apple tree, and he said he'd rather tell a thousand lies than cut down one apple tree.

SPRING DAYS IN BURLINGTON.

DOWN where the wake-robin springs from its slumbers,
    Opening its cardinal eye to the sun;
Come the dull echoes of far away thunders
    Heavy and fast as the shots of a gun.
Up on the hill where the wild flowers nestle,
    Like new fallen stars on the green mossy strand;
There come the dead notes of the house-cleaning pestle—
    The sound of the carpet is heard in the land.

Up! for the song birds their matins are singing;
    Up, for the morning is tinting the skies;
Up, for the good wife the clothes-prop is bringing
    Out to the line where the hall carpet flies.
Up, and away! for the carpet is dusty!
    Fly, for the house-cleaning days have begun!
Run! for the womanly temper is crusty;
    Up and be doing, lest ye be undone!

Late, late; too late. Just one moment of snoring.
    He wakes to the sound of the tumult below.
O'er the beating of carpets he hears a voice roaring,
    "Breakfast was over three hours ago!"
See, he is plunged in the front of the battle;
    Where dust is the thickest they tell him to stand;
Where suds, mops and scrub-brushes spatter and rattle,
    And the sound of the carpet is heard in the land.

"HAWKEYE" SANCTUM.

LIFE IN THE "HAWKEYE" SANCTUM.

THE *Hawkeye* has just got into its new editorial rooms, and it is proud to say it has the finest, most comfortable, complete, and convenient editorial rooms in America. They are finished off with a little invention which will be of untold value to the profession of journalism when it is generally adopted; and we know that it will rapidly come into universal use as soon as its merits are understood and appreciated. We believe it is fully equal, in all that the term implies, to the famous Bogardess Kicker, less liable to get out of order, and less easily detected by casual visitors. It is known as "Middlerib's Automatic Welcome." The sanctum is on the same floor as the news-room, being separated from it by a partition, in which is cut a large window, easily opened by an automatic arrangement. The editor's table is placed in front of that window, and near the head of the stairs; and on the side of the table next the window, directly opposite the editor, the visitor's chair is placed. It has an inviting look about it, and its entire appearance is guileless and commonplace. But the strip of floor on which that chair rests is a deception and a fraud. It is an endless chain, like the floor of a horse-power, and is operated at will by the editor, who has merely to touch a spring in the floor to set it in motion. Its operation can best be understood by personal inspection.

One morning, soon after the " Middlerib Welcome " had

been placed in position, Mr. Bostwick came in with a funny story to tell. He naturally flopped down into the chair that had the strongest appearance of belonging to some one else, and began in his usual happy vein: "I've got the richest thing—oh! ah, ha, ha!—the best thing— oh, by George! I can't—oh, ha, ha, ha! Oh! it's too *good!* Oh, by George, the richest thing! Oh! it's *too* loud! You must never tell where you got—oh, by George, I can't do it! It's *too* good! You know—oh, ha, ha, ha, oh, he, he, he! You know the—oh, by George, I ca—" Here the editor touched the spring, a nail-grab under the bottom of the chair reached swiftly up and caught Mr. Bostwick by the cushion of his pants, the window flew up, and the noiseless belt of floor gliding on its course bore the astonished Mr. Bostwick through the window out into the news-room, half-way down to the cases, where he was received with great applause by the delighted compositors. The window had slammed down as soon as he passed through; and when the editorial foot was withdrawn from the spring and the chair stopped and the nail-grab assumed its accustomed place, young Mr. Bostwick found himself so kind of out of the sanctum, like it might be, that he went slowly and dejectedly down the stairs, as it were, while amazement sat upon his brow, like.

The next casual visitor was Mr. J. Alexis Flaxeter, the critic. He had a copy of the *Hawkeye* in his hand, with all the typographical errors marked in red ink, and his face was so wreathed in smiles that it was impossible to tell where his mouth ended and his eyes began. He took the vacant chair, and spread the paper out before him, covering up the editorial manuscript. "My keen vision and delicate sense of accuracy," he said, "are the greatest crosses of my life. Things that you never see are

mountains in my sight. Now here, you see, is a——."
The spring clicked softly, like an echo to the impatient movement of the editor's foot, the nail-grab took hold like a bulldog helping a Burlington troubadour over the garden fence, the chair shot back through the window like a meteor, and the window came down with a slam that sounded like a wooden giant getting off the shortest bit of profanity known to man; and all was silent again. Mr. Flaxeter sat very close to the frosted window, staring blankly at the clouded glass, seeing nothing that could offer any explanation of what he would have firmly believed was a land slide, had he not heard the editor, safe in his guarded den, softly whistling, "We shall meet but we shall miss him."

Then there was a brief interval of quiet in the sanctum, and a rustling of raiment was heard on the stairs. A lovely woman entered, and stood unawed in the editorial presence. The E. P., on its part, was rather nervous and uncomfortable. The lovely woman seated herself in the fatal chair. She slapped her little gripsack on the table, and opened her little subscription book. She said: "I am soliciting cash contributions—strictly, exclusively, and peremptorily cash contributions—to pay off the church debt, and buy an organ for the Mission Church of the Forlorn Strangers, and I expect——." There are times when occasion demands great effort. The editor bowed his head, and, after one brief spasm of remorse, felt for the secret spring. The window went up like a charm; the reckless nail-grab hung back for a second, as if held by a feeling of innate delicacy, and then it shut its eyes and smothered its pity, and reached up and took a death-like hold on a roll of able and influential newspapers and a network of string and tape, and the cavalcade backed out into the news-room with colors flying.

The chair stopped just before the familiar spirit who was washing the forms; and, as the lovely woman gazed at the inky face, she shrieked: "Merciful heavens, where, where am I?" and was borne down the gloomy stairway unconscious; while the printers whose cases were nearest the wicked window heard the editor singing, as it might be to himself, "Dearest sister, thou hast left us."

An hour of serenity and tranquillity in the editorial room was broken by a brisk, business-like step on the stairs; the door flew open with a bang that shot the key half-way across the room, and a sociable-looking, familiar kind of a stranger jammed into the chair, slapped his hat over the ink-stand, pushed a pile of proof, twenty pages of copy, a box of pens, the paste-cup, and a pair of scissors off the table to make room for the old familiar flat sample case, and said, in one brief breath: "I am agent for Gamberton's Popular Centennial World's History and American Citizens' Treasure Book of Valuable Information sold only by subscription and issued in thirty parts each number embellished with one handsome steel-plate engraving and numerous beautifully executed wood-cuts no similar work has ever been published in this country and at the exceedingly low price at which it is offered $2 per vol——."

The spring clicked like a pistol-shot, the window went up half-way through the ceiling, the nail-grab took hold like a three-barreled harpoon, and the column moved on its backward way through the window, down through the news-room past the foreman, standing grim and silent, by the imposing stone, past the cases, vocal with the applause and encouraging and consolatory remarks of the compositors, on to the alley windows, over the sills— howling, yelling, shrieking, praying, the unhappy agent was hurled to the cruel pavement, three stories below, where he lit on his head and plunged through into a cellar, where he tried to get a subscription out of a man who was shoveling coal.

THE LANGUAGE OF FLOWERS.

IT was a Mt. Pleasant girl. No other human divinity could play such a heartless trick on an admiring, nay, an adoring and adorable, young man. He always praised the flowers she wore, and talked so learnedly about flowers in general, that this incredulous young angel "put up a job" on him—if one may be so sacrilegious as to write slang in connection with so much beauty and grace. She filled the bay window with freshly potted weeds which she had laboriously gathered from the sidewalk and in the hollow under the bridge, and when he came round that evening she led the conversation to flowers, and her admirer to the bay window. "Such lovely plants she had," she told him, and he just clasped his hands and looked around him in silly ecstasy, trying to think of their names.

"That is *Patagonia influenses*, Mr. Bogundus," she said, pointing to the miserable cheat of a young ragweed; "did you ever see any thing so delicate?"

"Oh!" he ejaculated, regarding it reverentially; "beautiful, beautiful; what delicately serrated leaves!"

"And," she went on, with a face as angelic as though she was only saying "Now I lay me down to sleep," "it breaks out in the Summer in such curious green blossoms, clinging to long, slender stems. Only think of that—green blossoms." And she gazed pensively on the young man as though she saw something green that probably never would blossom.

"Wonderful, wonderful indeed," he said, "one can never tire of botany. It continually opens to us new worlds of wonders with every awakening flower and unfolded leaf."

"And here," she said, indicating with her snowy finger a villainous sprout of that little bur the boys call "beggar's lice," "this *Mendicantis parasitatis*, what——"

"Oh!" he exclaimed, rapturously, "where did you get it? Why, do you know how rare it is? I have not seen one in Burlington since Mrs. O'Gheminie went to Chicago. She had such beautiful species of them; such a charming variety. She used to wear them in her hair so often."

"No doubt," the angel said dryly; and the young man feared he had done wrong in praising Mrs. O'Gheminie's plants so highly. But the dear one went on, and pointing to a young jimson weed, said:

"This is my pet, this *Jimsonata filiofensis*."

The young man gasped with the pleasure of a true lover of flowers, as he bent over it in admiration and inhaled its nauseous odor. Then he rose up and said:

"This plant has some medicinal properties."

"Ah!" she said.

"Yes," he replied, stiffly, "it has. I have smelt that plant in my boyhood days. Wilted on the kitchen stove, then bruised and applied to the eruption, the leaves are excellent remedial agents for the poison of the ivy." He strode past the smiling company that gathered in the parlor, and said sternly, "We meet no more!" and, seizing her father's best hat from the rack, he extinguished himself in it, and went banging along the line of treeboxes which lined his darkened way.

SPRING TIME IN AMERICA.

DEAR, faded, flowers, they bloom again,
   Like echoes of the spring time gone;
And mossy hillside, shadowy glen,
   Break out in beauty like the dawn.
In regal beauty, leaf and bud
   Bend 'neath the kisses of the breeze,
And "Spanish Mixture for the Blood"
   Smiles from the fences, rocks and trees.

Dear, smiling Spring, what tender hope
   Breathes from the life-awakening soil;
How "Bolus' Anti-bilious Dope,"
   And "Dr. Gastric's Castor Oil"
Bid frightened nature wake and smile;
   For spring time's blossoms fill us less
With thoughts of pansies than with vile
   "Panaceas" for "Biliousness."

If to the wooded nook we stray,
   Where every swelling germ is huge
With life; each gray-browed rock will say,
   "Use Philogaster's Vermifuge."
If from these sylvan bowers we fly,
   We fly, alas, to other ills;
And farm-yard gates and barn-doors cry,
   "Take Ginsengrooter's Liver Pills."

Each blue-eyed violet hides a "Pill,"
   There's scent of "Rhubarb" in the air;

"Rheumatic Plasters" line each hill,
  And "Bitters" blossom everywhere.
With "Ague Cures" the eyes are seared;
  The air is thick, or thin, I meant,
For Nature's face and clothes are smeared
  With "Universal Liniment."

WOODLAND MUSIC AND POETRY.

BUT Mr. Middlerib's greatest delight, escaping from his daily wrangle with phlegmatic Peorians, was to seek some cool, sequestered spot, where the air was vocal with the song of birds, there to read, and ponder, and doze, and blend with the melody of the woodland warblers wrathful objurgations of the gnats, and flies, and mosquitoes, and hard-backed bugs that nobody knew the names of. But his poetical nature rose above all these minor distractions, and he enjoyed his seclusion and its sylvan delights. One lovely morning he sat in a vine-embowered porch, with four cages of canaries hanging above his head, and the trees around fairly alive with the wild birds, and as he listened to the varied, melodious passages of the wild-wood orchestra, he grew enraptured, and in a moment of enthusiasm gave himself up to poetry for Mrs. M.'s benefit. He opened the book in his hand, and in a lull of the music he began:

"A cloud lay cradled near the set——"

"Tweetle, tweetle, twee twee tweedle dee tweet tweet!"

broke in ear-piercing chorus from the four cages, "twee, twee, tweedle de deedle, twee twee!"

"What a delightful interruption," said Mr. Middlerib, sweetly; and, with a tender smile wrinkling his placid face, like the upper crust of a green apple pie, he waited for the music to cease, and resumed:

"A cloud lay cra——"

"Twee, twee, twee-ee-ee, tweedle, tweedle, tweedle! Tweet-te-deet-deet, tweet tweet! Tweedle-de-deedle, tweetle, tweetle tweet tweet!"

"A poem without words," said Mr. Middlerib, softly, glancing from his book toward the cages wherein eight yellow throats were manufacturing music of the shrillest key that ever developed an ear-ache or woke up a deaf and dumb asylum. Presently he got another chance, and resumed once more:

"A cloud lay cradled near the set——"

"To-whoot! To whoot! Whootle-te-toot-toot!" came from a bird in the nearest hickory, a solemn-looking bird with a brown back and a voice like a wooden whistle. Mr. Middlerib paused and glanced toward the tree, while the benign smile which made his face look like a damaged photograph of one of the early Christian martyrs, faded away like a summer twilight. He resumed:

"A cloud lay cra——"

"Too-toot too doodle toot-te-doot! Wheetle de deetle, tweet tweet tweetle tweet, twee twee whoot de doot too too, chippity-wippity, cheep-cheep-cheep, whoot, squack squack!" went off the whole chorus, cages and trees, supplemented by a visiting party of cat-birds, all aroused into indignant and jealous protest by the obtrusive solo of the wooden-whistle bird, who appeared to be an object of general dislike. Mr. Middlerib, thinking he would read down opposition, went right on :

"——dled near the setting sun,
A gleam of crim——"

" K-r-r-r-r-r-r ! "
A woodpecker tapped his merry roundelay on the roof of the porch, and Mrs. Middlerib sprang from her chair with, " Mercy on us! what is that?" Mr. Middlerib made a cutting remark about people who had no appreciation of the beautiful in nature or art, and remarked:

" A gleam of crimson tinged its——"

" Twee-ee, twee, deedle-eedle-odle twiddle twoddle, twoot, too too tweedle oot! Teedle idle eedle odle, twee twee, twee! Pe weet, pe weet! Whootle ootle tootle too, squack squack ! "
Mr. Middlerib elevated his voice to about ninety degrees in the shade, and roared:

"——tinged its braided snow,
Long had I wat——"

" Caw, caw, caw! Ca-a-a-aw!" came from the pensive crow, startled from its quiet retreat in the old dead cottonwood, and Miss Middlerib giggled. But Mr. M. inflated his lungs and roared on :

"——ched the glory moving on,
O'er the still radiance——"

"Tweetle de twootle, caw, caw, tweetle doodle tweet

tweet! K-r-r-r-r-r, krk, krk! twee deedle eet tweet! teedle idle, whoot, toot, twoot! who! squack, squack, k-r-r-r——"

"Shut up, ye nasty, squawking, yallipin', howlin' little beasts! Shoo! Light out o' this or I'll stone ye from here to Halifax! Scat with yer noise! Oh!" exclaimed the exasperated worshiper of nature as he hurled his book into the nearest tree and went off the porch to look for some stones, "If there is any thing in this world I hate more than another, its a lot of nasty, flittering, fidgety, yowping, howling birds! Ugh!" And he threw his shoulder nearly out of joint, and sprained his arm, in a herculean but futile effort to hit a black bird a mile and a half away, with a rock as big as a straw hat. He has dropped the sulphur baths for the present and taken to arnica.

BUYING A TIN CUP.

THE town was dozing in the drowsy sunlight of a dull August afternoon, when a dejected looking man, with the appearance of one who was making desperate efforts to appear unconcerned, stepped into a prominent and fashionable dry goods establishment up on Jefferson street. Scorning the proffered stool, he braced himself firmly against the counter, and looking the polite and attentive clerk fixedly in the eye, broke the impressive silence by abruptly demanding:

"Gimme tinkup!"

"We do not keep them, sir," smilingly replied the affable clerk, and the glare of suspicion with which that man regarded him was sufficient to chill the blood of a snake.

"Donkeep tinkups?" he asked, quickly and distrustfully.

"No, sir," replied the clerk, "we have no tin cups. This is a dry goods store. You will find the tin store farther up the street."

"Few donkeep notinkups—watchkeep?" demanded the man, imperiously.

"We have grenadines, calicos, bareges, gros grain ribbons, tarletan, velvets, moire antique, empress cloth, pongee and Japanese silks——"

"Shut her off!" ejaculated the man, "Puttit tup! Puttit tup!"

"He turned away with a dignified gesture, and walked away with stately, though uncertain strides, and dived into the Plunder store, where he startled the proprietor by the same urgent demand for the "tinkup," and he was finally piloted into Kaut & Kriechbaum's, where he bought his "tinkup," which he fell down on before he got to the Barret House corner, mashing it flat as a pie pan. He was helped into his wagon, and as he drove away the last the citizens saw of him he was holding the flattened tin cup before him, exclaiming ruefully:

"Devlofa—lookin—tinkupthatis!"

ONE OF THE LEGION.

A CITIZEN of South Hill,
   His visage bathed in tears,
His raiment streaked with rust and dust,
   His mind distraught with fears,
Was leaning up by the shattered gate,
   And his sad eyes gazed around
Where reckless ruin here and there
   With fragments strewed the ground.
But a drayman stood beside him
   To hear what he might say,
As he stretched him out his good right arm
   And waited for his pay.

The weeping mover faltered
   As he saw the drayman's hand,
And he said, " I haven't a red, red cent
   In all of this broad fair land.
I haven't a clothes to my aching back
   Save only these rags you see;
And all the furniture I have left
   Won't pay you half your fee.
There's a leg of the table in the street,
   And the lamp globes strew the stair,
And the stovepipe's flattened out like a **lath**,
   And the clock is not nowhere.

" Tell my wife, if you can find her,
   That when the job was done,

The furniture wasn't half so good
   As it was when we begun.
That the end of the bureau she's looking for
   Is down by the alley gate,
And the parlor mirror is bent so bad
   She never can pound it straight.
We broke the legs of the kitchen stove,
   And we smashed the Parian vase,
And the dray ran over her rocking chair
   And ruined its stately grace.

"Tell my sister, her darling new spring hat
   Was packed in a bag of corn,
And I never again can look in her face
   And meet her glance of scorn.
We spilled coal oil on her summer silk,
   And we tore her cashmere sacque,
For her dressing bureau fell off the dray
   And the horse kicked out its back.

"There's another, not a sister,
   In happier days gone by,
You'd know her by the savage light
   That glittered in her eye.
Too business-like for foolery,
   Too sharp for my excuses—
Ah me, I fear adversity
   Has naught but bitter uses;
Tell her, the last time you saw me—
   For ere the clock strikes ten,
I'll be at work on the 'Third Degree,'
   The happiest of men;
Tell her I said that she could go
   To the bow-wow wow-wow wows;

That I'd stay down town when lodge was out,
    And sleep at a boarding-house
Tell her she needn't sit up for me,
    And she needn't leave no light——'
And a voice came out of the hall and said,
    " You don't go to no Lodge to-night."

His voice was gone in a minute,
    He gasped and tried to speak;
He tried to swear, but the drayman says
    That he couldn't raise a squeak.

And his mother-in-law rose slowly,
    And calmly she looked down
On the green grass of the littered yard,
    With household treasures strewn.
Yes, calmly on that dreadful scene
    She gazed, and looked around,
And said to the weeping man by the gate,
    " Pick them things up off the ground."

A TACITURN WITNESS.

AN ordinary case of assault and battery was called in Judge Stutsman's court, and the prosecuting witness was duly sworn: Phelim O'Shaughnessy, a little, weazen-faced man, with a stubbly beard all over his jaws and a pair of bright eyes flanking the snubbiest of noses.

"Now, then, Mr. O'Shaughnessy," said the court, "tell what you know about this matter in as few words as you possibly can."

"Faix, thin, yer anner, an' I will do that same," replied the witness, with great volubility. "Av' there is ony thing I do be despisin' it's wan ov thim same whurrimurroo gabblers that niver know when they're through. When ye git troo pumpin, sez I, lave the handle; that's me. An' ye niver see an O'Shaughnessy in the wor-r-ld, yer anner, that wur a cackler. I mind me mither's own uncle that ever was, Tim the Croaker they used to be callin' him, though his name was Timothy Mahone O'Dubbleriggle Balbrigganainey, for be the token he niver wur known to say more nor wan wor-rud at a time, yer anner, an' that wan he said with a grunt. There was wan day, whin he wur gamekeeper fur my lord Donald McAlpin Clanargotty Callum O'Dowd, a Scotch gintleman that owned a bit av a shootin' box might be, in the north uv——"

"Well, there, there, there," interrupted the court, "that's enough about your ancestry; now tell what you know about this case of yours, and stick to the point."

"The p'int, is it, avick?" replied the witness; "Musha,

thin, it wur fwhat I wur comin' to, jist. It's what I sez to Mrs. O'Shaughnessy twinty times a day, an' she's the wor-r-rst talker between here an' Dublin bay. 'Norah,' sez I; 'Is it you,' sez she; 'Faix thin, an' who else wud it be?' sez I; 'An' phwat uv it?' sez she; 'Div ye mind me, now?' sez I; 'Sorra the wan uv me does,' sez she; 'Wait thin, till I tell ye,' sez I; 'Whisht, thin, go on with yer blarney,' sez she; 'Howld yer hush a minit, thin,' sez I, 'an' let's have a second av quiet;' 'What!' sez she, 'wid ye in the house?' 'Listhen,' sez I; 'Whisper, thin,' sez she; 'Well, thin,' sez I, 'kape to the pint. Av yez will do nothin' but talk from the peep o' mor-r-rn till the lasht wink uv night, kape till the p'int.' Ah, yer anner, it's the wan fur talkin', she is, is Norah. It isn't an O'Shaughnessy she is, yer anner, her father, rest his sowl, was ould Darby Muldoon, the solid man, an' he wur sint to Austhralia for twenty-sivin years panal sarvitude fur talkin' a thraveler to death whin he wur dhrivin' him from——"

"That will do," interrupted the court, sternly; "we've heard enough of your reminiscences. Now you tell what you know about this case, or I'll fine you for contempt. You have filed information against Morris McHogadan for assaulting you with a paving hammer, in the back yard of your own premises in Melrose Place, Happy Hollow, and knocking three teeth down your throat, breaking one of your ribs, and chewing your ear off. Now what have you got to say about it?"

"Is it me, avick?"

"Yes, you are the prosecuting witness; that is your own case, and you filed the information on which the warrant was issued."

"An' it says that Morris McHogadan bate me?"

"It does, and it is sworn to."

"Oh, the divil an' all; who shwore to that?"

"You did."

"Phwat?"

"You swore to all that."

"Oh, tower uv ivory! That Morris McHogadan bate me?"

"Yes."

"Wid a pavin' hammer?"

"Yes, so you declared."

"Oh-h-h, thundher an' turf! An' bate me teeth down the troat ov me?"

"So you averred."

"Oh, the bloody-minded villin; an' broke me rib?"

"That's what you said."

"Oh-h-h, bones of the martyrs; and chawed off the ear o' me?"

"So you told us."

"Oh, to the divil wid the informashin that says sich a pack o' lies. Morris McHogadan bate me? Och, Moses an' Aarin, its tearin' ravin' disthracted mad I am! Why, yer anner, it's a bloody-minded lie. He can't fip wan side o' me; why, the pig-eyed thafe ov the wor-rold, I clawed all the red hair out ov the ugly head of him and trowed him down the bank ov the crick, and welted him like an ould shoe wid a splinther ov timber I grabbed out of the crick. Him bate me? He can't bate nobody. I didn't lave a whole bone in his ugly carkiss, an' av he dares to say I did, yer anner, I'll ate off his other ear an' pound the flure wid him. Oh, the divil fly away wid sich infermashin. It's the beggar's own lie, an'——"

Here the witness was cut short by the court fining him $10.00 and costs for assault and battery, and Phelim, astonished into a terrific flow of volubility for such a taciturn man, went away with a policeman, arguing that it wasn't possible that he could be fined when he was the prosecuting witness, and declaring that the case never would have gone against him but for "the bloody-minded infermashin," which he firmly believed to be the evil work of the designing Morris McHogadan.

THE SEEDSMAN.

How doth the busy nurseryman
    Improve each shining hour;
And peddle cions, sprouts and seeds
    Of every shrub and flower.

How busily he wags his chin,
    How neat he spreads his store,
And sells us things that never grew
    And won't grow any more.

Who showed the little man the way
    To sell the women seed?
Who taught him how to blow and lie
    And coax and beg and plead?

He taught himself, the nurseryman;
    And when his day is done,
We'll plant him where the lank rag weeds
    Will flutter in the sun.

But oh, although we plant him deep
    Beneath the buttercup,
He's so much like the seed he sells,
    He never will come up.

CORNERING THE BOYS.

ONLY a few days before they moved the capital, a worthy lady of Peoria one morning detected her two sons laughing immoderately. Suspecting that she was the cause of their disrespectful mirth, the good woman involuntarily loosened her slipper and called up the young culprits.

"Thomas, what made you laugh?"

"Nobody made me laugh; I laughed on purpose."

"None of your impudence, sir. John, why were you laughing at the door just now?"

John (eagerly)—"Wasn't laughing at the door, I was laughing at Tom."

Tom—"And I was laughing at John."

The matron assumed a dignified attitude. "Now, my boys, what were you both laughing at?"

Boys (in a triumphant shout)—"We were both laughing at once!"

The good lady summoned all her energies for a final effort, and resolved to corner the boys by a settling question.

"Now, then, I want you to tell me, Tom, what made John laugh and you laugh?"

Tom—"John didn't laugh a new laugh; it was the same old laugh!"

Neither of the boys got whipped, the slipper slid back to its accustomed place, and to this day nobody knows what those boys laughed at.

SELLING THE HEIRLOOM.

SELLING THE HEIRLOOM.

ONE afternoon, about a week after the big Fourth of July, a hungry-looking man made his appearance down near the post office corner, carrying in his arms an old-fashioned clock, about four feet high, with some ghastly looking characters scrawled across the dial, like the photograph of a fire-cracker label with the delirium tremens. He set the clock down, and in loud tones called upon the passers-by to pause, as he was about to make a sacrifice that would break the heart of the oldest horologer living. He was going to sell that clock, he said. An old family heirloom, and a genuine curiosity of antiquity, which he would not ordinarily take thousands of dollars for, but which he sold now because he was out of work, penniless; and when his wife and children cried to him for bread, he could not say them nay when he had that in his possession that would, in any intelligent community, bring them food and plenty.

"Gentlemen," he said, "look at that clock. A relic of antiquity. One of the oldest Chinese clepsydras in the world. Bamboo case and sandal-wood running gear. Not an ounce of metal in its construction. Made in China by the eminent horologer Tchin Pitshoo, as near as can be ascertained, three hundred years after the flood. Worth a thousand dollars if it's worth a cent; but of course I don't expect to get half its value in these hard times. The inscription on the face is in the characters of the purest Confucian Chinese, and the interpretation of them is, "Time flies and money is twelve per cent." Now what are you going to give me for that clock? Who will buy this clock, and present it to the Iowa Historical Society or the Burlington Library? How much? Start her up; send her ahead at something, gentlemen; there's a woman and five children that haven't had a bite to eat for two days, and can't get a crumb till the money for this clock is in my pocket. A marvelous time-piece; never lost——"

A man in brown overalls and a dirty face lounged up to the clock, and after scratching the case with a pin, to assure himself that it was really a genuine Chinese clepsydra, bid ten cents.

"Ten cents!" roared the man, rolling his eyes—"Heaven, hold back your lightnings! Don't strike him dead just yet! Give him time to repent. Ten cents to buy food for a starving woman and five children. Ten cents for a d——" He choked with emotion, and could not go on for a moment. "Ten cents! Why, that clock only has to be wound once a month, and it records every minute of time; tells just how long it will take you to get to the depot; tells when the train starts, and when the children are late to school. This clock, gentlemen, will tell when the oldest boy has played hookey and gone off fishing; it tells how late the hired girl's beau stays Sunday night, and it will register the exact minute of our oldest daughter's arrival and departure at and from the front gate after ten o'clock at night. Why, after you've had it six weeks, you'll not take six hundred dollars for it. It runs fast all day and slow all night, giving a man fourteen hours' sleep in the Winter and sixteen hours' sleep in the Summer, without disturbing the accurate average of the day a minute. Ten cents for such a clock as that! Ten cents! Gentlemen, this is robbery; it's cold-blooded murder. At ten cents; at ten, at ten, atten, atten, attenat-tennit-tennit-tennet-tenatenatenaten a-a-t ten cents only am I offered, twenty do I hear? At ten—"

An old rag man, after a critical examination of the marvel, bid fifteen cents, and was instantly regarded as a mortal enemy by the first bidder.

"Fifteen cents!" exclaimed the seller. "Gentlemen, knock me down and rob me of my clothes, strip me naked if you will, but don't plunder a gasping, starving woman and five weak, helpless babes. Don't rob the dying. Fifteen cents. Why, I've suffered more than three hundred dollars' worth of privation and sorrow and misery, rather than sell this clock at all. Fifteen cents. Why, you set that clock where the sun shines on it, and it will indicate a rain storm three days in advance, and will tell where the lightning is going to strike. Why, you could make millions by buying this clock to bet on. It will tell, just three weeks before election, who is going to beat. It's a credit to any household, and will run the whole family on tick. Fifteen cents! why, it won't pay for the shelf you stand it on. Fifteen cents for a clock that used to be owned by an emperor! Fifteen cents. Oh, kill me dead. At fifteen cents, fifteen, fiftn, fiftn, fift, nfift, nfift, nfiftnfiftnfift, ta-a-a-t fifteen cents for a clock that can't be duplicated this side of the Yang tse Kiang. At fifteen ce—thank you sir, twenty cents I have; twenty cents to feed a starving family of seven souls; twenty cents for a barefooted woman and five ragged children that haven't tasted food since Monday morning; twenty cents, from a city of thirty thousand inhabitants, for a starving family; there's Christian philanthropy for you. Twenty cents from the commercial capital of Iowa, for a clock that would be snapped up anywhere else in the world at hundreds, merely for its antiquity; there's intelligent appreciation of the arts and culture for you. Gentlemen, I can't stand this much longer; my heart is breaking. Twenty cents, twenty cents, twenty, twent, twen, twen, twentwentwen, and sold—a thousand-dollar clock, starving woman, dying children, heart-broken man, and all to the second-hand-store man for twenty cents."

He took his money, a ragged shinplaster and two street car nickels, and walked away with a dejected, heart-broken air. He stopped in at a bakery with frosted windows and transient doors, to buy bread for his starving wife and babes, and his voice was husky with emotion as he said to the natty-looking baker, whose diamond pin glittered over the walnut counter,

"Gimme a plain sour."

THE ROMANCE OF THE CARPET.

BASKING in peace, in the warm Spring sun,
   South Hill smiled upon Burlington.

The breath of May! and the day was fair,
And the bright motes danced in the balmy air,

And the sunlight gleamed where the restless breeze
Kissed the fragrant blooms on the apple trees.

His beardless cheek with a smile was spanned
As he stood with a carriage-whip in his hand.

And he laughed as he doffed his bob-tailed coat,
And the echoing folds of the carpet smote.

ROMANCE OF THE CARPET.

And she smiled as she leaned on her busy mop,
And said she would tell him when to stop.

So he pounded away till the dinner bell
Gave him a little breathing spell.

But he sighed when the kitchen clock struck one;
And she said the carpet wasn't done.

But he lovingly put in his biggest licks,
And pounded like mad till the clock struck six.

And she said, in a dubious kind of way,
That she guessed he could finish it up next day.

Then all that day, and the next day too,
The fuzz from the dustless carpet flew.

And she'd give it a look at eventide,
And say, "Now beat on the other side."

And the new days came as the old days went,
And the landlord came for his regular rent.

And the neighbors laughed at the tireless boom,
And his face was shadowed with clouds of gloom;

Till at last, one cheerless Winter day,
He kicked at the carpet and slid away,

Over the fence and down the street,
Speeding away with footsteps fleet;

And never again the morning sun
Smiled at him beating his carpet drum;

And South Hill often said, with a yawn,
"Where has the carpet martyr gone?"

Years twice twenty had come and passed,
And the carpet swayed in the autumn blast;

For never yet, since that bright spring time,
Had it ever been taken down from the line.

Over the fence a gray-haired man
Cautiously clim, clome, clem, clum, clam;

He found him a stick in the old woodpile,
And he gathered it up with a sad, grim smile.

A flush passed over his face forlorn
As he gazed at the carpet, tattered and torn;

And he hit it a most resounding thwack,
Till the startled air gave its echoes back.

And out of the window a white face leaned,
And a palsied hand the sad eyes screened.

She knew his face—she gasped, she sighed:
"A little more on the under side."

Right down on the ground his stick he throwed,
And he shivered and muttered, "Well, I am blowed!"

And he turned away, with a heart full sore,
And he never was seen, not none no more.

SODDING AS A FINE ART.

ONE day, early in the Spring, Mr. Blosberg, who lives out on Ninth Street, made up his mind that he would sod his front yard himself, and when he had formed this public-spirited resolution, he proceeded to put it into immediate execution. He cut his sod, in righteous and independent and liberty-loving disregard of the ridiculous city ordinance in relation thereto, from the patches of verdure that the cows had permitted to obtain a temporary growth along the side of the street, and proceeded to beautify his front yard therewith. Just as he had laid the first sod, Mr. Thwackery, his next door neighbor, passed by.

"Good land, Blosberg," he shouted, "you'll never be able to make any thing of such a sod as that. Why, its three inches too thick. That sod will cake up and dry like a brick. You want to shave at least two inches and a half off the bottom of it, so the roots of the grass will grow into the ground and unite the sod with the earth. That sod is thick enough for a corner stone."

So Mr. Blosberg took the spade and shaved the sod down until it was thin and about as pliable as a buckwheat cake, and Mr. Thwackery pronounced it all right and sure to grow, and passed on. Just as Mr. Blosberg got it laid down the second time, old Mr. Templeton, who lived on the next block, came along and leaned on the fence, intently observing the sodder's movements.

"Well now, Blosberg," he said at length, "I did think you had better sense than that. Don't you know a sod will never grow on that hard ground? You must spade it all up first, and break the dirt up fine and soft to the depth of at least four inches, or the grass can never take root in it. Don't waste your time and sod by putting grass on top of such a baked brick-floor as that."

And Mr. Blosberg laid aside the sod and took up the spade and labored under Mr. Templeton's directions until the ground was all properly prepared for the sod, and then Mr. Templeton, telling him that sod couldn't die on that ground now if he tried to kill it, went his way and Mr. Blosberg picked up that precious sod a third time, and prepared to put it in its place. Before he had fairly poised it over the spot, however, his hands were arrested by a terrific shout, and looking up he saw Major Bladgers shaking his cane at him over the fence.

"Blosberg, you insufferable donkey," roared the Major, "don't you know that you'll lose every blade of grass you can carry if you put your sod on that dry ground? There you've gone and cut it so thin that all the roots of the grass are cut and bleeding, and you must soak that ground with water until it is a perfect pulp, so that the roots will sink right into it, and draw nutrition from the moist earth. Wet her down, Blosberg, if you want to see your labor result in any thing."

So Mr. Blosberg put the sod aside again, and went and pumped water and carried it around in buckets until his back ached like a soft corn, and when he had finally transformed the front yard into a morass, the major was satisfied, and assuring Mr. Blosberg that his sod would grow beautifully now, even if he laid it on upside down, marched away, and Mr. Blosberg made a fourth effort to put the first sod in its place. He got it down and was going back after another, when old Mrs. Tweedlebug checked him in his wild career.

"Lawk, Mr. Blosberg, ye musn't go off an' leave that sod lying that way. You must take the spade and beat it down hard, till it is all flat and level, and close to the ground everywhere. You must pound it hard, or the weeds will all start up under it and crowd out the grass."

Mr. Blosberg went back, and stooping over the sod hit it a resounding thwack with his spade that shot great gouts and splotches of mud all over the parlor windows and half way to the top of the house, and some of it came flying into his face and on his clothes, while a miscellaneous shower made it dangerous even for his adviser, who, with a feeble shriek of disapprobation, went hastily away, digging raw mud out of her ears. Mr. Blosberg didn't know how long to keep on pounding, and he didn't see Mrs. Tweedlebug go away, so he stood with his spade poised in the air and his eyes shut tight, waiting for instructions. And as he waited he was surprised to hear a new voice accost him. It was the voice of Mr. Thistlepod, the old agriculturist, of whom Mr. Blosberg bought his apples and butter.

"Hello, Mr. Blosberg!" he shouted, in tones which indicated that he either believed Mr. Blosberg to be stone deaf or two thousand miles away.

Mr. Blosberg winked violently to get the soil out of his eyes, and turned in the direction of the noise to say, "Good evening."

"Soddin', hey?" asked Mr. Thistlepod.

"Trying to, sir," replied Mr. Blosberg, rather cautiously.

"'Spect it will grow, hey?"

Mr. Blosberg, having learned by very recent experience how liable his plans were to be overthrown, was still noncommittal, and replied that "he hoped so."

"Wal, if ye hope so, ye mustn't go to poundin' yer sod to pieces with that spade. Ye don't want to ram it down so dad binged tight and hard there can't no air git at the roots. Ye must shake that sod up a little, so as to loosen it, and then jest press it down with yer foot ontwil it jest teches the ground nicely all round. Sod's too thin, anyhow."

So Mr. Blosberg thrust his hands into the nasty mud under his darling, much abused sod, and spread his fingers wide apart to keep it from breaking to pieces as he raised it, and finally got it loosened up and pressed down to Mr. Thistlepod's satisfaction, who then told him he didn't believe he could make that sod grow any way, and drove away. Then Mr. Blosberg stepped back to look at that sod, feeling confident that he had got through with it, when young Mr. Simpson came along.

"Hello, Blos, old boy; watchu doin'?"

Mr. Blosberg timorously answered that he was sodding a little. Then Mr. Simpson pressed his lips very tightly together to repress a smile, and let his cheeks swell and bulge out to the size of toy balloons with suppressed merriment, and finally burst into a snort of derisive laughter that made the windows rattle in the houses on the other side of the street, and he went on, leaving Mr. Blosberg somewhat nettled and a little discouraged. He stood, with his fingers spread wide apart, holding his arms out like wings, and wondering whether he had better go get another sod or go wash his hands, when a policeman came by, and paused. "Soddin'?" he asked, sententiously.

"Yes, sir, a little," replied Mr. Blosberg, respectfully.

"Where'd you get your sod?" inquired the representative of public order.

Mr. Blosberg dolefully indicated the little bare parallelogram in the scanty patch of verdure as his base of supplies.

"You're the man I've been lookin' for," replied public order. "You come along with me."

And Mr. Blosberg went along, and the Police Judge fined him $11 95, and when Mr. Blosberg got home he found that a cow had got into his yard during his absence and stepped on that precious sod five times, and put her foot clear through it every time, so that it looked like a patch of moss rolled up in a wad, more than a sod. And then Mr. Blosberg fell on his knees and raised his hands to heaven, and registered a vow that he would never plant another sod if this whole fertile world turned into a Sahara for want of his aid.

THE AMENITIES OF POLITICS.

"THERE is one thing," said Mr. Leatherby, as he was walking down town one drizzling, disagreeable morning during the last presidential campaign, "that disgusts me with politics, and that is, the violent and abusive tone in which our daily papers conduct the discussion of every issue and question which they touch upon."

"Indeed you may well be disgusted at it," replied old Mr. Bartholomew, who had just joined him. "It is as much as a man can do to lift a newspaper off his door step with a pair of tongs. Time and again I throw the paper down half read, and I have seriously thought of stopping it altogether, for I consider its presence in my family a contamination."

"It is, in truth," replied Mr. Leatherby; "it is worse

than a contamination. It is corrupting; it has a degrading, brutalizing influence, that is, I am convinced, undermining the foundations of our moral structure. The daily press of to-day is one great engine of abuse, defamation, bad grammar, worse language and worst morals."

"I can not see, for my part," said Mr. Bartholomew, "why men can not discuss politics as freely, as earnestly, and as entirely free from acrimonious expressions and feeling, as purely exempt from abusive language of any kind, from any heat and anger, in fact, as they could discuss the grade of a street or the style of a coat."

"And so think I," said Mr. Leatherby. "I can not, for my part, conceive of an intellect so warped and narrow, a mind so shallow, that it can not carry on a discussion upon any question in politics without falling into the asperities, vulgarity, abusive detraction, and shameful slander that is the reproach and disgrace of the newspaper press."

"It is a form of idiocy, I believe," replied old Mr. Bartholomew. "It is an indication of a feeble mind that looks upon abuse as an argument, and bullying as logic. I am and always have been a Republican, but I can express my disapproval of many Democratic measures in a gentlemanly manner; and if I had not mind enough to keep my temper, I would consider that I had no right to talk politics."

"You are perfectly correct," rejoined Mr. Leatherby, earnestly; "and while we disagree on some points in political controversy, I being a life-long Democrat, yet we can freely and with mutual pleasure, and, I trust, profit, meet and discuss our differences in a friendly way, without giving way to the insane and detestable exhibition of temper, ignorance, and prejudice which marks the tone of the morning paper."

"I had not noticed it so much in the *Hawkeye*," replied Mr. Bartholomew, with a show of awakening interest in the conversation; "but when that trashy Democratic sheet that pollutes the evening air is brought to me by my neighbor, an ignorant dolt who can neither read nor write, but takes the paper as a party duty, and asks me to read it for him, I am amazed that the gods of truth and decency do not annihilate the infamous, puerile sheet with their thunderbolts."

"You must bear in mind, however," rejoined Mr. Leatherby, speaking a trifle louder than was necessary in addressing a companion whose hand was resting on his arm, "the *Gazette* has such a tide of corruption, such an avalanche of political bigotry and villainy to rebuke, that its voice must be raised in order to be heard; and it must speak boldly, defiantly, and in the thunder tones of righteous denunciation, to startle the people into a realizing sense of the peril which threatens the country from Republican misrule and tyranny."

"By George!" shouted Mr. Bartholomew, "the Republican party is the last, the only bulwark between the republic and eternal ruin. I tell you, sir, once let the Democratic party obtain control of this government, once let that infamous organization of political thieves, knucks, outlaws, and castaways take charge of our political machinery, and we will find ourselves in the hands of a horde of the most abandoned profligates, the most utterly unprincipled, the most vicious, demoralized, unconscionable, diabolical set of scoundrels that ever cheated the gallows."

"By the long-horned spoon!" roared Mr. Leatherby, jerking his arm away from Mr. Bartholomew's hand; "if the satanic and infernal plans of the Republican party were carried out, with all their attendant knavery and debauchery, this government would be a rule of branded malefactors and convicts, a government of felons, a penal colony in which the most hopelessly irreclaimable, graceless villains would administer the law. The bad faith of the Republican party, its ignominious record, its vicious tendencies, has shocked the Christian world, and——"

"You're a liar!" yelled Mr. Bartholomew, "and you are just like the rest of your besotted, low-lived, ignorant class—a low, mean, pitiful, beggarly, unscrupulous and treacherous set, whose impudence in asking for the votes of honorable men is only equaled by your rapacious and unbridled greed for office; your——"

"You are an old fool!" howled Mr. Leatherby; "a censorious, clamorous, scurrilous, foul-tongued old reprobate, and I disgrace my name when I talk to you on the street. You mistake vituperation and abuse for argument, and you reply to a simple plain statement of facts with malignant and defamatory slander and calumny, because you can't answer."

"Shut up!" shrieked Mr. Bartholomew. "Don't you say another word to me, or I'll slap your ugly mouth! By George, I'll kick your head off!"

"You can't do it!" roared Mr. Leatherby, pulling off his coat, and dancing around Mr. Bartholomew. "I can lick the whole Republican party, from the big whisky thief and ring master in the White House down to the sneak thief that picks pockets at mass meetings! I can——"

"You're a fighting liar, and you daren't take it up!" howled Mr. Bartholomew, pulling off his coat.

Then Mr. Leatherby ran up and kicked him twice while he was struggling in the arms of his coat, but the old gentleman got loose in a flash and hit Mr. Leatherby a resounding thwack on the nose with his cane, and when Mr. Leatherby stopped to hold a handkerchief over his bleeding proboscis, Mr. Bartholomew got in a couple more real good ones with his cane; then Mr. Leatherby went for the rocks in the macadamized street. He broke two windows in a grocery before he hit Mr. Bartholomew, when he caught the old gentleman on the side of the head and dropped him. Then Mr. Bartholomew took to the stone pile and hit a young lady on the other side of the street, and Mr. Leatherby hurled a tremendous big rock, which missed the old gentleman and blacked the eye of a policeman who was coming to separate them, but was so incensed that he arrested them, and they were each fined $10 and costs for fighting in the street. And they both firmly believe that the unbridled hatred and unreasonable recriminations and abuse of the daily papers are iniquitous in their influence, and should be suppressed for the good of society.

It was a sad scene when the authorities took a poor man from Happy Hollow, and sent him out to the poor house. The parting between the poor man and his eleven dogs, which he distributed among his sympathizing relatives, was affecting in the extreme. We believe the man had a few children, too, but not enough to make a fuss about.

A BASHFUL young man, while out driving with the dearest girl in the world, had to get out and buckle the crupper, and hesitatingly exclaimed that "the animal's bustle had come loose."

A THRILLING ENCOUNTER.

IT happens, once in a while, that even the ordinary routine of the editorial sanctum is broken by incidents and scenes that are fairly dramatic in their character. As we write, there comes back to us the reminiscence of a quiet, sleepy Summer afternoon, only a few short years ago. The very flies in the sanctum buzzed lazily about the room, oppressed by the heat and the quiet loneliness of the place, when the door opened with a quick, sudden snap, and we turned and saw a woman stepping into the room. She was not old, and her face, haggard with care and seamed with trouble, still bore traces of great beauty. She came into the office with a quick, nervous tread, and there was a hunted look in her eyes that betrayed the fugitive. She closed the door behind her, and turned the key in almost the same motion, with the quick instinctive manner of a person who had fallen into the habit of isolating herself from observation and pursuit at every opportunity. She refused to sit down, but said:

"I can tell you all you will want to know about me in very few words—I am a fugitive."

We told her we had guessed as much, and we besought her to confide nothing to us. We could not help her, we said; our duty as a journalist would not permit us to extend any aid to a person flying from the law. She said:

"I do not want you to aid me in farther flight; I am tired to death. My own conscience, more pitiless than the minions of the law, has pursued me for years with a whip of scorpions. I can not escape its terrible lashings. I can not fly from my punishment if I would, and I am anxious it should be over. Death would be a welcome relief, if it would but come."

Again we told the panting, weary creature to tell none of her story to us, and advised her to go to the police headquarters and give herself into the hands of the law, which would deal justly, and, we had no doubt, in view of her sufferings and remorse, mercifully with her.

"I can not!" she exclaimed, covering her face with her hands, and breaking into convulsive sobs; "I can not, I can not. You do not know there are other hearts would ache if I gave myself up and told all. I want to tell my story to some one who will pity me and advise me. There are those whose hands are as dark with ineffaceable stains as mine are, but who do not suffer the mental agony that oppresses me. Shall I, in order to escape the lashings of my own conscience, consign these, whose lives are happy and whose hearts know no remorse, to the same punishment for which I yearn?"

We asked her (for our curiosity conquered our caution) if it was possible that one so young and fair was the center of a wide-spreading circle of crime that held in its horrid entanglements so many others beside herself?

"Aye," she said, bit'erly. "If I went to the gallows through a court of justice, I would lead with me, held by the same terrible links of evidence, a guilty train of men hardened in crime, and their hands steeped in innocent blood!"

"Woman, woman!" we exclaimed, in horrified tones, "in the name of heaven, who and what are you?"

"Oh, heaven help me!" she shrieked, in a voice that chilled our marrow—"I am old man Bender!"

A weird, wild whoop rent the silence of the sanctum—

and the woman was alone. There was a sound as of a rising journalist scrambling up through the narrow copy tube, and the next instant a bare head, with a quill over one ear, burst through the hatchway in the roof, and, followed by a complete set of editorial anatomy, emerged, and running briskly to the rear wall of the building, disappeared down the lightning-rod, and was seen no more until the next day at three P. M.

We never saw the woman again, and wis not where she is, but we smile in bitter derision whenever we read that the police have arrested an old man answering the description of old man Bender.

FIVE WOMEN.

ONE afternoon five women went out on South Hill in a street car. One of them was a fat woman in a black dress, with a cameo pin as large as a stucco ornament. She breathed at a high pressure, about 103 to the minute. A woman with a thin, long neck, and sad eyes, and a Paisley shawl, sitting on the other side of the car, said, in a feeble voice:

"Good afternoon, Mrs. Waughop."

"Oh, (puff) Mrs. Dresseldorff, (puff, puff,) how do (puff) you do?" (Puff, puff.)

"Oh, I ain't feeling well at all. I've had so much trouble with my lungs, and nothing seems to do them any good. I've tried onion gargle, and three kinds of expectorant, and Wine of Tar, and two of Doctor Bolus's prescriptions, and one of Dr. Bleadem's, and a

GOBLIN GATE.

See page 148.

new kind of ointment, but nothing seems to have any effect on them. How do you feel to-day?"

"Oh," groaned Mrs. Waughop, "I'm not getting on at all. My asthma is worse every day (puff, puff), and I can't sleep at night, and I'm afraid I'll have to give up entirely (puff, puff). I could hardly get out to-day (puff, puff, puff). I went to Greenbaum and Schroder's and around to Guest's and down to Carpenter's (puff, puff), and into Parsons' and up to Mrs. Voorhees' (puff, puff), and down to Wyman's and up to Wesley Jones' and into Gus Dodge's and (puff, puff, puff) down to the express office, and then by the time I had made a couple of calls out on North Hill and went to the doctor's, I was as tired as though I had walked a mile (puff, puff, puff). I don't know what's going to become of me, I'm sure. How are you, this afternoon, Mrs. Dinkleman?" she continued, turning to the next woman, a lonesome looking female with a wart on her chin, who smiled dismally on being addressed and paused in the midst of a search for a street car nickel in the bottom of a black reticule as big as a hair trunk.

"I'm about half down with the chills," she said, with a prolonged sigh; "I have such a fever every night, I don't get two hours' sleep out of the twenty-four, and I'm afraid I'll be down sick before I get through with it. My eyesight is failing, too, and I have a constant headache that worries me nearly to death. I am glad, Mrs. Mulligan," said Mrs. Dinkleman, turning to the fourth woman, "to see you able to be out."

Mrs. Mulligan bowed feebly to the rest of the ladies. "Indeed I oughtn't to be out," she groaned, "I ought to be in bed this minute. I haven't had this flannel off my throat for three weeks, and I'm afraid I'll lose my voice entirely. I've had a misery across my back since I don't know when, and I had to have three teeth pulled this blessed afternoon. I was that bad with the rheumatiz all last week I didn't dare stir out of the house, and I've got a felon coming on my finger just as sure as I'm a living woman. What appears to be the matter with your face, Mrs. Gallagher?" she asked the last woman in the car.

"Neuralagy of the eyes," the last woman, who wore black glasses and green goggles, remarked, in such lugubrious tones that they cast a gloom over the entire community, and the masculine occupants of the car wondered if there was a well woman in America.

THE GOBLIN GATE.

WE once knew a most worthy man, whose irreproachable life was at one time threatened with mental and physical wreck, all on account of his front gate. He lived out on North Hill, with his charming wife and seven lovely daughters. He was a pale-faced, anxious-looking man, who moved about and looked and spoke as though he supped with sorrow seven times a week. . He has, with all those seven lovely daughters, only one front gate, and that's what made him pale. In one Summer he spent $217 repairing that front gate—putting in new ones, and experimenting with various kinds of hinges; and after all that, the gate swung all through the Winter on a leather strap and a piece of clothes-line—and there was peace in the household, and the man grew fat. But when the April days were nigh, it soon became apparent to the man that his troubles were at hand, and anxiety soon drove the roses from his damask cheeks and robbed his ribs of their substance. He used to climb over the back fence, to avoid calling attention to the disreputable looking old gate; but his self-denial was of no avail. One evening his eldest daughter, Sophronia, said:

"Pa, that horrid old gate is the most disgusting thing on Fifth Street. If you can't afford to have it fixed, I'd take it away and put up a stile."

And pa only groaned. But an evening or so later, his youngest daughter, Elfrida, came in and said, with considerable warmth:

"Pa! I wish you had that beastly old gate tied to your neck; that's what I wish!"

And she dissolved in tears, and evaporated up stairs in a misty cloud, while her sisters followed slowly, casting reproachful glances at pa. And the next evening, his third daughter, Azalea, came bouncing into the room, about 9:30 P. M., with her gloves in a condition to indicate that she had been patting gravel, and said, with some energy, that if pa had no feeling, other people had; and she wished she was dead, she did; and she hoped that the next time pa went out of that hateful old gate, he'd fall clear from Fifth Street to the bridge, so she did. And she broke down, and disappeared with a staccato accompaniment of sobs and sniffles. And the next time pa went out of that gate, he found it prostrate between the two posts, and saw that the fragile strands of the clothes-line had parted, under some extraordinary pressure; and that was what ailed Azalea's gloves. Pa saw there was nothing for it but a new gate, and he groaned aloud as he viewed the dreary prospect of furnishing gates to support the manly forms of the best young men of Burlington for another Summer. It soon became evident that he was getting up a gate he could match against time. He pondered, and pondered, and pondered. He became the confidant of carpenters; he was often seen guiltily showing certain plans and drawings to blacksmiths and cunning workers in iron and·steel. And in due time he had a new gate up; a massive gate, with great posts, ornamental and substantial—and the seven sisters were pleased. They read the little brass plate, that informed them that a patent was applied for, and they saw the words, "For 130 pounds;" but they didn't know what it meant until the gate had swung on the uneven tenor of its way about a week.

One evening, the weather, though sufficiently cool to be bracing, admitted a test of the new gate. A murmur of voices arose from the vicinity of that popular lovers' retreat, as Sophronia swung idly to and fro on its heavy frame. Presently, a pale-faced, anxious-looking man, who was holding his hand upon his breast to still his beating heart, as he crouched in a dark corner of the porch, heard Rodolphus say:

"But believe me, Sophronia, my own heart's idol, between the touches of the rude hand of time and the unkind—— " As he began the word, he leaned forward and bent his weight upon the gate, and with a sharp click a little trap-door in the side of the post flew open, and a gaunt, many-jointed arm of steel, with an iron knob as big as a Virginia gourd on the end of it, flew out, and, with the rapidity of lightning, hit Rodolphus two resounding pelts between the shoulders, that sounded like a bass drum explosion.

"Oh-h-h! gosh!" he roared, "I'm stabbed! I'm stabbed!" and, without waiting to pick up his hat, fled, shrieking for the doctor; while Sophronia rushed into the house, crying, "Pa! pa! pa! Rodolphus is shot!" and swooned. The pale-faced man said nothing, but shrank still further back into the shadow, and thrust his handkerchief into his mouth to stifle a smile. Pretty soon he knew the voice of his daughter Azalea at the gate, saying "Good night." But a rich, manly voice detained her; and the measured swing of the gate was again heard in the distance. Soon he heard Lorenzo say, as he made ready to climb upon the gate:

"But whatever of sorrow may await our future, dear one, I would it might fall upon me———"

And just as he lifted his last foot from the ground, the trap opened, and the gaunt arm reached out and fell upon him, with that big knob, four times; and every time it reached him, Lorenzo shrieked:

"Bleeding heart! Oh, mercy, mercy, Mr. Man! Oh, murder!"

And as he ambled away in the starlight, wailing for arnica, Azalea fled wildly to her home, shrieking, "Oh pa, pa, pa! somebody is murdering Lorenzo!" And on the porch a pale-faced man thrust the rim of his felt hat into his mouth, to reinforce his handkerchief, and hugged himself in placid content. Pretty soon the man's fifth daughter came home from a party, and she, too, perched on the gate; and, in a moment or two, Alphonso said:

"But, my own Miriam, would I could tell you what I feel for you———"

But he didn't; for, just as he leaned upon the gate, the gaunt arm reached out and felt for him with about seventy-five pounds of iron, and knocked his breath so far out of him that he couldn't shriek until he had run half a mile away from the house. And Miriam ran into the house, screaming that Alphonso had a fit.

And the pale-faced man rose up out of the shadow and emptied his mouth; and as he stood under the quiet starlight, looking at the gate whose powerful but delicate mechanism repelled every ounce of weight over 130 pounds, a look of ineffable peace stole over the pale face, and the smile that rested on the quiet features told that the struggle of a life-time was ended in victory—and a gate had been discovered that could set at naught the oppressions of thoughtless young people.

THE AUTOMATIC CLOTHES-LINE REEL.

NO one who lived in Burlington that year, can ever forget the first practical test that was made of the famous "Domestic Automatic" clothes-line reel. It was a curious and powerful bit of mechanism, and was the invention of a man who lived on Barnes Street. This man used to be grievously afflicted because the Scandinavian lady who superintended the weekly wash day ceremonies at his house always took great pains to leave a net work of clothes line spread all around his back yard. And when he made complaint to her about it she addressed him in the musical accents of Christine Nilsson's native language, and overwhelmed him with a torrent of eloquence that he could not understand. And when he remonstrated with his wife and daughter about it they laughed him to scorn, and his daughter, who was educated at Vassar, and can hustle her terrified parent out of the house with one hand, told him if he interfered any more in that department around that house he'd get drowned in the wash tub. So this man suffered. One bitter cold Winter morning he ran out to the wood-shed after some kindling, and the first line caught him under the chin and pulled his neck out till it was a foot long, and he ran into the house and frightened his wife into fits by his terrible appearance, and she threatened to apply for a divorce if he ever made faces at her that way again. It was nearly three hours before his neck shrunk back to its natural size. And a few nights after that, he was all dressed to go to a party with his family, and he went bounding down the back yard to see that the alley gate was fastened, and a slack line caught him amidships, let him run out the slack, and then when it hauled taut, just picked him up, tossed the breath out of him, turned him clear over, and chucked him down on his back, splitting his coat from the tail-buttons to the neck. And he couldn't move, and he couldn't speak, and he couldn't even breathe, only about thirty cents on the dollar, so he couldn't answer his wife and daughter when they screamed to him that they were ready, and they concluded that he had run away to avoid going with them, so they went off without him, and never came back till eleven o'clock, and the man lay out in the back yard all that time, trying to die. And one time after that, he was jogging across the back yard with his arms full of about three hundred pounds of hard wood, and he was laughing like a hyena at something he had read in *The Hawkeye*, when a clothes prop slipped just as he passed under the line and dropped on his head, raising a lump as big as an egg, and as he fell forward, another line caught right in his mouth, and sawed it clear back to his ears, so that when he smiled the top of his head only hung on a hinge.

Well, these things naturally weighed on his mind and depressed him, but they set him to thinking, and he went to work and invented a patent clothes-line reel, which was inclosed in a heavy cast-iron box, and was worked by a powerful automatic arrangement. You only had to wind up the box and set it for a certain hour, just like an alarm clock, and at that hour the reel would go off, and pull on the line like a team of mules, the spring hook at the other end of the line would let go its hold, and that line would be rolled up at the rate of a thousand miles a minute. He said nothing about his invention, but put up the box and told some lie about it to his family, which is a way men have, and he set it for 7 o'clock P. M., and wound it up strong. Then he watched Miss Nilsson's compatriot run out the line and adjust the hook, and he went away.

About 7 o'clock that evening, while he was toasting his feet at the fire and reading the almanac, the family were disturbed by unmistakable indications of a fight going on in the back yard between a hurricane and an earthquake, in which the earthquake appeared to be getting a little the best of it. The affrighted family rushed to the back door and looked out upon a scene of devastation and anarchy. The air was full of fragments of linen, and cotton, and red flannel, while shirt buttons, clothes pins, and little brass buckles, were flying like hail. The reel in the iron box was making about 60,000 revolutions a minute, and was whirling around like a thrashing machine, and the line was tearing around the posts like a streak of runaway lightning, and the clothes were trying to keep along with it, and around the posts they were ripping, tearing and snapping more than any cyclone that ever got loose, while where the line shot into the hawse-hole in the iron box, the striped stockings and white shirts and things, and flannels, and yarn socks, and undershirts and more things, and aprons, and handkerchiefs, and sheets and things, and pillow slips, just foamed and bulged, and tossed wildly, and ripped, and tore, and scraped, until the yard and air were so full of lint that it looked worse than an arctic snow storm. Oh, it was dreadful. It was terrible. Everybody shrieked in dismay.

"Somebody's at the clothes line!" screamed the man's daughter.

"Good heavens!" yelled the man, "hadn't you taken the clothes in?"

"No!" chorused the women.

The man thought he would save what was left. He sprang at the clothes line. He caught the flying hook at the end with both hands, and the next instant, before the terrified eyes of his shrieking wife and daughter, he was jerked through the hole in the iron box, a quivering mass of boneless flesh, while his glistening skeleton fell rattling upon the porch.

They gathered his frame work off the porch, and unlocked the box and drew out his covering. He was not dead, so deftly and quickly had he been removed from his framework. They sent for the doctors, but their skill could not avail to get the man together again, and now he sits, limp and boneless, in a high-backed easy chair, smiling sadly at his grinning skeleton, which sits in a chair on the opposite side of the fire-place, grinning sociably at its counterpart, and rattling horribly every time it crosses its bony legs, or scratches the top of its glistening head with its gaunt, fleshless fingers. And thus that poor man will have to drag out a dual existence until death comes to both of him. It is a painful, expensive life, for the skeleton eats just as much as the flesh, and the flesh has taken to smoking ten cent cigars, and the skeleton can't sleep a wink unless it has a big hot whisky every night at bed time. And all this is the result of wicked, wicked carelessness. A terrible warning to women who leave the clothes-line up after dark.

INSPIRATIONS OF TRUTH.

EVERY year, so oft as the 22d of February comes, the day sacred to the memory of the father of his country is faithfully celebrated by two good boys of Burlington, who, if their lives are only spared, will yet be second editions of the immortal G. W. Last year, it was noticed by every one about the house, they were unusually good. They stayed home all the morning, and talked about Washington, and how he broke the mule and girdled the sassafras tree, and how good he was, and what a pity it was he had no middle name. Along in the afternoon their mother sent them to the church, where there was to be a festival, with a basket filled high with sweet home-made bread, and cold boiled ham, and roast chicken, and one thing and another. They took hold of the basket and plodded soberly and goodily toward the church. As they started down Division Street they saw a boy coming toward them whom they knew. He was the son of a neighbor, the blacksmith's boy, with whom they had a feud of long standing; for on divers occasions he had caught these good brothers out, separately, and had rudely assaulted them, and fairly pounded the hair off their heads. He was a little too healthy for either of the boys alone, but the pair had sworn to make it lively for him if ever they lighted upon him together. So soon as they saw him they put down the basket and gave chase. He girded up his loins and fled, but the boys got themselves up and pursued after him and pressed him hard, and after a rattling chase of about two blocks, they encompassed him round about in a vacant lot, and fell upon him, and smote him insomuch that he begged for mercy and screamed for succor until he was black in the face. Then the victors, joyous returning from the fray, with light steps sought their long abandoned train. Imagine their dismay when, through the gathering twilight gloom, they saw somewhat less than one hundred and fifty thousand dogs, half buried in the basket, dividing and devouring the sutler stores contained therein. There was precious little left when the dogs were driven away, and the boys went home exceeding sorrowful, but hopeful. Their mother met them at the door, and took the empty basket from their hands.

"Who did you give the basket to?" she asked.

"Mrs. Featherstone, dear ma," replied the elder George Washington.

"And what did she say?" asked their mother, for Mrs. Featherstone is an authority in church festivals.

"Oh," chorused both George Washingtons, "she said it was the nicest basket that had come in all the afternoon."

"And," added the younger George, feeling that he wasn't doing himself justice if he didn't get in an independent statement, "Mrs. Lamphreys said she would give anything in the world if she could make such white bread as yours — she said it was wonderful how you done it."

"Now, did she say that?" cried the delighted woman; for at the last sociable Mrs. Lamphreys said her bread was like bass-wood slabs.

"And Mr. Middlerib," cried the elder G. W., fearful lest his younger brother should find favor and be exalted over him, "said there wasn't such chickens anywhere in the State of Iowa outside of that basket."

And then the younger held the age again, and the

older chipped one, and the younger saw him and raised him, and then the older came in, and the younger stayed right by him, and they told all manner of things and compliments about and from all manner of people who were at the church, until the good woman, astonished and delighted at her sudden popularity, determined to go to the sociable, although she had not intended to do so. She went, and she looked in vain for her cake and ham and chicken. She returned home at an early hour, and roused her young George Washingtons from the sweet, innocent sleep of childhood. Then she took a skate strap, and after a brief but pointed cross-questioning on the evidence already brought forward, proceeded——. The rest is too awful.

SPIRIT PHOTOGRAPHY.

IT must have been nearly three years ago, as nearly as we can remember, just about the time Monfort and Hill got to photographing ghosts, that a tall, pale man, with piercing black eyes and long hair, came to Burlington and opened a photograph gallery. He was a spirit photographer, and when his sitters received their pictures, for which they were expected to pay very roundly, lo, the spirit faces of dear ones who had gone before clustered around the face of the party whose photograph had been taken from life. There were plenty of people in the learned city of Burlington who were as fond of believing in supernatural things as are the outside barbarians. So, credulous men and women thronged to the spirit artist's studio, the spirits came up to be photographed around their mortal friends by squads and platoons, and worldly dross, in the shape of a fluctuating and irredeemable currency, poured into the artist's coffers, and he was happy. Among others who went to his studio, was a sad-eyed young man who is a genius. He never used to get home till two o'clock in the morning, because he was down in his office, he told the folks, burning the midnight oil, and committing the yearnings of a restless and ambitious genius to paper. He was supposed to be writing a book of poems, and, consequently, the fair ones who were privileged to enter the circle of his dreamy acquaintance, doted on him. When he went to have his photograph taken, the dearest girl in the world, the one who tells him what nice hands he has, and who rubs his head when his long hours of lonely study make it ache all the next day, accompanied him. He told her on the way down that he expected when his counterfeit presented itself on the albumenized card, the spirit faces of Byron, and Hood, and Macaulay, and Shakspeare, and Tom Moore, and Shelley would rise and cluster around him. She gasped hysterically, and, looking proudly at him, said she believed they would too, and wouldn't it be nice? But he only sighed gloomily, as genius always sighs, and they entered the studio.

While the young man was posing himself the Professor told him that those who were nearest and dearest to him in his lonely hours would gather around him and kiss the clustering curls on his marble brow, and that no earthly power could keep them out of the camera. The young lady reiterated her opinion in regard to the "niceness" of such an arrangement, the young man put on a look of genius and gazed into the camera with the air of a man who is wondering where he can borrow three dollars; the artist dived under the cloth and in due time he stepped to the front with the picture and exhibited it to the poet and the adoring girl.

Spirits?

One or two of them. Right in the center was the young poet, gazing dreamily out into vacancy. And the spirits who cheered him in his lonely hours of study, and assisted him in the conflagration of the midnight oil, gathered around him, and never stirred or faded, not even when the poet ejaculated, " Oh lying horrors!" nor yet when the young girl shrieked and fell fainting with her hair caught in that forked thing the artist stands behind the subject to hold his head steady. For on the right of the poet there stood a spirit with a long slim neck whose name appeared to be " Whisky Cocktail," and on the left there was a short, squatty spirit who was announced as just plain " Gin," and then, clustering all around the young poet's head, like an aureola, were " Straights," whatever they are, " Grasshopper Punch," " Log Cabin Cocktail," " Old Tamarack," " Eye Openers," " Appetizers," " Night Caps," " Can't Quits," " Corpse Revivers," " Coffin Nails," " Indian Cocktails," " Mountain Dew," " Benzine," " The New Drink," " Fly Poison," " What Killed Dad," " The Same," " Fast Freight," " Bran'an Wa'r," " Sherri'neg," " Sudden Death," " Crusade Drops," " Commissary No. 3," " Old Crow," " Tangleleg," " Forty Rod," " Grim Death," " Jimson Juice," " Chain Lightning," " Twelfth Resolution," " That's on Me," " Temperance Tract," " Quinine," and several other spirits who were too far in the back ground to show their cards very distinctly.

The young man didn't take another sitting, and he has since spent more time trying to convince " her" that this spirit photography is the greatest humbug that ever deluded a credulous people, than he ever spent with the spirits who share his lonely hours of midnight toil.

WRITING FOR THE PRESS.

PROF. MATTHEWS, in his delightful book, "Hours With Men and Books," devotes a chapter, and a very instructive chapter too, to advising and directing people who are determined to write for the press what to write and how to say it. But even in that special chapter Prof. Matthews has overlooked quite a number of important points which we, in our experience with occasional newspaper contributors, have come to look upon as absolutely essential to good correspondence. We have had, even in the usually infallible *Hawk-eye*, some complaint, once in a while, from occasional correspondents about mistakes which have appeared in their articles when they come out in print. We are aware that in many cases the fault was our own, but we are confident all such trouble could be remedied if correspondents would pay a little more attention to the preparation of their manuscript. Printers are not always infallible, and proof readers do sometimes make mistakes, but we have prepared a few practical hints and instructions, and if people who write occasionally for the papers will only observe the following simple and practical rules, which are much easier to observe than Prof. Matthews', they may be assured that their articles will always command the highest market price, which is seldom less than two cents a pound:

Never write with pen or ink. It is altogether too plain, and doesn't hold the mind of the editor and printers closely enough to their work.

If you are compelled to use ink never use that vulgarity known as the blotting pad. If you drop a blot of ink on the paper, lick it off. The intelligent compositor loves nothing so dearly as to read through the smear this will make across twenty or thirty words. We have seen him hang over such a piece of copy half an hour, swearing like a pirate all the time, he felt that good.

Don't punctuate. Editors and publishers prefer to punctuate all manuscript sent to them. And don't use capitals. Then the editor can punctuate and capitalize to suit himself, and your article, when you see it in print, will astonish even if it does not please you.

Don't try to write too plainly. It is a sign of plebeian origin and public-school breeding. Poor writing is an indication of genius. It's about the only indication of genius that a great many men possess. Scrawl your article with your eyes shut, and make every word as illegible as you can. We get the same price for it from the rag-man as though the paper were covered with copper-plate sentences.

Avoid all painstaking with proper names. All editors know the full name of every man, woman and child in the United States, and the merest hint at the name is sufficient. For instance, if you write a character something like a drunken figure "8," and then draw a wavy line, and then write the letter M and another wavy line, the editor will know at once that you mean Samuel Morrison, even though you may think you mean "Lemuel Messenger." It is a great mistake to think that proper names should be written plainly.

Always write on both sides of the paper, and when you

have filled both sides of every page trail a line up and down every margin, and back to the top of the first page, closing your article by writing the signature just above the date. How editors do love to get hold of articles written in this style. And how they would like to get hold of the man who sends them. Just for ten minutes. Alone. In the woods, with a gun.

Lay your paper on the ground when you write; the rougher the ground the better. A dry goods box or the side of the house will do if the ground is too damp. Any thing rather than a table or desk.

Coarse brown wrapping paper is the best for writing your articles on. If you can tear down an old circus poster and write on the pasty side of it with a pine stick, it will do still better.

When your article is completed, crunch the paper in your pocket, and carry it two or three days before sending it in. This rubs off the superfluous pencil marks and makes it lighter to handle.

If you can think of it, lose one page out of the middle of your article. The editor can easily supply what is missing, and he loves to do it. He has nothing else to do.

If correspondents will observe these directions, editors, in most instances, will hold themselves personally responsible for every error that appears in their articles, and will pay full claims for damages when complaint is made. We shall never forget the last man who complained at the *Hawkeye* office under this rule. We can never, never, although we should live a thousand years, forget the appalling look he turned upon us while we were pulling his lungs out of his ear with the nail-grab. Our heart seemed to turn to ice, under the influence of that dumb beseeching look, while we tore him to pieces.

We have never torn a man to pieces since without feeling the hot tears spring to our eyes as we think of that man. We have been tempted, time and again, to break ourselves of this habit of tearing men to pieces for trivial causes. But we digress. We were merely saying we are always happy to receive complaints and correct any errors for which we are responsible.

DANGERS OF BATHING.

AS the warm weather raises the waters of the creeks and rivers to the temperature so inviting to the boys of the republic, a few instructive and general suggestions relative to bathing in the streams may prove the means of saving some juvenile lives. Boys are proverbially rash and reckless in almost everything they do, and are so apt to overdo whatever they undertake, except sawing wood or fastening the front gate, that too much wholesome advice on the benefits of abstinence can never be amiss in their cases. And especially is such advice necessary in regard to bathing, for when a boy makes up his mind to "go swimming," he thinks of nothing in the world except getting into the water. And every year so many precious lives are endangered, and so much pain and misery caused by boyish carelessness and thoughtlessness in this respect, that it is a solemn and important duty of journalism to warn the boys of the dangers that wait upon bathing parties, and instruct them how to avoid them. We therefore give a few rules, culled from the pages of personal experience, which, if properly observed by the boys of America, may save them no one can tell how much misery and suffering.

1. Always ask your mother if you may go down to the river with the boys to hunt carnelians. Mention the names of Sammie Johnson, and Robbie Gregg, and Ellis Haskell and Johnnie Chalmers, and Charlie Austin, and Wallie Colburn, and Dockie Worthington, all well-known "good boys," who wash their faces every morning, keep their clothes clean, wear white collars, and don't say bad words, as the young gentlemen who are to comprise the party. A judicious and strict adherence to this rule has often obtained the necessary parental permission to visit the river shore, which would otherwise be sternly denied, especially if it should appear that Bill Slamup, and Tom Dobbins, and Jim Sikes, and Butch Tinker, and Mickey McCann, were the alternates who were confidently expected to represent the first named delegates in the convention.

2. Avoid going into the river in the vicinity of a lumber yard. The temptation to take pine boards from the lumber piles to swim on is too strong for many boys to resist. It is very pleasant, we know, to swim around on a nice broad plank, but the lumbermen do not always like it, and we have known a rough board, abruptly drawn from beneath the horizontal figure of a kicking, paddling, laughing boy, to fill him with remorse and slivers to an extent that would appear incredible were it not for the fact that the boy who loses his plank in this way has plenty of time to count his slivers as he pulls them out.

We knew a boy, twenty years ago, who swam off a plank in this way, and immediately afterward sat down on the sandy shore, and amid the unfeeling laughter and mocking sympathy of his colleagues, withdrew from his cuticle, beginning at the chin and ending at the toes, three hundred and seventeen well-developed average slivers, and four of a larger variety, denominated snags. And sometimes we wake up in the night, from happy dreams of childhood's guileless days, and half believe we didn't get all those slivers out then.

3. Avoid putting a bar of kitchen soap in your pocket before you leave home. It frequently gives the bather away entirely, being quickly missed from the sink, and readily detected about the person. And even if you get it safely to the river, and the first boy who "soaps himself" does not lose it in twenty feet of water, the "strocky" appearance of your hair, on your return home, instantly betrays the recent and extravagant use of resin soap, and grave consequences are apt to follow. Besides, you do not really need the soap, as is attested by your well-known aversion to it at home.

4. If convenient, bathe very near a railroad bridge. Then, when a passenger train comes thundering by, you can rush out of the water and dance and shriek on the bank. Travelers like this; and if your uncle Jasper, from Waterloo, or your father returning from Creston, should happen to be on the train and recognize you, they will tell you what the passengers said about it, and your father will be so pleased that he will assist you in a little physical exercise, so essential to the health after bathing. And then the next time you go in swimming you can show the boys your back—a spectacle in which they will take fiendish delight, which they will exhibit by imitating, in most expressive pantomime, the contortions, gestures, and outcries in which you were supposed to have indulged while your father was putting that back on you.

5. If you desire to get up a crowd to go swimming, signify your wishes by holding up your right hand, with the first and second fingers erect and spread apart like a

letter V, and as many good boys as are ready, willing and anxious to run away and go with you, will respond by the same sign, and the party can easily be made up without fear of detection, in the presence of the unsuspecting preceptor, who is a graduate of a private school, and never had any fun.

6. Should any boy be so lost to honor as to desire to leave the water before the rest of the crowd wish to do so, he may be easily induced to return to the liquid element by gently tossing a handful of dry sand or dust upon his back, as nearly between the shoulders as may be. If there is a really good, unsophisticated boy in the crowd whose habit of wearing a white collar and carrying a clean handkerchief pronounces him a haughty aristocrat, the bad boys, by getting dressed first and judiciously applying the sand to him as often as he "comes out," can keep him in the water until his father comes to look for him. Then, the next afternoon he goes down with you to the river, you can look at his back, and have your revenge.

7. If a boy lingers in the water too long, it is sometimes advisable, in order that he may learn to abstain from indulging himself to such an intemperate extent in the future, to tie each sleeve of his shirt in a most terrific hard knot, right at the elbow. When this knot is dipped into the water, and a boy gets at each end of the sleeve, braces his feet and pulls for life, it may be drawn so tightly that it can not be drawn out with a stump machine. The boy who belongs to that shirt, after many vain endeavors, is either compelled to cut off the sleeves, or, *multis cum lachrymis*, go home with it buttoned around his neck and hanging down his back like a drunken apron. This gives him away, bad, and the appearance of that weeping boy, plodding timorously and apprehen-

sively homeward through the gloaming, and the variegated aspect of his back the next night, produce such a pleasant impression upon you, that for two weeks afterward, as your dear mother looks in at your room door, and sees you smiling in your sleep, she thinks the angels are whispering to you.

8. The most approved method of drying the hair is to shake it up rapidly with a pine stick. Never comb your hair smoothly before going home, no matter who offers to loan you a pocket - comb. A slick head of hair excites suspicion in the family circle on sight.

9. If, at the supper - table, the dreadful discovery is made by your mother or sister that your shirt is wrong side out, the best way to do is to own right up. Excuses are useless; and no mother or father of ordinary intelligence was ever misled by the assertion, however solemnly made, that the shirt was turned by reason of the boy too suddenly climbing a fence instead of going through the gate.

10. To get water out of your ears, lean your head over to one side, and kick out violently with one leg, while you pound your head smartly with the palm of your hand. It is an exploded fallacy that holding a warm stone to the ear will bring out the water.

There are some other rules which might be added to the above, but they are comparatively unimportant, and are so generally known that you can learn them by applying for information to the first bad boy you meet.

THE POWER OF DIGNITY.

THE human heart, in all its expansive, limitless capacity for enjoyment, takes greater pleasure in nothing than in witnessing a portly, solemn-visaged man, the embodiment of natural dignity, importance in clothes, administer a scathing rebuke to some "smart" petty government official. One morning just such a personification of innate dignity loomed up at the stamp window of the post-office, and glared in gloomy and majestic displeasure at the busy clerk who registered a letter before he sprang to the window and asked the stately customer what he wished. The great man did not answer for several moments. He gazed steadily and impressively over the clerk's head, and then asked, in ponderous tones:

"Is there any one hear-r-r-e who attends to business?"

The embarrassed clerk blushed, faltered for a moment, then, recovering himself, said, with characteristic and national cheerfulness, becoming an official of the Republic:

"I will see, sir."

And he disappeared. He went into the other departments, tortured a carrier with an original conundrum, and heard a good story in the mailing room, and came back.

"Yes, sir," he said to the great one, "there are, in addition to myself, three clerks in the letter department, one in the mailing room, four carriers, three route agents, the mail driver and a janitor."

"Ah-h-h! I am glad there are so many. I may in all that number find one who is at his post."

And then he looked as impressive as a special agent, and was silent for three minutes, while the humbled clerk awaited his orders, and impatient men behind him fidgeted and grumbled. Finally, the great man said with deep solemnity:

"I wish one three-cent stamp."

The clerk tore off the stamp and held it, waiting for the consideration. The great man made a somewhat longer pause than usual; he felt in his various vest pockets; he gradually lost his look of impressive rebuke; his chest caved in, and he assumed the aspect of an ordinary frail mortal, and he said:

"Ah — the fact is — I'm sure — ah — in short, I find that I have carelessly left my purse at home — can you kindly —"

The clerk, with the faintest suggestion of triumph in his eye, brusquely waved the great man aside with —

"Sorry for you, sir; but the clerk who sells stamps on credit is not in. What does the next man want?"

And the great man, as he backed through the smiling crowd who stood around with money in their hands, felt somehow that his rebuke had been thrown away, and feared that if the case went to the jury without argument it would very probably bring in a verdict for the Government.

A CANDID CONFESSION.

THERE used to live down on Washington Street, a good man, who endeavored to train up his children in the way they should go, and as his flock was numerous he had anything but a sinecure in this training business. Only last Summer the elder of these male olive branches, who had lived about fourteen wicked years, enticed his younger brother, who had only had ten years' experience in boyish deviltry, to go out on the river in a boat, a species of pastime which their father had many a time forbidden, and had even gone so far as to enforce his veto with a skate strap. But, the boys went this time, trusting to luck to conceal their depravity from the knowledge of their pa, and in due time they returned, and walked around the house, the two most innocent looking boys in Burlington. They separated for a few moments, and at the expiration of that time the elder was suddenly confronted by his father who requested a private interview in the usual place, and the pair adjourned to the wood shed, where, after a brief, but highly spirited performance, in which the boy appeared most successfully as "heavy villain" and his father took his favorite role of "first old man," the curtain went down and the boy, considerably mystified, sought his younger brother.

"John," he said, "who do you suppose told dad? Have you been licked?"

John's face will not look more peaceful and resigned when it is in his coffin than it did as he replied,

"No, have you?"

"Have I? Come down to the cow yard and look at my back."

John declined, but said:

"Well, Bill, I'll tell you how father found us out. I am tired of acting this way, and I ain't going to run away and come home and lie about it any more. I'm going to do better after this, and so when I saw father I couldn't help it, and went right to him and confessed."

Bill was touched at this manly action on the part of his younger brother. It found a tender place in the bad boy's heart, and he was visibly affected by it. But he asked:

"How did it happen the old man didn't lick you?"

"Well," said the penitent young reformer, "you see I didn't confess on myself, I only confessed on you; that was the way of it."

A strange, cold light glittered in Bill's eye.

"Only confessed on me?" he said. "Well, that's all right, but come down behind the cow shed and look at my back."

And when they got there do you suppose John saw the first mite of Bill's back? Ah no, dear children, he saw nothing bigger than Bill's fists, and before he got out of that locality he was the worst pounded John that ever confessed on anybody. Thus it is that our coming reformers are made and trained.

BURLINGTON NOVELETTE.

A BURLINGTON NOVELETTE.

CHAPTER I.

"MARGUERITTE!"

"Bertrande Hautville Montaigne du Biffington!"

And the soughing of the September wind swept through the tremulous leaves like the whisper of memories, ghosts of the far away had been. Each star that lit the azure dome with glittering ray—er, ah—er—er—with glittering ray. Ray.

It looked like rain.

CHAPTER II.

Margueritte Hortense Isana l'Erena del Imperatricia du Calincourt Johnson was an orphan.

Her father was dead.

And, also, by the way, her mother.

Her great grand parents were not living. Alas, no. The cold clods rattled on the coffins of those estimable people when Margueritte was young. She was not acquainted with the fact until the good people had been dead some seventy-five years.

Then kind friends, whose hearts were torn and rifted with sympathy, broke the news gently to her.

She sat like one stunned. Over her marble face there passed no trace of the emotion which raged like a high fed cyclone in her soul. She said:

"Did they leave me anything?"

And they told her, "Not a stiver, dear, not a lone nickel; not a street car check; not a solitary red, red cent. Only an old photograph album with the covers torn off and the pictures lost. You are badly left."

And then the fountains of the deep were broken up and she wailed in the bitterness of her agony.

"Why, oh, why did they die? Why did they die? Why did they die and leave me,— leave me — leave me nothing?"

A deep manly voice, resonant as a vesper bell when it is peeling for the fray, answered from the next room.

"I give it up."

Let us draw a veil over the dreadful scene.

CHAPTER III.

Bertrande Hautville Montaigne du Biffington was not an orphan.

He was an Ancient and Excepted Odd Fellow.

He was of a noble and numerous parentage. He had one mother, and she was a Chicago princtess. She used to hold brevier cases on *The Daily Tomahawk*. She had ten divorces, neatly framed, hanging up in her parlor, and Bertrande, whose own original father had died of an hereditary attack of arsenic in the soup while his divorce suit was pending, was successively flogged by an illustrious line of paternal incumbents, and acknowledged the sway of one father, full rank, and ten fathers by brevet. He loved the lonely orphan, who had no parents whatever, from a sense of natural duty and justice, to kind of even the thing up and strike an equitable average.

CHAPTER IV.

There is only one place where nature does not abhor

a vacuum. That is under a Congressman's hat.

CHAPTER V.

Night had come. It got in on the evening train, and was late, as usual. The drowsy bat was on the wing; or rather, the wing was on the drowsy bat. Both wings, in fact, were on the d. b. Down in the mossy glade, where deepening shadows mock the starlight's gleam, she waits. Her Italian marble brow is clouded with a weight of sorrow. Her finely-chiseled chin is still; the plastic chewing-gum, pasted on the trunk of a rugged oak, cools and hardens in the evening air. The firm tread of a manly No. 9 comes crashing through the woodland.

'Tis he.

"Bertrande!"

"Margueritte!"

They said no more. They could not. They had forgotten the rest of each other's names. They sat in the deeping shadows of the gloaming, holding each other's hands, and trying to think of something nice to say.

Suddenly his delicate nostrils quivered and trembled with a startled light.

"Margueritte!" he exclaimed, "we must fly! I hear the sound of native applejack upon the evening air! M'ff! m'ff!"

"Oh, hevings!" she cried, "it is, it is me long lost fathyer!"

"Then," he exclaimed, drawing a United States regulation cavalry saber from his bosom, "I am lost!"

"Oh, no, not lost;" she said in earnest tones, "go straight ahead till you come to the *Hawkeye* office, then turn up Market Street two blocks and follow the street car track south until you smell beer. Then you will know where you are. Fe-ly! Fe-ly! Me fathyer comes."

"Methought," he said, pausing in his flight, and speaking sternly, "Methought thou haddedest not a father."

"I haive, I haive," she shrieked, "and it is he!"

And as she spake a fatherly looking man parted the bushes and stood by her side. He was clad in a dark blue cut-away coat, with a button-hole bouquet, white vest, lilac kids, lavender pants, a pink neck-tie, waxed mustache, and a high hat. His boots were four and a half; his snowy handkerchief was perfumed with jockey club, and his breath with whisky sour. He was twenty-one years of old.

Bertrande regarded him sadly, and said to her he loved:

"It seems to me your father is rather juvenile."

"Dear Bertrande," she said, laying her head upon her father's shoulder, "he married awful young."

"Ah," said Bertrande, bitterly, "I thought may be you had adopted him."

And turning on his heel he was gone.

*　　*　　*　　*　　*　　*　　*

A REMINISCENCE OF EXHIBITION DAY.

"WELL, no," the boy said, "the thing didn't go off exactly as I expected. You see, I was the sixth boy in the class, that was next to the head when the class formed left in front, and I was pretty near the first boy called on to declaim. I had got a mighty good ready and had a bully piece too. Ah, it was a rip staver."

And the boy sighed as he paused to lift a segment out of a green apple, and placed it where it would do the most good, for a cholera doctor. We asked what piece it was.

"Spartacus to the Gladiators," he said. "Just an old he raker of a piece. I got it all by heart, and used to go clear out to the Cascade to rehearse and hook strawberries. Old Fitch" — Mr. Fitch was the boy's preceptor, one of the finest educators in the state — "he taught me all the gestures and inflections and flub drubs, and said I was just layin' over the biggest toad in the puddle——"

"Excelling all your competitors, probably Mr. Fitch said," we suggested.

"Yes," the boy replied, "he's a toney old cyclopedia on the patter, is old Fitchy. But him and me was both dead sure I was goin' to skin the rag off the bush——"

"Win all the honors," we gently corrected.

"Yes," he said, "and the way it went off was bad. You see, I didn't feel easy in my Sunday clothes on a week day to begin with. And my collar was too tight and my necktie was too blue, and I was in a hurry to get off early, so I only blacked the toes of my boots, and left the heels as red as a concert ticket. And the crowd there was in the school-house. Jammed. Every body in their good clothes and every body looking solemn as Monday morning. When my name was called something came up in my throat as big as a foot-ball. I couldn't swallow it and I couldn't spit it out. And when I got up on the platform — oh, Godfrey's cordial! did you ever see a million heads without any bodies?"

We felt ashamed of our limited experience while we confessed that we could not recall having witnessed such a phenomenon.

"I never did till then," the boy went on, "but they were there, for a fact, and I began to remember when these heads danced round and round the room that I had been forgetting my piece in the last five minutes just as fast as I ever forgot to fix the kindling wood at night. But I commenced. I got along with 'It had been a day of triumph in Capua' and 'Lentulus returning with victorious eagles' and all that well enough, but when I got on into the heavy business, I was left, sure. If Spartacus had talked to the gladiators as I did, they would have thought he was drunk and hustled him off to bed. It was awful. I stumbled along until I came to 'Ye stand here now like giants as ye are. The strength of brass is in your rugged sinews, but to-morrow some Roman Adonis, breathing sweet perfume from his curling locks, will with his dainty fingers pat your red brawn and bet his sesterces upon your blood?'"

"That was excellent, capital," we said, applauding, for the boy had growled off the last sentence like a first heavy villain.

"Oh yes, is it though?" he said, with some asperity. "Well, that's the way I was going to say it that Friday, but what I did say was, 'The strength of brass is in your rugged sinews, but to-morrow afternoon (you see I got to thinking of a base ball match) some Doman Aronis breathing sweet perfumery from his curly socks, will pat your bed rawn and bet his sister sees your blood.'"

"Did they laugh?" we asked.

"Oh no!" he replied, with an inflection that type won't take. "Oh, no; they never smiled again; *they* didn't. It was when I got down a little that they felt bad. When he says, 'If ye are beasts, then stand here waiting like fat oxen for the butcher's knife.' I told them, 'If ye be cat fattle, then wait here standing like a butcher for the carving knife.' And I got worse and worse until it came to this, 'Oh, Rome, Rome, thou hast been a tender mother to me. Thou hast taught the poor timid shepherd boy, who never knew a harsher tone than a flute note, to gaze into the glaring eyeballs of the fierce Numidian lion, even as a boy upon a laughing girl. Thou hast taught him to drive the sword through rugged links of mail and brass and warm it in the marrow of his foe!'"

"Bravo!" we shouted.

"Cheese it," he said, sententiously; "I didn't say it just that way. I said, 'Oh Rome, thou has ten a binder mother to me. Thou hast taught the poor boy who never knew a sheep note to glare into the laughing ear of a fierce Numidian eyeball even as a lyin' boy at a girl. Thou hast taught him to mail his ragged brass through swords of link, and marry it in the warmer of his foe.'"

"And then?" we asked.

"I cried," he said, "and went down Everybody was cry'n'. They all had their faces in their handkerchiefs or behind fans, and were shaking so it nearly jarred the school house."

"You should practice elocution during vacation," we suggested, "and you will not fail again."

He bolted the rest of the green apple, threw his bare feet up in the air, and walked around on his hands in little circles. "Don't have no speakin' in vacation," he said.

And we knew that, boy-like, he was going to let the day and the morrow take care each of its own evils, and we wondered as we came away how many fathers would recognize their own boys in the hero of this sketch, and if dear old Fitch, the oldest boy, with the clearest head and the tenderest heart we ever knew, would remember him.

MR. OLENDORF'S COMPLAINT.

YOUNG Mr. Olendorf used to board at a nice boarding house out on North Hill, a little this side of the North Pole. It was a good way out; but Mr. Olendorf always was fond of pure air and pedestrian exercise, and as his business hours were easy, he preferred the comforts of a home in the suburbs to the excitement and clamor of a down-town hotel. A mild-looking, meek-faced, soft-voiced young man was Mr. Olendorf, as ever you could wish to see. He rarely complained about anything, and he never spoke harshly of any one. He would sit on his trunk, when the family had carried his chair down to the parlor for the convenience of invited guests; and he would patiently sew on his shirt-buttons with a darning-needle and carpet thread, rather than

OLENDORF'S COMPLAINT.

intimate to his washer-lady that it wasn't just the thing to run fine shirts through a corn-sheller to wash them. Many a time he crawled into a bed that looked like the crater of an extinct volcano, rather than report the hired girl for neglecting to make it up. And six times a week he cleaned his grimy lamp-chimney with his fingers, as far as they would reach, because, he said, in the fullness of his charitable soul, the girl had so much to do she hadn't got round to it. And the seventh night in the week, the lamp being empty and dry as a flat bottle on a hunting expedition, he would undress by the dim religious light of a match. He used to wash with a piece of soap four inches long and two inches thick, as brown as varnish, and so hard it chipped the edges of the wash-stand when it was carelessly dropped; and often and often, when his eyes were full of soap, and he reached out his imploring hands, groping for the short, thin towel that was seldom there, he had to feel his way to the bed, abrading his shins against things that he couldn't see and didn't know the names of, and dry his face and hair on the pillow-slips. But he never murmured. He used to find bright streaks of red by the dozen in his pomade, and go down to the breakfast table with his own coal-black locks as dry as good advice, and marvel at the exceeding glossiness and slickness of the hired girl's bright auburn cranium. But he said never a word. And the drouth used to strike his perfumery bottles once in a while, and leave them as empty as a lecturer's head; and he would wind his modest nasal horn in a handkerchief that smelled like a washtub, and when his landlady's daughters sailed scornfully past him, perfumed for all the world like the ghosts of his toilet bottles up stairs, he never looked suspicious, but only smiled apologetically, as though it was wrong in him to leave temptation in their way. And once, when he had an attack of cholera morbus, and sent out for a quart of brandy, and took a tablespoonful of it, and came back at night to find the bottle very empty, and the landlady's husband very full, and lying in Mr. Olendorf's bed with his boots on, young Mr. Olendorf only agreed with the landlady that it was very singular, and that the old man must be ill. So you see Mr. Olendorf was inclined to be rather peaceable and meek, and when he did complain there must be some reason for it.

One evening Mrs McKerrel, his landlady, approached the young man for the purpose of securing the weekly dole which he paid for the comforts of a home, and bracing himself up by a desperate effort, Mr. Olendorf, for the first time in his life, complained.

"It's the hash, Mrs. McKerrel," he said plaintively. "It's too monotonous. It's good hash. I can't say that it isn't good. It is more nutritious than chopped straw, and a prize candy package doesn't equal it for variety. But I want change. I like hash for breakfast. But when you give us baked hash for dinner, and put boned hash on for supper, and give us plain hash again for breakfast, and serve stuffed hash again for dinner, it isn't a square deal. I believe you impose on us. I never heard of 'stuffed hash' before I came here, and the only difference between it and the common kind is that it is thinner. The last 'stuffed hash' you gave us you made us eat with steel forks, and it was as thin as soup, and how is a strong man going to make out a dinner when he has only twenty-five minutes in which to eat soup with a three-tined fork? And I don't think you do the fair thing by us on what you call 'boned hash.' It's hardly right, Mrs. McKerrel, to make a hash of sardines and herrings and then call it 'boned.' It's just like eating a shoe brush. Now there ought to be, once in a while, a change. Not too often, you know; I don't expect you to keep a French restaurant for seven dollars a week, but just often enough to keep the bill of fare from growing tiresome. Say once every seven years. For instance, you may have 'boned hash' to-morrow for dinner, which, it being Sunday, you will. Well, then, you might have 'boned hash' every day until 1882, and then give us a roast, or a car-spring chicken. And so with 'stuffed hash,' and 'hash a la mode,' and 'hash a la Mayonnais,' 'Lady Washington hash,' 'hash on toast,' 'spring hash, with mint sauce,' and 'hash a la mortar,' and the other hashes on your bill of fare. By serving them up once every seven years, you have enough kinds to run clear into a Centennial."

The landlady, looking aghast, made an effort to speak, but young Mr. Olendorf motioned her to silence.

"And if you would speak to Mrs. Muldoon, dear Mrs. McKerrel," he went on, "and tell her that, while I am not proud, I do not consider the hickory shirts which the estimable Mr. Muldoon wears while he is developing the railroad resources of the United States exactly the things to wear to church; and even if I had no other scruples against attending public worship in a section hand's shirt, torn all the way across the shoulders and fastened at the neck and cuffs with horn buttons, Mr. Muldoon's are five sizes too large for me, and I would rather she would send me my own. And if you can bribe her to put the starch in my collars instead of my handkerchiefs, I feel that it will improve the appearance of my neck, and spare the feelings of a lacerated and tender nose. No man, Mrs. McKerrel, can wipe his nose on a sheet of tin and do the matter justice."

Mrs McKerrel placed her hands on her hips and stood

up, but Mr. Olendorf begged her to be patient just a moment, while he went on :

"And do you think, if I made a chalk mark on them, that your domestic could learn the difference between my hair brush and my shoe brush? And if I made her a little present, might she not be induced to look up something else to black the stoves with instead of my shoe brush? It is dreadfully mortifying, Mrs. McKerrel, to black your shoes after night and get clear in church the next morning before discovering that your feet are glistening in all the glory of 'Plumbago's New Silver Gray Luster,' and everybody is laughing at you. And then, Mrs. McKerrel, I don't know how my things get so full of snuff. I never use snuff, and I don't want to complain, but——"

Here the exasperated matron could restrain herself no longer. Hastily thrusting her snuff-box back in her pocket, she bade Mr. Olendorf pack. What he wanted, she said, was a Fifth Avenue hotel for seven dollars a week, and he couldn't have it in her house. He was too particular for such a plain woman as her; if he didn't like the ways of plain people, he would have to go where they were nicer. He was too stuck up and fussy to live in her house. Boarders she had kept, of the very best people in the highest classes in society, and this was the first time she had ever heard a word of complaint in her house.

And that is the way Mr. Olendorf happened to call around at the Gorham and ask Andrews for a nice room, a long ways up. And Andrews gave him a key and told him to climb till he knew he was lost, and then crawl into the first bed he saw.

RURAL FELICITY.

MR. PHILETUS R. THROOP is a well known insurance agent of Burlington. He is a perfect steam engine to work, and every Summer, when he feels about worn out by his labors, he goes out to the farm of his Uncle George and rests a couple of weeks. He went out last Summer, as usual, but he only remained a couple of days, and on his return he was heard to say that he would never, never, never, go into the country again if he died for a breath of fresh air. The causes which led to this determination were as follows:

You see, he got a late start on his last trip out into the country, so that when he reached his Uncle George's farm it was about nine o'clock in the evening, and the family, after the good old-fashioned custom, had gone to bed; not a light was visible about the house. Mr. Throop got out of the wagon in which a neighboring farmer had brought him, before they reached the house, so that the noisy wheels would not apprise any waking member of the fact that a visitor had come. Then he climbed over the fence and skipped briskly across lots to reach the house, and give Uncle George and the family a good surprise. Mr. Throop was not so familiar with the farm as he ought to have been to attempt such a nocturnal expedition. He had not gone twenty steps before he stepped into a great ditch, and had time to say all he could remember of the child's prayer, "Now I lay me," before he reached the bottom, and then had plenty of time to compose and repeat a much more appropriate and longer one before he crawled out again. After that he went more slowly, picking his steps with the greatest care, and straining his eyes as he peered into the darkness to distinguish noxious objects. But it was very dark, and of course appearances were unusually deceitful. He would walk around a patch of young clover or luxuriant turf, his heart standing still the while with the terror of having so narrowly escaped walking into a great well, and the next minute he would, after peering ahead of him until his eyes ached and sparks of fire danced before them, walk with the greatest confidence and composure into a pile of last year's peabrush seven feet high, knocking off his hat, scratching his face and tearing his clothes. And then such a time as he would have hunting for his hat, and all the imaginable and unimaginable things that he would pick up in mistake for that useful article of apparel, can be far better imagined than described. And once he ran into a fence and nearly put his eye out on the end of a great stake that was standing out like the point of a *chevaux de frise*. And just before he got to the barn-yard he was amazed to discern a creek flowing between him and the fence, and after vainly hunting in the dark for a bridge, he pulled off his boots and trousers, and, holding the bundle of clothes high in his arms, waded across a stubblefield! so dry, every foot of it, that he might have lighted a match on it anywhere. He thought every tooth he had would chatter out of his head before he could get into his clothes again. Then he got into the barn-yard. He knew it was the barn-yard after he got into it, because in less than a minute after he had climbed the fence, he fell over a slumbering cow, and before he could get up, the frightened animal rose to her feet and bucked Mr. Throop over her head. Then he heard a cow get up just before him, and another just behind him, and two or three to the right and left, and when a cow with a bell that could be heard two miles got up and began galloping around the yard stirring up the rest of the cows, Mr. Throop would have willingly given up the best risk he had ever taken for a lantern. It wasn't safe to stand still, so he took his hat in his hand and went along, swooping it around him in great circles, shouting "Swoosh! Hi! Hooey! Scat! Whish! Whoosh! Ste-boy!" as he went along. He only hit one cow with his hat, however, and the animal thus rudely assailed reached out and kicked him in the groin and doubled him up, and with a farewell flourish hit him on the side of the face with the end of a tail so full of cockle burs that it weighed twenty-seven pounds and knocked him so flat he thought he never would want to get up again. Then he saw what he supposed was the house, looming up black and quiet before him, and he thought his troubles were over. They had just begun.

The next minute he stepped under an open shed where the agricultural implements had been stored during the Winter. The first intimation he had of this was by falling over a plow. He scraped both shins, from the instep to the knee, across the edge of the share, and one of the handles caught him under the chin and jabbed his head up and back so suddenly that he heard his neck crack, and the other hunched him in the floating ribs and knocked enough breath out of him to start a tornado, in a small way but on a safe basis. He thought he never would get away from that plow, for he no sooner got one leg out of one entanglement of draught-irons, coulter, share and handles, than he got the other one snarled up in a still more hopeless maze of mould-board, clevis, sole-plate and beam, besides several other parts that he didn't know the names of. And when at last he vanquished the plow he lost himself in a cultivator, and wore himself out trying to crawl through the gang of coulters. When he got clear of that he fell in with a reaper and mower, and after prodding his instep into indescribable agony by thrusting it against the sickle guards as he fell, he caught hold of the reel, which, of course, immediately whirled with his weight. But it chanced that quite a large colony of barn-yard fowls had used the reel as their roosting place during the Winter, and as it whirled round the amazed and bewildered Mr. Throop rained down upon himself a terrific tempest of hens and roosters, Brahmas, light Cochins, ungainly Shanghais, and a variety of other breeds in such a tumult of squawkings and cacklings, and flappings of wings, and vague but vigorous clawings of feet, that he didn't care whether he got out alive or not, and, indeed, before he got through with the reel he knocked himself down with its vindictive slats seven times. Then he got away from that and impaled himself on a horse rake, and fell over the handle of a fanning mill, and nearly killed himself in the horse power of a thrashing machine, and finally got into the house yard, felt his way to the house, and fell exhausted and speechless against the front door with a diamond-shaped harrow hanging around his neck. And Uncle George, awakened by the thump at the door, opened an up-stairs window and demanded who was there, and receiving no answer shot twice at the recumbent form of Mr. Throop with his revolver. And when they came down with lights and opened the door, they were as greatly surprised as Mr. Throop could have wished.

THE GARDEN OF THE GODS.

THE people around Barnes Street well remember when Mr. Middlerib planted the "garden of the gods." He bought cartloads of rich earth for it, and loaded it with patent fertilizers, and ground and stirred and raked it until the soil was fine as corn meal. The seeds were received by express, and there wasn't a package that didn't have a full college course of Latin printed on the back, and Mr. Middlerib grew bald trying to pronounce the fearful and wonderful names of the seed, that were to make the garden of the gods the wonder of South Hill. When these germs of magnificent flora were planted the neighbors hung over the fence in silent admiration and listened to Mr. Middlerib's botanical lectures, delivered over every package that was opened. Where the *abolutus haciedendus microbulus* was imbedded, he erected a large trestle immediately, for that impetuous climber to ascend and ramble over. And where he implanted the *diocantanean psyttachineliensis psoddium*, he reared a tall, straight stick for that towering mass of blossom and foliage to shape itself against. He refused the most penetrating hints for a few seeds of the *bianthus geridian psottoliensis giasticus, floridens bilthus*, and the care and great gravity with which he earthed the germs of the *bibulus Burlingtoniensis giganteus* brought tears to the eyes of the women. And when the seeds were all planted, how zealously Mr. Middlerib watched and wrought and fought for their protection. He would get up in the night to chase the neighbors' cows around the house two or three times, and across the garden of the gods four or five times, and out of the front gate once, and return to his virtuous couch with profanity in his heart and mud on his feet, and one slipper down by the cistern and the other in the verbena bed.

All the cut-worms in the State of Iowa appeared to be attending a mass convention in the garden of the gods. When the tinner came to fix the spout, he stuck the ladder by which he ascended to the roof in that sacred ground, and the carpenter who patched the cornice set one of his trestles in the same place. Every tramp who came to beg, selected that one favored locality as the only spot in the world where he might assume the usual humble and respectful position, and rehearse the stereotyped application for provender. Mr. Middlerib nearly wore out his voice shouting at people and cows, and railing at cut-worms, and one Sunday morning he fell asleep in church, and Mrs. M. prodded him with her parasol just as the minister said, in impressive accents, "And here we are treading on sacred ground." "Git off of it!" yelled Mr. Middlerib, dreaming of the grocer's boy standing on the g. o. g., and using his oft-repeated phrase, "Scatter, or I'll bury ye in it!" And it raised such a church scandal that Mr. Middlerib was obliged to double his subscription to keep in good fellowship.

But after manifold troubles, the garden came along beautifully, only the plants acted a little queer. The climber refused to climb, save in a horizontal position, but after its own way; and in all general directions on a horizontal plane it manifested a disposition to crowd all over that part of South Hill. The *diocantanean psyttachineliensis psoddium* scorned the straight stick by which it was expected to brace itself, and grew out in crooked branches like a garden oak. But the tender care it received, and the rich earth in which it was planted, showed what wonders cultivation will do, and when, at last, Mr. Middlerib, after long and manfully holding out against the declarations of the envious neighbors and the hints of his wife and daughter, was obliged to sit down on the porch, one lovely Summer evening, and admit that he had wasted enough breath to make a tornado, and filled the air with vociferous and murderous threats and vituperations, and quarreled with three-quarters of his acquaintances, all for the sake of raising a jimson weed, it was nevertheless a jimson weed nine feet high, with blossoms as big as inflated sun-flowers. So he let the jimson weed stand, and argued with every one who came to the house that, with sufficient care and proper cultivation, it could be developed into a fruit-bearing tree. As for the *abolutos haciedendus microbulos*, as soon as he was morally and botanically certain that it was just chickweed, Mr. Middlerib one night secretly pulled it up and threw it away, and ever afterward professed to be heart-broken because some rascally, envious florist had come up from Keokuk and stolen the choicest climber in the Mississippi Valley. The *bianthus geridian psottoliensis giasticus, floridens bilthus* never showed itself until toward the latter part of June. Then it thrust up a delicate, fragile little sprout, drank in a little of the glad free air and pure sunlight, heard itself called by its full name, and drooped under the burden and died. The *bibulus Burlingtoniensis giganteus* came up and did well. It did not flower very abundantly, but it developed very marked qualities. The chickens came up and pecked at it, and then laid them down under the currant bushes and closed their eyes upon this world of sorrow and mysterious plants. The pigs got into the yard and rooted a little of it up, and their sudden demise gave rise to the rumor of the hog cholera, and the air of the hill was vocal for the next five days with the protests of healthy porkers against the popular modes of treating the hog cholera, such as boring holes along the spine with a red hot iron and splitting the ears and tail and rubbing in salt and cayenne pepper. And after Master Middlerib fooled with it and got some of it on his face, which immediately swelled up so that nothing was visible to his eyes, and his eyes were visible to nobody, for nearly a week, the wonderful plant was pulled up with the kitchen tongs and thrown into the alley, where the geese of South Hill found it, ate it, grew fat on it, and came around and asked for more. Nothing that grows under the heavens can kill a South Hill goose.

There were other plants in the garden of the gods that came up and grew to maturity and brought forth blossoms each after his kind, but as they turned out to be various species of rag-weed and dog-fennel, they were not considered worthy of mention by Mr. Middlerib. But he is disheartened with scientific gardening, and he only lives now for one object: to ascertain whether these Latin names are really the scientific names of those plants which they set forth, or he was swindled by the traveling seed agent.

A TRYING SITUATION.

THERE was a time when Mr. Bilderback was almost persuaded to cut off his pew rent, renounce his religious convictions, and become an atheist or a pagan, he wasn't very particular which. He was for many weeks in great distress of mind, and professed the greatest hatred of all churches, on general principles. This state of affairs, which fortunately was not permanent, was brought about by a very annoying, though perfectly innocent occurrence. One beautiful but rather warm Sunday morning he was dozing comfortably in his pew, in the church of which he is one of the main sleepers, when he became aware of an apparition gliding solemnly down the aisle with a collection basket in its hand. Mr. Bilderback braced up into an erect posture, cleared his throat in a ponderous tone of Roman firmness, as one who should say, "Who's been asleep?" And as the basket was extended toward him, he felt in his trousers pocket for his wallet. It wasn't there, and as he withdrew his hand, and felt in the other pocket, he felt that the eyes of the congregation were upon him, and that was all he felt, for he certainly didn't feel any pocket-book. He nodded the basket man to wait a second, and leaned over to the left while he felt in the right inside pocket of his coat, from which in his growing nervousness he drew half a dozen chestnuts which rolled over the floor with a rattle that sounded in his hot ears like the thunders of the Apocalypse, and made him warmer and more nervous than ever. Then he leaned over the end of the pew and felt in the other inside coat pocket and drew out a bundle of letters, a lot of postal cards, a circus ticket, a photograph of an actress, a funny story printed on a card, a pocket comb and a long string, and his face grew so warm his breath felt like a hot air blast. Then he squared his elbows and went for his vest pockets, and strewed the pew cushion with quill toothpicks, newspaper scraps, street car checks, a shoe buttoner, some lead pencil stubs, and crumbling indications of chewing tobacco, a bit of sealing wax, a piece of licorice root about an inch long, and three or four matches. Then he leaned forward and, stung to madness by the smiles which were breaking out all around that church worse than the measles in a primary school room, dived into his coat tail pockets, and drew forth a red silk handkerchief, two apples, a spectacle case, a pair of dog skin gloves, an overcoat button, and a fine assortment of bits of dried orange peel and lint. Then he stood up, devoutly praying that an earthquake might come along and swallow up either him or the rest of the congregation, he didn't much care which, and went down into his hip pockets, from which he evolved a revolver, a corkscrew, a cigar case, a piece of string, a memorandum book, and a pocket knife. By this time Mr. Bilderback's face was scarlet clear down to his waist, and he was so nervous and worked up that he nearly shook his clothes off, while the man with the basket couldn't have moved away, if he had died for staying. And when Mr. Bilderback, in forlorn despair, once more rammed his hand into the trousers pocket where he began the search, the congregation held its breath, and when Mr. Bilderback drew forth the very pocket-book which he had missed in his first careless search, and had since all but stripped to find, there was a sigh of relief went up from every devout heart in that house. But Mr. Bilderback only dropped into his seat with an abruptness that made the windows rattle, and registered a mental vow that he wasn't going to come out to church again to be made a fool of by a man with a long handled darning basket.

MR. BILDERBACK LOSES HIS HAT.

"NO," Mr. Bilderback said, "it wasn't." He put it there last night, the last thing before he went to bed, he remembered most distinctly. It wasn't there now, and he didn't know who had any business to move it. Somebody had done it, and he hoped to gracious that it would be the last time. Somebody was always meddling with his things.

Mrs. Bilderback, coming down stairs with a weary air, asked if he had looked in the closets?

"Closets?" Mr. Bilderback snarled, "Kingdom of Ireland! Does any sane man put his hat in the closets when he wants it every time he goes out? No. I hung it up right here, on this very hook of this particular rack, and if it had been left alone, it would be there now. Some of you must have moved it. It hasn't got legs and couldn't get away alone."

Master Bilderback suggested that it wouldn't beavery surprising if it felt its way along fur a little ways, for which atrocities he was rewarded with a wild glare and a vicious cuff from his unappreciative parent. Then Mr. Bilderback said, "Well, I suppose I can walk down town bareheaded."

Well, that was the usual formula. Every body knew just what it meant, and as soon as it was said the family scattered for the regular morning search. Mrs. Bilderback looked in all the closets with the air of John Rogers going to the stake, and then she went into an old chest, that had the furs and things put away in it, and was only opened twice a year, except when Mr. Bilderback's hat was lost, which occurred on an average three times a day. She shook pepper or fine cut tobacco or camphor out of everything she picked up, and varied her search by the most extraordinary sneezes that ever issued from human throat, while ever and anon she paused to wipe her weeping eyes and say that "well, she never." Mrs. Bilderback's search for the lost hat never got beyond that chest. She would kneel down before it and take the things out one by one, and put them back, and take them out, and sneeze and sigh, and wonder occasionally "where the hat could be," but her search never went beyond that old moth proof chest.

Miss Bilderback confined her search to the uncut pages of the last *Scribner*, which she carefully cut and looked into, with an eager scrutiny that told how intensely interested she was in finding that hat. She never varied her method of search, save when the approaching footsteps of her father warned her that he was swinging on his erratic eccentric in that direction, when she hid the magazine, and picking up the corner of the piano cover looked under that article with a sweet air of zealous interest, exclaiming in tones of pretty vexation, "I wonder where it can be?" And it was noticeable that this action and remark, both of which she never failed to repeat every time her father came into the room, had the effect of throwing that estimable but irascible old gentleman into paroxysms of the most violent passion, each one growing worse than its predecessors, until they would culminate in a grand burst of wrath in which he ordered her to quit looking for his hat. Then she would retire with an injured air and tell her mother, between that indefatigable searcher's sneezes, that "one might wear one's self out slaving and looking for pa's hat in every conceivable place, and all the thanks one got for it was to be scolded." Master Bilderback, he helped hunt, too. His system of conducting a search was to go around into the back yard and play "toss ball" up against the end of the house, making mysterious disappearances, with marvelous celerity, behind the woodpile or under a large store box, so oft as he heard the mutterings of the tempest that invariably preceded and announced his father's approach.

But Mr. Bilderback. His was a regular old composite system of investigation; it combined and took in everything. He raged through the sitting-room like a hurricane; he looked under every chair in that room, and then upset them all to see if he mightn't possibly have overlooked the hat. Then he looked on all the brackets in the parlor, and behind the window curtains, and kicked over the ottoman to look for a hat that he couldn't have squeezed under a wash-tub. And he kept up a running commentary all the time, which served no purpose except to warn his family when he was coming and give them time to prepare. He looked into the clock and left it stopped and standing crooked. And he would like to know who touched that hat. He looked into his daughter's work-box, a sweet little shell that "George" gave her, and he emptied it out on the table and wondered what such trumpery was for, and who in thunder hid his hat. "It must be hid," he said, peering down with a dark, suspicious look into an odor bottle somewhat larger than a thimble, "for it couldn't have got so completely out of sight by accident." If people wouldn't meddle with his things, he howled, for the benefit of Mrs. Bilderback, whom he heard sneezing as he went past the closet door, he would always know just where to find them, because (looking gloomily behind the kitchen wood box) he always had one place to put all his things (and he took off the lid of the spice-box), and kept them there. He glared savagely out of the door, in hopes of seeing his hopeful son, but that youthful strategist was out of sight behind his intrenchments. Mr. Bilderback wrathfully resumed his search, and roared, for his daughter's benefit, that he would spend every cent he had intended to lay out for winter bonnets, in new hats for himself, and then maybe he might be able to find one when he wanted it. Then he opened the door of the oven and looked darkly in, turned all the clothes out of the wash-basket, and strewed them around, wondering "*who* had hid that hat?" And he pulled the clothes-line off its nail, and got down on his hands and knees to look behind the refrigerator, and wondered "who *had* hid that hat;" and then he climbed on the back of a chair to look on the top shelf of the cupboard, and sneezed around among old wide-mouthed bottles and pungent paper parcels, and wondered in muffled wrath "who had *hid* that hat?" And he went down into the cellar and roamed around among rows of stone jars covered with plates and tied up with brown paper, and smelling of pickles and things in all stages of progress; every one of which he looked into, and how he did wonder "who had hid *that* hat." And he looked into dark corners and swore when he jammed his head against the corners of swinging shelves, and felt along those shelves and run his fingers into all sorts of bowls, containing all sorts of greasy and sticky stuff, and thumped his head against hams hanging from the rafters, at which he swore anew, and he peered into and felt around in barrels which seemed to have nothing in them but cobwebs and nails; shook boxes which were prolific in dust and startling in rats, and he wondered "who had hid that *hat?*"

And just then loud whoops and shouts came from up stairs, announcing that "here it was." And old Bilderback went up stairs growling, because the person who hid it hadn't brought it out before, and saw the entire family pointing out into the back yard, where the hat surmounted Mr. Bilderback's cane, which was leaning against the fence, "just where you left it, pa," Miss Bilderback explained, "when we called you into supper, and it has been out there all night.". And Mr. Bilderback, evidently restraining, by a violent effort, an intense desire to bless his daughter with the cane, remarked with a mysterious manner, that "it was mighty singular," and putting on the hat, he strode away with great dignity; leaving his wife and daughter to re-arrange the house.

MIND READING.

ONE morning, about the middle of the Spring term, Master Bilderback made his appearance at school with a subdued manner apparent in all his actions, while a cast of sadness mingled with traces of pleasant memories overspread his countenance. It was, in short, that general expression of penitence which people assume after a holiday of more than usual hilarity. His quiet manner astonished the scholars and alarmed his teacher, who feared that it was a portent of some unusual mischief, and kept her eye upon the lad in consequence. He did not appear to be conscious of the surveillance under which he was placed. He bent no pins, he chewed no gum, he fired at the adjacent scholars no projectiles of masticated paper during the morning; no dismal but subdued cat-calls were heard from the vicinity of his seat; no grotesque grimaces made his neighbors laugh with uncounterfeited glee; restful were his feet, and quiet the fingers which were wont to drum on the desk four minutes out of every five. Master Bilderback was either in some deep affliction or he was ill. There was something wrong about him.

It transpired, along toward noon, when Master Bilderback's spirits began to rise a little, that he had indeed passed under the rod, with his father at the other end of it, during the evening previous. The waters of affliction had gone over his soul, and his back had gone under the sole of his mother's slipper. It seems they had company at Mr. Bilderback's that evening, quite a large party, in fact, and the conversation turned on mind reading. The discussion became very spirited, Mr. Bilderback being the leader of the party which avowed its belief in mesmeric influences. The usual arguments of learned length and thundering sound were hurled back and forth, Mr. Bilderback winning especial distinction by the clearness with which he proved that, in certain esthetic conditions of the mental and physical systems, the peculiar psychic forces which always existed in a latent state, were roused into an active condition; and the action of the intellect upon the cerebrum was felt in the cerebellum, and transmitted by mesmeric condition to the candelabra, where the psychomatic transfusion of the occipital parietis made the Ego as cognizant of the mutation and genuflexions of the non-Ego, as though the psychic modifications really impinged upon the same ganglion; and the nerve waves along the ganglia of the two systems, transmuted by a touch of the hand, were, and could only be, identical. And Mr. Bilderback's party said, "Yes; what could you say to that, now?" And the other party shook their heads and said, "Yes; but that was only a theory, after all; they would like to see the hypothesis demonstrated." And at that critical juncture, Master Bilderback, who had been an attentive listener, spoke up, in his rough, horrid style, and declared that "that wasn't nauthin';" that they tried it at school, an' he could let the boys hide things and then lead them right to the place where they were hid. The excitement ran high for a few moments, and Master B. was closely catechised, but he never varied from his original story; and they finally determined to try him.

Mr. Tweesdle, a young fellow who dotes on poetry and Miss Bilderback, was the first subject. He announced that he was thinking of a certain object, and by the way he looked at the mind reader's sister, everybody thought they knew what it was. But Master Bilderback seized him by the hand, led him out in the hall and up to the hat-rack, followed by the entire company, and reaching his hand into Mr. Tweesdle's overcoat pocket, drew forth a paper bag containing a pound of sausages, half a dozen eggs, and a couple of rusks, remarking, "There, that's what you're thinking of." And just at that moment he certainly was, although he shook his head in an idiotic manner and laughed feebly, while all the rest of the people never smiled, but only looked at each other and said, "Why, how funny!"

This sad affair cast a gloom over the entire community for a few moments, but the people rallied and demanded another test. There was a general reluctance on the part of the visitors to take a hand in it, and so Mrs. Bilderback was prevailed upon to be a subject in the course of scientific experiments. As soon as she had assumed a pensive expression and announced that her mind was wholly occupied with one subject, to the exclusion of all other terrestrial things, the boy grasped her by the hand, and away they went, sailing up stairs, followed by the entire congregation. The mind-reader marshaled them into a room, and leading his subject straight to the bureau, drew from a small drawer a set of false teeth and a bottle of hair dye. Mrs. Bilderback shrieked, the company looked grave, and some of the ladies declared to each other that well now, they never did.

There was another brief season of gloom, which was dissipated by Mr. Bilderback declaring that as neither of the subjects in the two experiments they had just witnessed had denied the accuracy of the mind-reader's judgment, he would submit to the test himself. Great applause greeted this determination, and as Mr. Bilderback, with a glance that threatened a massacre if there were any tricks played on him, placed his hand in that of his son, the congregetion rose en masse to follow where the mind-reader might lead. Master Bilderback placed his hand against his father's forehead for a moment; then he placed it against his own and remained for several seconds in a thoughtful posture, and then led his reluctant parent, followed by the company, out of doors, and calling for a lantern, which was provided, they went into the wood shed, where the mind-reader, despite several stealthy nudges from his parent, reached his arm behind a pile of hickory knots, and drew forth a whisky bottle nearly a foot long, flat as a board, and about half full. Then a shadow fell upon the community that not even the cordial good nights that were exchanged at the door could dissipate, and after the footsteps of the last reveler had died away in the distance, Master Bilderback held two separate private seances with his parents, the remarkable manifestations of which occasioned the subdued state of mind and unusual depression of spirits which were so painfully apparent in the young man the following day.

A SAFE BET.

ONE night, last Winter, old Mr. Balbriggan, who lives out on Columbia Street, had occasion to make a journey out to the wood shed to get the hatchet. It was very dark, and as there was no lantern about the house, Mr. Balbriggan took a kerosene lamp, and shading it very carefully with a big tin pan, started out to the wood shed. The wind was rather uncertain and gusty, and Mr. Balbriggan had some misgivings about his getting out to the shed without accident; and every time the lamp flared, his mind misgave him. "I'll bet a dollar that lamp'll blow out," he muttered when the first gust came, but he shied the tin pan around with great promptness, and the lamp steadied down. There came another gust and a bigger flare, and the chances for the lamp going out improved so decidedly that the old gentleman promptly raised his first stake. "I'll bet a dollar and a half," he muttered, "that lamp blows out." Then the wind lulled a little, and as he hurried on toward the shed it was so quiet that, while he didn't quite lose all confidence, he began to hedge a little; "I'll bet fifty cents," he said, "it'll go out before I get back." Another gust and a flare. "I'll bet two dollars that lamp blows out," muttered the old gentleman again, chipping a little higher as the chances seemed to grow better; but again he saved the light by the timely interposition of the tin pan. "I'll bet three dollars," he cried with great earnestness, as the next gust came, "this lamp'll blow out;" but there were no takers and the lamp rallied again. But a still stronger gust fairly lifted the flame out of the top of the smoked chimney; and the old gentleman hissed in a hoarse, suppressed whisper, "I'll bet five dollars this lamp'll blow out." But it settled down to work once more, and did very well until Mr. Balbriggan got very close to the woodshed; when the wind rallied and came at the lamp from two or three directions at once, and the old gentleman fairly shouted, "I'll bet ten dollars this lamp'll blow ——" and just then the door of the woodshed blew violently open, hitting the lamp and the tin pan, knocking them both out of Mr. Balbriggan's hands, and striking the old gentleman a terrible blow in the face that made him see more lights dancing in the air, for about a second, than even the lamp could send forth. And while he held his nose with one hand and groped around with the other to find where he was, there came from the house door the voice of the eldest juvenile Balbriggan, falling through the darkness like a falling star: "Raise him out, pa, raise him out; make it a hundred dollars; you've got a dead sure thing on it!"

THE LAY OF THE COW.

SWITCH engine Louisa, "B., C. R. & M.,"
    Was slowing up Front Street about three P. M.,
When the stoker looked out of the window to say,
"There's a cow going 'cross the t-r-a-c-kay."

Pensively halted the cow on the track,
Burs on her pendent tail, bran on her back;
Dreaming of Summer, she seemed not to see
The approach of the switch e-n-g-i-n-e.

Once more spake the stoker, "There she is now,"
"Bully," the engineer quoth, "for the cow."
And reversing his engine he cried, "Shoo! Oh, shoo!"
Said the stoker, "Oh, shoo't the see-oh-doubleyou."

Shrilly the whistle shrieked for its alarm,
And the stoker threw firewood and coals in a swarm;
But the cow never heeded, nor thought that her star
Was setting at four miles an h-o-u-r.

The switch engine struck her about amidships,
And her Summer dreams met with a total eclipse;
It mangled her carcase, most shocking to see,
And threw her down Front s-t-r-double-e-tea.

Sadly the engineer drew in his head,
And "pulled her wide open," as onward he sped;
But the stoker smiled gayly, "Old fellow," said he,
"There's some cheap porterhouse s-t-a-k-e."*

   * That isn't the way to spell porterhouse steak, but the right way wouldn't rhyme.

YOUNG MR. COFFINBERRY BUYS A DOG.

PEOPLE lifted their eyes above their mufflers one raw November morning as they walked down Jefferson Street, and smiled and grinned, and laughed even unto hysterical weeping, as they watched the toilsome and uncertain progress of a patient young man who had bought a dog and was leading his property home. It was a nice enough kind of a dog, one of the kind of dogs whose mouth begins back close to the shoulders. It had dreadfully long legs, this dog, with great knobs of knees, and its restless tail had a dejected droop, as though the dog was just heart-broken at the idea of leaving his old home. The young man was leading the dog along with a very long string, one end whereof was tied around the dog's neck. The only trouble with the dog was that he was young. He had not attained the years of discretion. He couldn't trot placidly along thinking of things. He couldn't walk at his master's heels with a face as solemn as though he expected to be sausage before Thanksgiving Day. He was a nervous, fidgety, inquisitive dog, and he tried to read all the signs, and crawl under all the wagons, and dive between every body's legs as he went along. And the first thing he knew, he had a contract on hand that was much too big for him, and he was just about crazy over it, for he wasn't the dog to give up, if he was young, and he stuck to his work like a Trojan. And this was what made people laugh. The young man who was leading him had just lifted his hat to some lady acquaintances who were passing when the dog, looking up, misunderstood the motion and thought his master was going to hit him a diff with that hat. With the natural instinct of self-preservation, the shy, timid young thing dashed between the young man's legs and ran to the length of his tether; then he gave a terrified howl and darted back in the opposite direction, going outside the young man's right leg. Then, with a frightened yelp it sprang back between the legs again, circled around and came down outside the left leg. Then it ran rapidly around the young man, dived through his legs again and ran around him once and a half in an opposite direction, and his last maneuver closed the performance, for it wound the dog completely up, with his frightened face laid close against the young man's knee. Mr. Coffinberry blushed to his ears, and replacing his hat, began the task of extricating himself from the toils that artful dog had cast around him. But the animal's confidence was not yet entirely restored, for at every movement of Mr. Coffinberry's hands, he squirmed and writhed and pulled back on the string until he was choked, and coughed and gasped in a manner most terrifying to the people not thoroughly acquainted with the symptoms of hydrophobia, and the young man was naturally as badly frightened, when these paroxysms became very lively, as was the dog itself. It was fifteen minutes before the snarl was disentangled. Then before they had gone half a block further, that dog, after having rushed into and been forcibly, and in some instances rather petulantly, dragged out of every doorway on the line of march, incontinently shot down a cellar grating, where he was immediately clawed and scalped by a cat as big as a soap box, and was also nearly garroted by his master drawing him up out of the cellar by the cord, for all the world as though he was a well bucket. About thirty steps further on, the dog ran between a clergyman's legs, got frightened and ran around him once and then dived between his master's legs, then rushed out toward the curb stone, but changing his mind, circled back and scooped in a blushing school teacher, and then gazed upon the mischief he had wrought, with hideous howls. The bystanders thought they never could get out of that entanglement. The minister declared alternatively that "he never did" and moreover that "well he never;" the blushing school teacher remarked "good gracious," and suggested also, "dear me," and, furthermore, "well, now;" and the young man said something about the dog being damp, which was highly improbable as the morning was very raw. By dint of a great deal of persuasion and pulling and hauling, however, in which they were greatly assisted by the dog, the unhappy trio were finally separated and went their way, making ineffectual efforts to look unconcerned. Then the dog wrapped himself up around a lamp post; then he got through the hind wheel of a grocer's wagon five or six times, back and forth, around a different spoke every time, while his master was talking to the grocer, and the latter drove off before the young man noticed what arrangements his dog had concluded with the wheel, and Jefferson Street was edified by the spectacle of a dog wound up to a wagon wheel and revolving rapidly with it, while a young man of pleasing address ran alongside the wheel and added his agonized appeals to the half-stifled wails of the hanging pup. They got the wagon stopped and got the pup loose, and the young man, wearied with the long struggle, resolutely turned toward the store, and walked rapidly away, the unhappy dog lying prone on his back, gasping and pawing the air, while the boys who witnessed the strange procession made the welkin ring with cries of

"Dog's a chokin! mister, yer dog's a chokin!" But young Mr. Coffinberry knew that so long as his dog was helplessly sprawled on his back he couldn't wrap the inhabitants of Burlington up in perspiring, distracted groups, so he kept on the even tenor of his way, and when he finally untied the string from the animal's neck and turned him loose in the store, there wasn't so much hair on that dog's back as would make a tooth brush.

A MODERN GOBLIN.

A DREARY, cheerless Christmas Eve. The dead hour of day, when the pale twilight falls over the earth, still and colorless as a shroud. Down the long vistas of deserted streets but here and there the feeble rays of some struggling light gleams through the gray twilight, pale as the glitter of a jewel on the brow of death. Across the dull waste of sky the ghostly clouds fly before a piercing wind, which whirls and tears their edges into fluttering fringes. The gloaming fades slowly and almost imperceptibly into night. Away back from the town, out on the bleak hillsides, the leafless trees toss their bare arms, gaunt shapes against the pallor of the sky, the swaying branches answering their mocking shadows, dancing like specters on the frozen ground; while the withered leaves rustle like very shudders.

The hour, neither light nor darkness, neither day nor night, that, with its weird, indescribable magic, draws you from the cheery grate to press your face against the cold window, and dream out into the gray light, peopled with specters and visions—often grotesque, but never merry—that come trooping from every shadow. Comes a rosy little face, framed in tangled tresses—ah, long, long unfolding years must roll back to take you to the time when the laughing eyes looked into yours; to-night you remember—dear child—the dimpled hands were crossed on the pulseless breast, when you were a boy; and the cheerless winter landscape, the dreary hills of snow, and the leafless forests stretch away, mile after weary mile, between your home and where the Christmas winds sigh plaintive monodies over her little grave. There comes a thoughtful, earnest face, manly and noble; a playmate of your boyhood, a college classmate and friend; the man who stood for your ideal of all that is brave and true, and virtuous and generous. As you look at it, you remember, to-night, that when you saw the real face, so little time ago, it was worn and old and haggard, and stamped with the leprous mark of vice. You shudder at the recollection; but the pleading look of the vision goes to your heart as it fades away; and other faces, long forgotten, crowd before you. One, furrowed with marks of patient suffering and care, with silver bands in the brown hair drawn so smoothly away from the brow, mother-love glistening in the tender eyes, mother-love in the quivering, heart-reaching eloquence of the tremulous lips, mother-love in the caressing gesture of the gentle hands—what wonder that it lingers long, and fades only when you crush the burning tears that blind your eyes and veil the vision from your sight? And comes one sweeter, dearer than all—your heart throbs more quickly as you see a shadow rise in the deepening twilight — a face glowing with blushes and wreathed in smiles; a face that shone into your life like sunshine, in its bright springtime days; a face that has remained constant while everything else has changed—your old heart grows tender and young with dear recollections, and you thank God that although years have set their mark upon this dear vision, it is still yours, loving, faithful, and powerful to bless and charm in every mood and at all times. It is gone; and looming through the deepening shadows another form of familiar presence rises before you. The silvery tones of memory-bells chime like a Christmas choral through the bleak wind shaking so angrily the noisy shutters. It is the milkman, and he jangles all your sweet dreams out of tune, sending the ghosts your retrospect has raised back to the shadowy past. And as your visions disappear, you dismally watch the female vassals of the neighborhood sallying forth in answer to the tinkling summons, bearing all possible manner of squatty tinware and corpulent yellow bowls, in which to receive lawful but attenuated measures of that peculiar aqueous fluid of cerulean hue with which, under the ghastly appellation of "cream," our best society dilutes its table beverages. And when this amusement ceases to be longer interesting, you leave the draughty window and seek the more congenial companionship of the black, close-shut gas-burner, which out of respect to your conceit and the conventionalities of the Christmas time, we have designated a "cheery fire-place," with an incipient cold in your otherwise empty head.

For the shadows have beckoned and reached to each other, and joined their giant hands, and danced until the light is frightened away. In heavier volumes rolls the black smoke from every chimney, indicating that the estimable and respectable business men of the city, having left their clerks with orders to save gas and not waste the coal, and to close the store only when the last lingering, possible chance of securing one more belated customer has faded into hopelessness, are now at home, enjoying the unspeakable luxury of heaping the stove with coal their wives have carried in, and driving the other members of the family to madness by monopolizing the privilege of poking the fire. Gas lights twinkle in the streets, for the faithful almanac in the gas company's office has been mislaid, and they do not know there will be a moon quite late in the morning. A ruddy glow of firelight and lamplight streams out into the gathering darkness when a door is opened, men are hurrying home, their faces averted, and their bodies bowed against the howling wind, or else scudding briskly before it. The city was hurrying home to enjoy its Christmas Eve in the bosom of its several families, and to scold the children and pack them off to bed, if they romped and made too much noise. Everybody knows what city it was, so there is no use wasting time describing it. It was just the same old city, only they had strengthened the little brick house down below the corner where the blacksmith lived, with a coat of whitewash. Just the same old city.

And everybody knows the hill on the street, where it turns to wind up the bluff and go to the rich folks' houses on top of the long hill that stretches around behind the town like a great horse shoe, and looks down on all the business, and bustle, and noise, and hurry, and work, and fatigue that have made the city so rich and powerful. And just at the time we were speaking about a gentleman was making devious headway up this hill, just as the street leaves the business of the city and goes scrambling up to the quiet and rest on top of the hill. A discouraged looking gentleman, who seemed to have begun his Christmas at the wrong end, and so got nearly through with it before it had really commenced. The gentleman's Napoleonic head was covered, part of the time, with a glossy silk tile, which art had shaped into the fashionable, uncomfortable cylinder which adorns the caputs of our Best Young Men, but accident, oft recurring, and too many vigorous slappings on and pattings down by the officious but ill-directed zeal of many friends, and too frequent steppings on by the owner as the last means of checking its mad career in a race with the wind, had graced this glossy cylinder with many alternate elevations and depressions, giving it that corrugated effect so attractive, natural, and useful in the washboard and concertina, but very repugnant and ungraceful in the silk hat. The gentleman's eccentric style of buttoning his overcoat, three holes over the same button, lent an air of abstraction to his general appearance, while his knitted brow told of intense mental conflict and exertion. He made little forays from the sidewalk to the middle of the street, returning to his pathway by devious and angular ways, as though striving to baffle some unseen pursuer. From time to time he made vicious, impulsive, startled clutches at the streaming ends of his necktie, fluttering in the blast, which he regarded with a vague uncertain terror, and, when he had seized them, he laughed in hollow, hysterical accents. The smell of coffee was heard in the distance as he passed, and ever and anon, as the restless earth raised itself in precipitous terraces before him, he lifted his feet high in air and with lofty steps essayed to scale the treacherous mirage. He paused in his circuitous progress to shake hands with the last friendly lamp-post on that thoroughfare, expressing his confidence in that faithful municipal lighthouse as a "goo'role feller," who was, under any and every possible combination of circumstances, " all ri'." At times he felt for his hat with both hands, and having secured a firm grip upon its uncertain brim, he removed it from his head with great caution, and swinging it violently in the air, proceeded with great enthusiasm and heartiness to " hurrah for" somebody, but invariably forgot who, when he came to the name, and contented himself with assuring himself that that was " al' ri'," after which with gravity he felt for his head, found it, and with much deliberation got the hat up on top of it, generally sideways or upside down, and with great physical effort, crushed and pulled it on. At length, having parted company after affectionate and prolonged adieus, with the last friendly lamppost, the young gentleman loudly announced that he was a " total wr—hic!—creck " and proceeded furthermore to declare that he would not and could not by any means be induced to seek the shelter of his mother's roof again until smiling morn should hail and deck the hills with gold, and the rosy-fingered hours should herald the coming of the god of day. And singing this true statement in a rich baritone, a kind of a wheelbarrow tone, in fact, possessing more volume and hoarse wheeziness than we would admire in Nilsson's chest tones, he made a vigorous but ineffectual effort to fall up the hill, and angrily ejaculating, " Ju know who yer pushin'? " he shot over the curbstone with frenzied gestures that seemed to proceed at least from ten pairs of legs, and disappeared in the gloom of the gutter, where he lay, and whence his stertorous breathing startled the nervous passers-by.

Had the fallen man kept on the uneven tenor of his way a little farther he would have encountered a mysterious being that would have transformed his snores into sounds of deeper intonation. The street, where it turned and led up the hill, was not a cheerful one. On the west side the bluff rises abruptly as a wall, and on the opposite side it sinks away into a dark, gloomy ravine, that has an uncanny look at the best of times, and the sidewalk is provided with a wooden railing, to keep careless or belated passengers from plunging down the hill-side. A little stream winds along the ravine, endeavoring, in a despairing kind of way, to find its way to the river, which it never does. It starts, but from the time the city was first settled there has been no record that the little stream ever got clear through; nobody knows what becomes of it, where it goes to; but certain it is, that all trace of it is lost before it gets half way to any where. But we have naught to do with this forlorn little country brook that comes purling through pleasant meadows, and bubbling over white pebbles, and wrangling around great bowlders, to get bewildered and lost in the entangling mazes of the drains and gutters and sewers and culverts of the city.

Seated on the railing of the sidewalk was an apparition of far less cheerful mien than the gentleman who, when we left him, had just wrapped the curbstone about him and laid down to snore the Christmas hours away. This figure wore a snow-white mantle, much too airy and summery for the season and very decidedly out of style, which fell from his angular shoulders in graceful folds, a portion of its light tissue being folded over his osseous head after the most conventional style of his class. As he swung his legs carelessly to and fro, they struck the lower boards of the railing with a strange rattling sound like muffled castanets, and his manner of whistling " Down Among the Dead Men," under his breath in that weird, ghostly place, with the bluff rising black and abrupt before him, and the ravine lying deep in impenetrable shadow behind him, had that awful touch of the supernatural in it that would make one's blood run cold to contemplate. A ghostlier ghost never chose a ghostlier time or place for his ghastly recreations.

He ceased his hollow whistling and stilled his nervous legs as he heard approaching footsteps on the sidewalk, and dropped from his easy perch on the railing as a young man and a lovely maiden came toward him, toiling up the slope down which the December zephyr roared and swept into a fury that would make an Ulster overcoat feel sick. The young man's arm was wound tenderly about his companion's shrinking seal-skin cloak, while he hoarsely whispered words into her ears, which were rosy with the exhilarating influence of twenty-eight degrees below zero. The ghost stepped in front of them.

"Excuse my hoarseness," he said, with a winning smile that extended over the entire width of his finely-chiseled face, "but I had the very disagreeable misfortune to have my throat cut in this exceedingly romantic spot about a half a century since, and my voice has since been affected to such an ex ——"

The very wind paused in its noisy bluster to listen to the wild shrieks that were piercing the darkness like acoustic arrows, and the rapid patter of two pairs of Arctic over-shoes that were pounding the bosom of the frosty earth far down the hill, away from the shadow of the bluff, away from the dreadful blackness of the ravine, in the direction of the gleaming street lamps of the city.

The ghost leaned upon the railing and sighed as he said:

"This was not the style of responding to an apology when I dwelt among men. Perhaps my voice, which I have not used before for fifty years, has that in its mouldy accents which is disagreeable, startling, and possibly repulsive, to mortal ears. I will modulate my intonation."

He paused to observe the figure of a portly man, looming vaguely through the night, as, with many asthmatic puffs, the well-fed citizen essayed to beat up the hill against the wind.

"He looks," said the specter, musingly, "very much like an honest old settler I used to know, who sold whisky to and stole furs from the Indians, the year after I first came to what is now this city."

The panting citizen came alongside and was passing by, when the ghost dropped his bony hand noiselessly in the hollow of his arm.

"A thousand pardons, my dear sir," he began, "but I observe a most extraordinary resemblance in—— "

" Oh-h-h-h-h, Lord!"

And again the ghost was alone. As the echoes of the excited and grossly misapplied remark of the citizen died away in the mocking echoes of the dreary solitudes, the ghost walked across the street and carefully examined the face of the bluff, in which direction the portly mortal had made his unceremonious and abrupt exit.

"No," the specter remarked, after a critical inspection, "it is very evident that he did not plunge through the hill; he certainly ran over its summit. The celerity with which he accomplished this undertaking at his time of life, and in his condition of superfluous flesh too, smacks almost as much of the marvelous to me as I did to him. I would be willing to bet my boots, now," he added, with a ghastly wink at his bare feet, "that the portly old party can not come here to-morrow noon and get over that hill inside of twenty-five minutes."

"Passenger travel on this street," he continued, resuming his station on the sidewalk, "is livelier than it was in my time. As I remember, the two gentlemen who performed the surgical operation on my windpipe, which has so disagreeably affected my voice, had to wait here for me five hours in the cheerless gloom before my other business engagements permitted me to come along and make an involuntary and unwilling third in their interesting little surprise party. And I sat on a stump near this very spot, and watched my lifeless remains nearly two days before the coroner found them and gave them the customary inquest with a fearful and wonderful verdict, followed by Christian burial. Yes, yes, the village has been prosperous since then, and now — but soft, a young man — a lover, too, or I'm no ghost. I will befriend him and he will love me."

A goodly young man he was indeed, as ghost or girl would wish to see. Torture racked his soul when, at every step, his dainty boots, a size and a half too small, touched the ground. And even the snowy expanse of linen cuffs, weighted with moss-agate sleeve buttons, failed to conceal the fact that his flame-colored kids would not button. Though the piercing wind chilled him to the very marrow, his overcoat was opened and thrown back from his throat to display the blue necktie that graced his paper collar. The elaborate and painful costume betrayed his errand. You might wring bergamot out of the air when he passed along, and there was jockey club on his handkerchief, and his breath smelled a little of sozodont, some of trix, and a great deal of something else. The ghost looked after him, as he passed by, with as much friendly admiring interest as he could throw into his rather open countenance, and then gathering his robe about him followed swiftly and silently at the limping heels of the nice young man, who toiled painfully but very patiently and exquisitely properly up the hill until he reached the summit of the grade, and pausing before a mansion of pretentious appearance, proceeded to investigate the ever changing mysteries of a front gate.

Properly constructed, the front gate is more fearfully and wonderfully made than the architect who designs or the carpenter who builds it. No other created or manufactured thing in the whole wide universe can equal or rival it for original perversity and malignant obstinacy. A patient man, whose soul is melting within him from chronic and exaggerated meekness, will fall from grace and relieve his tortured soul in a burst of giant powder profanity after fifteen minutes' struggle with a front gate, and then he will shower a tempest of abuse upon the unknown man who contrived such a diabolical and outrageous gate, and he will cease to struggle with it and will climb over the fence and disintegrate his raiment on the pickets, and abrade his cuticle all the way down his back as he slides off, and then his soul will be tossed into a very sirocco of passion and mortification when he sees the dog of the mansion come trotting along and open the gate with a simple push of his nose. Or a woman, full of a woman's love and yearning tenderness, will take hold of a gate and tug at it, and pull and haul and jerk until she nearly drags the solid posts up by the roots, and when all the blood in her system is boiling in the top of her head, and her eyes are starting from their sockets, and she dissolves in tears of utter, abject wretchedness and rage because she is debarred by virtue of her sex from the ecstatic privilege of swearing at the gate and the pirate who made it, a grinning boy will open the barrier by merely pulling it the other way. Men with real, living ideas, and lofty aspirations, and soaring ambitions, and grand, illimitable thoughts, swelling and groaning and throbbing in heart and brain, have stood before an orthodox front gate and manipulated its fastenings, moving that piece this way and this one that, and all of them the other, until the pot-metal securities have assumed the vexed and perplexing varieties and dimensions of a Chinese puzzle with the delirium tremens or a Centennial election table. And then, when at last with a despairing groan he lets go of it, and raises his hands to heaven to call down its righteous judgment upon the unregenerate mocker who made that gate, it slowly swings open by its own weight, and the distressed Christian discovers to his unspeakable amazement that he has had it open twenty times within the last fifteen minutes. And all these troubles are magnified after night. Hook and staple connect the swinging gate and the immovable post where hook and staple there were none before. The most trifling and ordinary bolt has a way of acquiring a double action after dark, so that whatever is loosed at one end is immediately fastened up as tight as a candidate at the other. Nails, too, appear, driven in the post immediately above the latch, and finally, when all other ties are sundered, lo, a strap hugs the whole structure in its binding embrace. It is a work of ten minutes to find the buckle, and when found it is a knot, tied when the strap was wet, and now firmer in its clinging folds and more intricate in its appalling entanglements than the famous knot which Gordius of Phyrgia tied in his chariot harness, a knot which baffled even the sublimest efforts of the Chicago divorce lawyers. Even the simplest form of a gate latch known to man, composed of a round hole in a post into which a stick is thrust athwart the gate, is a snare, a vanity, a vexation of the spirit and a mortification of the flesh; for no living man ever opened a strange gate of this genus that the stick did not come out with a jerk, rasping the abraded knuckles along the rude edges of the pickets.

With a gate which presented, or rather concealed, and successively developed, like masked batteries, all the modern combinations of baffling elements and inventions, the young man has all this time been expostulating. A good young man, for while he has been laboring with that remorseless gate with all the intensity of purpose and earnestness that fires the blood of youth, he has only relieved his impatient swelling soul by saying from time to time that "he *would* be dad binged," once or twice varying the tense, as the future suddenly seemed to break upon him with all the fullness of time, to declare that he *was* "dad binged," and several times, as though conscious of some degree of uncertainty attending the whole matter, devoutly hoping that, at some indefinite time in the vague hereafter, he *might* be "dad binged." Once he passed suddenly to the imperative and passive, appealing to some unknown quantity to "dad bing the dad binged old gate," a confusion of mood, tense and voice that was absurd, and even the ghost, which stood in the porch of the mansion watching his movements with that all-absorbed interest which visitors from another world display in terrestrial matters, shook his head gravely, as if doubting the advisability of a needless waste of power in dad binging that which was already declared dad binged. But the ghastly visage relaxed in a grim smile, as with one last tremendous effort, the adolescent raised the barrier from its fastenings, hinges and all, and fell forward to the gravel walk with the fiendish gate clasped in his arms, reaching the ground in a rattling chorus which roused all the dogs this side of the moon.

Disengaging himself from the chaos into which the

gate had fallen, the young man reached the porch with a halting step, and as he stood near the door, brushing gravel off his clothes with his tattered kids, the ghost gathered his bustle and train about him, slid deftly through the key hole, and flattened himself against the door on the inside. The tinkle of the bell had scarcely sounded in the hall when a light footstep was heard in echo to its clamor, and a beautiful young girl hastened to the door. She opened it, but the ghost stepped before her and faced the smiling, blushing, bowing young man, threw his gaunt arms around his neck, and in a hollow whisper began,

"Darling! I have watched so long for——"

A terrific yell rang through the corridors like almost any other yell would ring under similar circumstances. A rush of hasty feet along the gravel walk, a stumble, a crash and a dismal howl at the site of the fallen gate; then the dying echoes of fleet, pattering footsteps in the distance, and then silence, dispossessed of her curtained throne for one brief moment, resumed her noiseless reign, and the smiling ghost, after a vain effort to dig himself in the ribs, chuckled with dismal jollity and hid his shadowy form in the recesses of the porch.

The young girl stood spell-bound, gazing out in the direction of her vanished lover, and shaking her lovely head in mute, astonished negations, in response to the hurried and excited inquiries of the family, who came swarming into the hall in all possible stages and degrees of amazement and terror, propounding with great volubility all the conundrums which would naturally suggest themselves in consequence of such an astounding and unheralded and unprovoked outburst of human voice.

"I cannot imagine what did ail him," she said at length, when her stern father, in mild reproof, had laid his heavy hand upon her rounded shoulder, and oscillated her lithe form to and fro until her back hair was in her hands, and the floor was strewn with hair-pins and samples of curls, thick as autumnal leaves and one thing and another strew the brooks in Vallambrosa and vicinity. "I opened the door, and before I could say 'Good evening,' he opened his mouth to its fullest extent, and with a look of horror, fled from my presence, leaving no token save an amount of noise altogether incommensurate with his size. I can't imagine what he could have seen to affect him so. I was afraid at first that I hadn't rubbed the pearl powder out of my eyebrows, but I had."

Every member of the convention offered a suggestion or an explanation of the mysterious affair, but they were all overruled by paterfamilias, who, venturing the gruff opinion that the young man was in the habit of placing himself exterior to sundry and various decoctions dispensed at those retail drug stores which are, by law, closed on Sundays, and had merely incurred that peculiar form of mental distemper in which the patient keeps a private menagerie on exhibition in his boots, drove his wondering family back to the parlor.

But youth is buoyant. Its sorrows are transient and its tears are April rain, flecked with the sunshine even while they fall; its fears are short lived as its sorrows, and die away when the thought or scene that gave them birth is gone. So he who flew from the hideous shadow that had veiled the fairy figure of his love from his fond gaze, blushed in the darkness at his nervous fancy, and re-arranging his wardrobe, retraced his steps with more of that native grace and innate dignity peculiar to the young man of the nineteenth century, than he had displayed while making his presence seldom. Again he passed the wreck of the demolished gate, and once more he rang the bell, and listened for the echoing footfall, while the attentive specter came and stood demurely at his elbow.

"You horrid boy," murmured a sweet voice through the keyhole, "I have a great mind not to let you in. What made you act so perfectly ridiculous?"

"Dearest," the young man said, "it was a foolish, horrible fancy; I will never frighten you again."

"It was perfectly dreadful," she replied, "horribly, dreadfully awful. How could you be so perfectly horridly dreadful? But you may come in this time."

And with coquettish deliberation she opened the door, to see the ghost, bending his smiling gaze upon her colorless face and staring eyes.

"Thank you," he said, in hollow tones, "since you insist upon it, I will come——"

"Oo-oo-*ee*-E-E-E-E!"

And thump! She dropped to the floor with a velocity and abruptness that even astonished her ghost. Dumb with amazement, her lover stood gazing at her form, lying prone upon the new hall carpet, emitting a series of long-drawn shrieks. He recoiled, as again the members of the family came pouring and buzzing out of their rooms, like hornets from their domicile on a swaying apple tree bough, jarred rudely by the unconscious granger's towering head. The angry father caught a glimpse of the trembling, half-stupefied, and thoroughly mystified youth, standing near the door-way, appealingly and timorously offering his explanations. The parent, with a few hurried words, disappeared up stairs. Quickly he returned, bearing in his hands a ponderous shot-gun, at the sight of which the young man, without pausing to explain, fled quite as precipitately, and with as little ceremony, as he had sauntered away from the embrace of the ghost.

"Because," he remarked to the wind, which was vainly trying to keep pace with his flying movements as he cleared the fallen gate with a bound, and waltzed airily down the road, as though tight boots were a vision and an unreal dream, "because the old man appears to be a trifle impatient to-night, and I would not cross him in his sadder moods. He might do that to-night for which to-morrow I might mourn."

And deftly passing from twelve to fifteen linear feet of solid earth beneath each foot, oft as he raised it from the ground, with swift evasion he transferred himself to healthier climes and more congenial scenes.

The indignant father, meanwhile, had stepped out on the porch, and holding his warlike weapon a-port, peered angrily into the gloom for a glimpse of the flying figure, whose distant, echoing footsteps he could faintly hear.

"Thou art so dear," he said, "and yet so far."

To him the silent ghost approached. Standing by his unconscious side, the specter leaned his bony elbow upon the mortal shoulder, resting his hollow cheek upon his attenuated hand. Then, with a graceful motion and an easy gesture, of which a ballet dancer might be proud, he drew aside the lower portion of his drapery, disclosing to view a pair of emaciated shins of which a ballet dancer would most certainly be ashamed. Crossing one of these specimens of anatomical curiosities in front of the other, he rested the bended limb upon the toes, and stood thus for a moment, in that elegant and charming pose so much affected by our best young men at the opera and theater, who place themselves on exhibition for the untaught multitude upon every possible occasion.

For a few brief moments he stood thus, wrapped in admiration of his refined and elegant appearance, then dropping his face and turning it until his breath, if he had any, would have swept the cheek of his unconscious companion, he said:

"Let me entreat you, dear sir, to do nothing rash. Let me implore you to put by your murderous weap——"

Bang! bang! Two loads of death-dealing buckshot perforated the roof of the porch, and the howl of an elderly voice mingled with the crashing, discordant echoes that rose clattering through the darkness. The slam of a door, and the rush and scramble of many feet succeeded, followed by the clanging of locks and bolts; the subdued hubbub of many voices could be heard, detailing in many exaggerated phrases, extravagant narratives, and with a smile of grim amusement playing across his expressive features, like a telegraphic line from one ear to the other, the specter learned, as he listened at the keyhole, that while the master of the house had been standing on the porch, a pale blue light suddenly clove the night, accompanied by a sulphurous smell, in the midst of which appeared, rising out of the ground, a colossal body with five heads, and with hideous gashes yawning in its throats, from which the welling blood flowed down, and splotched and streaked the long white robe with horrible carmine stains. Its many eyes, the patrician said, glared like burning coals, and its hair twined and wreathed itself in fantastic shapes, like living serpents.

The specter assumed a thoughtful look as he listened to these terrible revelations.

"It is barely possible," he said, "that I am a maligned apparition. From his vivid powers of imagination, and a slight tendency to exaggerated word coloring in narration, one would take this elderly party for one of the gifted prevaricators who deal in political prophecies in the presidential year. I may not be a very handsome ghost, but I do most profoundly believe that this portly

Ananias who, I see, is just now leaving the room to learn how his daughter is coming on, has most foully traduced my personal appearance. And while there is no one in this apartment save that comfortable-looking old lady, who has been terrified and mystified into motionless silence, I will quietly step in and settle this vexed question by consulting the pier glass."

With that graceful, easy manner which is characteristic of a well-bred ghost, he slid through the keyhole, and a moment later, stood singeing his bloodless shins before the blazing grate, while he made a critical inspection of his visage in the mirror. After studying the picture for some moments in silence, he stroked his chin with a complacent air while a smirk of self satisfaction played over his features.

"Any mortal," he murmured, "who would flee in terror from such a face as that; any man who could detect any thing like an unearthly glare in those hollow eyes; any creature who can find it in his heart to announce the discovery of hair on that head, or find a trace of blood about that figure, from throat to heels, is a lunatic, and should be looked after. Be looked after," he added, in an absent way, "Looked after. Looked after."

"And," he continued, after a few moments' deliberation, "I should like to be appointed to look after him. He would then have a more faithful conservator than was ever appointed by a county court. I would interest and amuse him, and strive to divert his mind from the troubles which appear to have so disordered his imagination and distorted his vision and faculties of observation. I would keep him in a state of constant mental activity. I would help him around, and I would make myself useful to this family in a variety of ways. For instance, I would make this old gentleman so distrustful of that long walk up the hill after dark that he never would stay down town late at night, and could not be induced to attend lodge, or 'just step down to the post-office' after supper. I would imbue his very nature with such an utter abhorrence for dark places that he would never kiss the hired girl behind the cellar door. Never again; ne-ver, ne-ver. I would reform this man, and make this family happy, and this house should resound with manifestations of excitement and exclamations of astonishment, and indications of very dubious merriment, as it were. I see much good in this virtuous and happy project, and I will cultivate the acquaintance of this excellent lady of the mansion, convince her of the necessity of a protector for herself and her family, and carry my plans into operation. I have a conviction that this would be a most comfortable house to haunt."

He stepped to the side of the matron, and laying his icy fingers against her cheek to arouse her attention, and holding his throat shut with the other hand to prevent his voice escaping prematurely at the aperture which has been previously referred to, said, in a louder voice:

"You will pardon the abruptness of my speech, my dear madam, but I deem it my duty to inform you that it is my firm belief this part of town is haunted. Yes, ma'am, haunted. I shouldn't be surprised, indeed, if there was a ghost somewhere in this house this very minute. In fact I have every reason for believing——"

Thus far his auditor had preserved such a respectful silence that the speaker believed she was listening with rapt attention, and he fondly hoped that he had at last found a friendly, appreciative gossip who would not interrupt his remarks with ill-timed applause before he was half through. Looking at her face, however, at this moment, the expression of her countenance was such as chilled him with disappointment. She was not splitting the night air with blood-curdling, discordant shrieks, it is true, but it evidently wasn't her fault. Her eyes had left their sockets and were standing out on her cheekbones with nothing particular to do except to stare at each other across the top of her nose, each with an expression of blank amazement at seeing the other there. Her mouth was alternately closing with sudden jerks and distending with spasmodic gasps; noiseless, but all the more provoking on that very account. She appeared to be making strenuous efforts to rise, but as every attempt to assume an erect posture brought her closer to the ghost, she sank back helplessly in her chair after every effort, and resumed her dreadful staring and noiseless gasping.

"You had better scream, madame," said the disgusted ghost. "Pray, do not restrain yourself on my account. It is really painful for me to witness your suffering. If my presence here is distasteful to you, pray have the goodness to intimate the fact in the abrupt and startling manner so much affected by this family. You had better express your emotions, if you have any. If you have through any little passing thrill of excitement, temporarily lost the use of your voice, and find some difficulty in recovering it, perhaps I can assist you."

With a horrible leer he withdrew the drapery from his neck, and leaning back his head disclosed the gaping incision in his respiratory and swallowing apparatus which had compelled him to go into the ghost business. As he had shrewdly conjectured, that startling display developed the full action of the old lady's dormant vocal powers, and, for the next five minutes, Bedlam was a quiet, sequestered cloister in comparison with that house. For an instant the author of all the uproar paused to smile at the vociferous woman screaming till the chandelier trembled, and pounding a vigorous tattoo on the floor with her aged heels, and then he left the house, merely stopping as he went to look in on the kitchen, and by one genial wink at the servants establish a first-class English opera chorus in that department of the household.

He then passed out into the chill air, and gliding slowly along the gravel walk, paused to contemplate the ruins of the front gate and speculate on the whereabouts of the handsome youth who had so lately enacted the part of a modern Samson, and had torn down the gates to Gaza little on the loved face which parental tyranny would thereafter conceal from his ardent gaze forever.

"It is ever thus," moralized the ghost; "at once the mightiest and the weakest being in created life, God's noblest work is the toy of bodiless phantoms. We tear down and we build up; we purpose and we prevent; we do and we undo; we overcome every real difficulty, and surmount every actual obstacle, and at last, when our object is all but accomplished — lo, a shadow terrifies us, and the courage and labor of an hour, a year, or a lifetime, are swept into ruins. At least, *we* used to do thus. I have left the firm, but the surviving partners carry on the business of life in pretty much the same old style. The world invents a great deal, but it doesn't improve very much. It is the same old world, after all. It has the locomotive and the telegraph, true; but the men who invented the locomotive and the telegraph loved, feared, hoped and lived pretty much as Cæsar's couriers and Dido's sailors used to. Men declaim against the remotest possibility of the spirits of the dead revisiting the glimpses of the moon, and yet my presence affects in the same unpleasant and turbulent manner alike the most skeptical and the most credulous and surperstitious. I believe, speaking of spirits, I will go down town to a certain house I wot of, where parties of my friends, the Spiritualists, hold frequent seances, at which they converse familiarly, though ungrammatically, with the spirits of their own deceased friends, and of the illustrious dead. They will be glad to see me, I know, because I am intimately acquainted with some of the parties whom they occasionally summon back to earth, and they will be glad too, because I can correct some of the erroneous ideas they entertain in regard to the present condition of some of these spirits who are constantly writing back, in such execrable English as would make a cultured, intelligent ghost blush, how happy they are, and how glad they are that they died, and how much they know. I am as contented a ghost as one can find under the republic, and I never was glad that I died, and I never write to any of my relatives, and never visit any of them, except," he added thoughtfully, " my dear haunt." And he chuckled grimly over his ghastly little joke.

In another moment he was seated comfortably beneath a table which was surrounded by a party of seekers after truth, who were patiently sitting up for the latest returns from the spirit world. The ghost was much touched by the anxiety displayed by a young man in very long hair and green spectacles to hear from his departed uncle. The spirit mails were snowed in, or intercepted by guerrillas, or held for postage, or suffering from some other cause of detention that Christmas Eve; for it seemed as though the young man never would receive so much as a postal card from his deceased relative. The ghost pitied him, and just as the medium, a beautiful young girl of forty-nine summers, was passing into another trance, he crawled out from under the table and bowed pleasantly to the anxious inquirer.

"I think I can allay any anxiety you may feel on account of your departed avuncular relative," he said; "I have met him several times, and although the peculiar and pressing nature of his engagements elsewhere prevents his attending in person social assemblies on this side of the ground, he is——"

He ceased speaking at this point, for his voice had long ¦ een drowned in the uproar of shrieks, and breaking furniture, and crashing glass, as the seance broke up along with the tables and chairs, and the anxious seekers after truth emerged into the night with window sashes hanging round their necks. Foreseeing that there would be trouble if he did not emigrate in order to permit the wanderers to return and resurrect the overturned stove, the messenger from the realm of shadows departed and once more sought his station on the hill. And again he whistled "Down Among the Dead Men" through his teeth, while he smiled pensively, and communed with his own pleasant thoughts.

"It's just as I said," he mused; "had I been that young man's uncle, whom he so earnestly desired to see, his terror would have been just as great. They rap and call for us, they implore us to come, and when we come they go. And they go very abruptly. Some of those people to-night got out of that room by edging through fissures that would squeeze the very breath out of the leanest ghost I ever saw. Believer or skeptic, it makes no difference. Saul was not more terrified at Samuel's ghost, which he was so anxious to see, than was the witch who accidentally raised the apparition. But these broken, interrupted interviews with terrified mortals are growing monotonous. I will stay out all night, because it is Christmas Eve and my night out, but I will spend the remaining silent hours in meditation, and let the wicked old world sleep in peace, unless, mayhap, some belated wayfarer should stray this way, when I will revenge myself upon him for the shabby treatment I have received at mortal hands to-night. I will frighten him so that he will not be through screaming when I come here again next Christmas Eve. I have tried to be agreeable to everybody to-night, and everybody has refused to be sociable, and has repulsed my courteous advances with the most hideous shrieks and uproar. And to the next hapless mortal who shall cross my haunt, I will be terrible."

He ceased speaking, and knotted his face with a series of horrible contortions and hideous grimaces, which he practiced until he acquired one which appeared to satisfy his fastidious taste. This one he exercised several times in order to fix it firmly in his memory, and then, folding his arms, he leaned against the railing and gloomily waited for a customer, as ill-natured and unhappy a ghost as could be found in all the haunts of men or specters.

His ghostship did not have long to wait for a subject, standing there in the gloomy street, with the cold, glittering stars occasionally peeping timidly through the rifted clouds sailing overhead. Before long a heavy footfall was heard ascending the lower part of the hill, and then, as it came nearer, the dismal one could hear the frosty earth creaking under the passenger's feet at every step he took. A voice which was marked by that peculiar intonation which we so frequently notice in close proximity to a pick or a hod, uttered, in sentences so profusely vaccinated with trilled r's that it sounded like a high school commencement, a wrathful objurgation upon the wind, as the winter zephyr well nigh lifted the speaker from his feet.

"Growl about that, will you?" muttered the ghost, with savage gleefulness, "I'll make you wish the wind had blown you into the moon before you get to the top of the hill. I wish he would walk more slowly," the specter went on, rubbing his fleshless hands in delighted anticipation; "I should like to have a few moments' quiet enjoyment in contemplating the possible and probable actions of the worst frightened man in America. I have been accused of frightening people before now, but those vile slanders against my considerate and pacific disposition and my reassuring physiognomy will all be retracted and atoned for after to-night. After this man's experience no man, no living mortal will dare stand up and say that any one was ever frightened prior to this date. Why, there won't be as much hair left on this individual's head, in about three minutes, as would make me a switch. All the doctors in America won't be able to get his eyes back into their proper places. He will howl and yell and shriek and pray to the day of his death. Scared? It isn't the word. It's too weak. Whistle, will you?" he continued, apostrophizing the approaching figure, "I'll make you wish you had a French horn fifteen feet long, with all the keys open and the mouth-piece cracked, to express your feelings through. Why," he said, arranging his robe and twisting his face into such a blood-curdling awful contortion that it raised a blister on the frozen ground and the very wind turned and blew up hill for dear life; "why, my unsuspicious republican, you'll be the worst demoralized community in about fifteen seconds that ever disturbed the holy quiet of midnight."

Stretching out his gaunt arm in a weird, ghostly

gesture, the white drapery falling away from it in conventional folds, the specter stepped out to the middle of the sidewalk to confront the coming man. A man of medium size, the new-comer, with bluff square shoulders, twinkling eyes, a nose that had been made of a remnant so that the unfinished end retreated toward the eyes, a mouth puckered up in a melodious whistle, the head covered with an abundance of closely-cut hair of the shade of St. Louis pressed brick; a ragged coat was buttoned close and the wearer carried under his arm a walking-stick of most benevolent aspect, the bulge on the end of which reminded one of an invitation to join the innumerable caravan. His whistle ceased as the ghost loomed up before him, not suddenly cutting off his tune in the middle of the note, but in a long-drawn diminuendo passage, commonly expressive of inexpressible astonishment.

The ghost slowly and impressively waved his extended arm in the direction of the gloomy ravine. The mortal shuffled uneasily toward the middle of the street in an effort to get round the unpleasant obstruction. The specter noiselessly glided before him and still confronted him with outstretched arm and hideous countenance, and both figures regarded each other in silence. The mortal was the first to open the conversation, who, after muttering under his breath, "The saints betune us and har-rum, an' phwat is he makin' thim faces at me for?" remarked in a brisk tone:

"Cool avenin'!"

Motionless as a statue, the ghastly figure glowered upon him in its frozen attitude and terrifying gesture.

"Is it Tim Moriarity, as died the year before I kim' over, I don' know?"

No reply and no change of posture on the part of the specter.

"Is it the Feenicks boys ye are thin, as kilt aich other the night ov the ball at the creek three years ago come nixt September an' jist two months lackin' six weeks after O'Flaherty's sisther dhrove the cow off the wagon bridge?"

Still the specter maintained its silence and its position.

"Ye 've a mighty familiar countenince, onyhow," continued the mortal, who kept up his cautious maneuvering for the weather gauge, in which he was steadily baffled by the ghost. "It seems to me I've seen the face av yez somewhare on a tombstone. Yer not livin' fur around here, mebbe?"

In hollow tones the ghost replied, "I am dead."

"Did, is it? Oh, the saints rist yer ristless sowl. An' phwat are ye doin' out here? Whaire do ye live — I mane, whaire are ye buried?"

"At the top of this hill," came in the same hollow tones.

"An' a mighty agreeable place that same is, to be sure," replied the mortal, in a conciliatory intonation, "shlapin' undher the grass, wid the cows and pigs browsin' and rootin' around all day long an' kapen' ye company nights. Born divil that ye air," he added, in a lower tone, "I wisht wan or the other of us wur thayre now, fur it's a onpleasant company ye air, anyhow. Well," he added, aloud and with great cheerfulness, "good night till ye. Be good to yerself."

"Stay," uttered the terrible monotone; "come thou with me."

"Oh-h, the dev — I beg yer par-r-don. I mane I can't think of it. Luk at the time it is, an' see the murdherin' cowld I have in me head already, along ov being out till midnight. The wife and childher 'll be did intirely wid sittin' up fur me, an'——"

"Follow me!" said the hollow tones of the ghost.

"Oh-h, tundher an' turf—I mane—I beg yer par-r-don, don't shpake of it; it's a married man I am. I can't sthay; besides, there's no use—ivery place in town is shut up, and sorra the wan ov me dhrinks av they wasn't. I wouldn't taste a dhrop av I lived in lashins ov it; I'm a whole Father Mathew society by myself."

"Come! Come!! Come!!!" The sepulchral tones boomed out like a bass drum solo.

"Aw-w-w! Millia murther! Go aisy now! Phwat du ye mane, divilin' the tin sinses out of me to come, whin ye see I want to go? By the mortial gob," he added, under his breath, "av I thought I cud find anything in yer head to feel it, avick, I'd make ye raisonable wid a welt ov this splinther av a sthick. Whist! ye bloody minded villin!" he roared, with suddenly increasing courage, as some wakeful Brahma in a neighboring coop startled the night with a stentorian crow, which was shrilly echoed by a bantam and a dozen or more obscure roosters of no particular strain, like the birds that crow at election times, "Do ye hear that? An' that? An' that agin? An' the wan afther that? Scat! ye bloody minded Banshee, or we'll crow the rags aff o' yer beggarly back!"

The ghost gave a hollow laugh, that sounded like water pouring out of a jug.

"You may crow," he said, more in his easy conversational style and tone than he had been using, "till you split your throats; this is an anniversary night with me, and I won't go home till morning."

His uneasy companion's face fell at this announcement, and he looked like a man who felt that he had prematurely committed himself. But he rallied again.

"A anniver-sary, is it? Do ye have it often?"

"About once a year."

"Is that all? An' just think ov yer makin' so much fuss about that! Kape on yer hat, or what iver ye call it, or ye'll have a cowld in the head. Good avenin', agin."

The ghost mildly protested against his haste. It was Christmas Eve, he said, a season devoted to sociability and good fellowship——

"An' a foine idee ye have of bein' sociable, too," interrupted his auditor; "Christmas is a nice enough saison, but a frayzin' hillside at midnight, wid the wind blowin' a jimmycane an' the thermomether twenty-sivin degrays ferninst Cairo, isn't the way I'm thinking to be sociable about it, jist."

"I am delighted to have met you under such——"

"Faix, thin, thayre's only wan of us that's feeling so delighted about it."

"——Favorable and pleasant circumstances. I should never have forgiven myself had I permitted you to pass by without speaking. I must insist——"

"Begorra, thin, it's too har-r-d ye wad be on yersilf intirely. It's me that wad give mesilf absolution fur a week av I had gone around the other way an' never heard ov ye in me life."

"——On your further acquaintance."

"Thrue for you, avick, an' the furdther it is the betther it wud shuit me. An' the quicker we star-r-t, don't ye see, the furdther we can make it before mornin'. I know I'll think betther ov ye whin I can't see ye. *Good avenin'.*"

"Stay," said the specter, detaining him as he sought to hurry by, "I have that to tell you, and that to show you, to-night, which will make you a rich man, and send me back to my narrow resting place——"

"Oh-h-h! hear 'im talk about it!"

"——Never to leave it again until the last dread trump shall summon me."

"Don't mintion it, don't; don't shpake ov it at all, at all."

"My tale is brief and sad."

"An' have ye a tail, thin?"

"Listen!"

"Shpake!"

"In early life——"

"Phwat's that?"

"——I plowed the raging main."

"An' was ye a Granger, thin?"

"Nay, I was a pirate!"

"Same thing; kape on; it's frazin I am."

"I steeped my wicked hands in human gore for many years. When my atrocious crimes had amassed me a princely fortune, I repented me of my evil ways."

"Musha, thin, it war you for knowin' whin to repint."

"I bade adieu to my evil companions, and taking my share——"

"Ah, did ye, though? An' it was a cautious ould reformer ye was, all the same."

"——of our ill-gotten spoils, I fled west—far to the inland—pursued by the stings of an avenging conscience and a sheriff's posse."

"It was thim as stirred up yer conshince."

"I reached this city in safety and hid my gold, stained with human lives, in yonder deep ravine. Oft as I needed money, I came here by night and got what I wished."

"Can ye get any ov it now, do ye think?"

"One winter night—a cold, bleak Christmas Eve—returning from such a visit to my hoard, I was waylaid by two men, who suspected my secret, on this very spot——"

"Good avenin'!"

"Stay yet one moment. They seized me, hurled me to the ground——"

"Here?"

"On this very spot where now we stand. They——"

"Let's walk furdther down the hill."

"Listen. They hurled me to the ground, and, as I struggled for my gold, they—slew me!"

"Phwat!"

"They cut my throat from ear to ear!"

"M-i-l-l-i-a m-u-r-d-t-h-e-r! An' did it hurt?"

"It haggled some, but——"

"An' did yez niver git over it?"

"I died!"

"Oh-h-h-h! Bones of the martyrs! GOOD avenin!"

"Stop a moment. I——"

"Ah yez, shtop a minit. It's yerself is the pleasant man to be shtoppin' wid, on a hillside at midnight. Go on, thin, for it's starvin' wid the cold I am."

"I died where I fell; and a coroner's jury, after due deliberation, returned a verdict, on my lifeless remains, that 'the alleged deceased came to his probable death in a fit of temporary inanition, induced by the administering of narcotic drug or drugs, by some visitation of Providence to the jury unknown.'"

"Wur that all, alanna? I thought ye said they cut the throat ov ye."

"They did. But the intelligent citizens who composed the coroner's jury could not see that that had anything to do with it. Since that time, once a year, on every anniversary of my untimely death, I am forced to leave my grave——"

"Oh, mortial man! don't shpake ov it at all, an' us out here in the dark an' could, and niver a dhrop ov anything to rise the cockles ov me heart wid nearer than town. But kape on."

"——and haunt this hill. My spirit can not rest in peace until the money which I left concealed from human gaze shall be given into hands fit to be entrusted with wealth."

"An' is that all, acushla? Go back to yer den, and dhraw yer stool in to the fire, an' be comfortable. Show me whare to dig jist, and sorrow light upon me av ye'll ever have any more nade to wake up an' worry about another cint as long as ye live—I mane, as long as ye don't live. Whare's yer bank? Divil be in me but thare'll be such a run on it in about ten minits they'll think thare's an ould-fashioned American panic broke loose in ghostland, for a truth. Can't shlape because ye can't give yer money away! Musha, thin, it's meself can't shlape often enough because I haven't ony to give away, or to kape, ayther. Show me yer threasury, avick; I'm yer oysther."

"Years ago I might have given it away, had men but known my secret. But the spell laid upon me——"

"A spell ov what?"

"——forbade me to reveal my hidden wealth until I should meet a man going home sober, on Christmas Eve, who would not be afraid of me. The condition was a hard one, for although in my annual hauntings I have met many men plodding up this hill too drunk to be frightened, you are the first sober man I have met on Christmas Eve since the city was an Indian trading post."

"Ah well then, it's small blame to them, for it's gettin' ready to shwear off New Year's day they are, the whole jing-bang ov thim. Troth, they do that every year."

"You did not manifest any fear at my sudden appearance. You were not, apparently, afraid of me; you ——"

"Afraid, is it?"

"I merely remarked that you were not afraid of me."

"Is it me?"

"I said, my quick-tempered friend, that——'

"Is it you?"

"Calm yourself, my bellicose mortal, I simply ——"

"Listen to 'im! Hear 'im talk about ony body bein ashkared ov an ould bag o' bones sthandin' in the dark makin' faces! Why, ye consaited old skeleton, is it comin' to Ameriky to be shkared wid you I'd be, whin we had a ghosht ov our own in the Ould Sod for more nor twinty years? A ghosht that wur worth bein' shkared ov, too."

"You surprise me," said the ghost. "Are you quite certain that your own family was favored with the permanent society of a ghost? You will pardon me for intimating that your appearance and dress do not indicate a station in life that calls for such a condition of things. For I am decidedly under the impression that we are permitted to haunt only aristocratic families, who inhabit large rambling houses, with long gloomy corridors and magnificent bay windows and lofty mansard roofs and heavy mortgages; full of dark corners and convenient hiding places for ghosts, and frequently so uncomfortable and dreary, especially on the occasion of a poor relation's visit, that no one but a ghost can enjoy living in them. I once knew a most respectable ghost, a specter of a most extraordinarily rugged constitution, who haunted one of these houses, and went to sleep in the spare room one night and was so laid up with the rheumatism that he was unable to get out of his grave——"

"The saints betune us! Don't mintion it!"

"—— for nearly six weeks. I took his place at the mansion during his indisposition. A dreary, frosty place enough, fitted up elegantly with a thousand-dollar piano, a costly mechanic's lien, Brussels carpets, a chattel mortgage or two, French plate windows, a tax title, and a few similar expensive luxuries. I did not wish to be laid up with the rheumatism, so I took preventives instead of cures. From being frosty and chilly, I made that house the warmest place this side of —— "

"Don't say it, alanna! Skip that!"

"—— the equator," pursued the ghost, quietly. "It soon became the most hospitable mansion on the street. It was full of company all the time, and poor relations came and got square meals and slept in the best beds and were made welcome. You can not imagine how I softened that old fellow's proud heart. And you must excuse me if I say that you do not appear to belong to that favored class which is honored with hereditary ghosts. A ghost, my unsophisticated friend, is an expensive luxury."

"Thrue for you, it is, thin. The wan we had was the most expinsive thing we wur ever throubled wid. He kim till the house in me father's time an' I dunno how long befoar."

"Did he look like me?"

"Sorra the wan ov him. He'd ate a rigimint ov yez in a minit. Shouldhers like a sailor an' a head set on 'im like a bull dog's. He wur a ghosht now that cud talk to ye about bein' ashkared ov him."

"Does he ever annoy — that is, entertain you now?"

"Faix, thin he doesn't. It isn't here he cud live at all, at all. It wur in the ould counthry he did be vexin' us an' teasin' the life out ov us from mornin' till night."

"Why, did he appear in the daytime, then?"

"It wur grace fur his bones that he did. Be the holy poker, alanna, it wur waitin' fur him in the dark twenty times a month we was. Catch an Irish ghosht comin' in the dark. He knowed whin to come."

"Did you ever try to lay the ghost?"

"Wanst. The byes laid him wid a blackthorn stick, an' sorra the wan of him throubled us agin fur six weeks afther."

"I don't understand. Why did he haunt you? What was——"

"Why did he? For the rint, av coorse. It was the thavin' ould landlord, bloody end to him. Talk about ghosts! The ould *boddagh Sassenagh* gev us more throuble in wan day than the whole jing-bang ov such thin-legged spooks as yerself cud make us in a week. Thare was wan time the ould swaddler kim down to Muldoonery's shebeen—ye knew the Muldoonery's?"

"The name is familiar, but I can not say that I ever had the honor of the family's acquaintance."

"The betther for you thin, for ye died wid a whole head——"

"But my neck was spoiled."

"Oh-h, by this an' by that, listen to him! Don't sphake ov it. The Muldoonerys was me father's own family. Ould Malachi Muldoonery, wan of the Killatalicks, thim as was own cousins to the O'Slaughtery's of Killgobbin— ah, thim was the high-toned wans fur ye; when it come to ould families, they lifted the pins, jist. They had a ghosht ov thare own, a rale wan, sphooky enough to frighten a horse from his oats, that wore a long night-shirt like yer own, an' carried his head undher his arm. Oh, Gog's blakey, but he wur the boss ghosht. He wur beheaded fur headin' a rebellyun three hundhred years ago. Ah, tare-an-ouns, the tussle me own uncle, who was an O'Slaughtery, had wid this same ghosht wanst. We heard the sphook thramplin' up an' down the hall, fur he always wore a shurt of armor undher his white dhress, an' me uncle got up an' wint out, an' peerin' down the dark hall, sees him.

"'Arrah!' sez me uncle.

"Sorra the word sez the ghosht.

"'Are ye thaire?' sez me uncle.

"The ghosht stopped walkin' and screwed on his head like the head ov a cane.

"'An' phwat av I am?' sez he.

"'Come out o' that, thin, ye bladdherhang,' sez me uncle.

"'I won't, thin,' sez the ghosht.

"'Ye'd betther,' sez me uncle.

"'I hadn't thin,' sez the ghosht.

"'Do ye know what this is, ye omadhawn?' sez me uncle, balancin his blackthorn.

"'None o' yer chaff,' sez the ghosht.

"'I wont lave a whole bone in yer carkidge,' says he.

"'I hwat!' sez the ghosht.

"'I wont!' sez he.

"'Yer a liar!' sez he.

"'Is it me?' sez he.

"'Show me yer head!' sez he.

"'Whoop!' sez he.

"'Hurroo!" sez he.

"Whack! wint the black-thorn, and wid that the whole house was roused wid a bellerin' an' roarin' that wud shame the bulls ov Bashan. It was me uncle, an' they found him out dures tied to the gate-posht wid a bed-cord half a mile long and knotted up that way that it tuk thim till after daylight to ontie him, for sorra the knot cud they cut. Oh, heavy heart go wid the ghosht that tied him out in the cowld that a-way. An' afther they got him untied he died."

"Immediately?" asked the specter.

"Och, the divil, no; about twenty-sivin years afther. But this isn't tellin' me about that famous bank ov yours?"

"True," said the specter. "we are losing time. To you, who have kept sober Christmas Eve, and have scorned to desecrate and profane the sacred memories of the season ——"

"Tower ov ivory!" whispered the exile of Killatalick, "av that isn't purty good for an ould cut-throat ov a pirate!"

"—— and have shown the integrity of your moral being —— "

"An phwat's thim, I wondher?"

"—— in that you feel no fear of visitants from the spirit world, to you I commit gold won by dishonest means, but which at last reaches honest hands that will devote it to worthy purposes. Come with me, and do as I tell you."

Crossing himself with an energy and rapidity that indicated a slight lack of confidence in the moral standing of his guide, the descendant of the Muldoonerys of Killgobbin followed his ghostly leader down the hill-side into the hollow and along the course of the bewildered and frozen brook, until they paused before an irregular wall of rock, long ago cut down by the action of the water. As they stood before this rude wall, the specter turned to his companion.

"If," he said solemnly, "you do not feel as though you could maintain the strictest silence, and not utter a word or an exclamation, no matter what wonders you may see, do not follow me farther. The charm which opens the care of my hidden wealth to your eyes, closes it in destruction on any violation of the spell under which I am held. Are you ready? On your life now, do not utter a sound."

The ghost touched the rock with his bony hand. It yawned like a door, and in the cavern behind the gloomy entrance they crept, crouching, along a narrow passage until the roof arched and they stood erect. An open chest lay at their feet; glittering jewels sparkled like stars in the gloom; precious stones in the mysterious coffer gleamed till their rays pierced the shadowy pall of the cavern with a pale, tremulous light. At a silent motion from the specter, the mortal, trembling with excitement and eagerness, bent down and seized the chest. Once, twice, thrice, he strained every muscle, and tugged until it seemed as though his eyes were bursting from their sockets, but the glittering fortune seemed immovable. He set every nerve for one tremendous effort; he braced his feet firmly, and once more grasped the handles of the coffer. It moves! The ransom of an empire is his!

"'S'matter 'ith you fellers? Hic! Watchu doin'? Hey?"

The blinding light, and the deafening crash that followed, lasted scarce the duration of the lightning's flash, and all was darkness and silence. When the gray light of morning quenched the beams of the paling stars, the exile woke to consciousness to find himself lying outside the spell-bound cavern, with the unbroken rock looming cold and pitiless beside him, and his dream of wealth was gone. A faint odor of stale whisky kissed the wintry zephyrs, and a shattered bottle in the near distance lay like a mournful memory of his happy dreams. When the unhappy man's friends discovered him, they took in all the conditions of the cheerless bivouac, and when in the cozy surroundings of his home he told his marvelous narrative, they were skeptical enough to declare that they believed all the story about the ghost and the cavern and the money chest was only the inspiration of that bottle before it was broken, and that the exile of Killgobbin saw the light and heard the crash when he staggered over the edge of the wall and broke his head. But he still believes that if the young fellow who went into camp on the hillside at the opening of this story had not finished his sleep and broke in upon them in such an untimely manner, he would never again have done a harder day's work than cutting off coupons from government bonds.

The rest of us know that this is true. And if any young man doubts the truth of this veracious chronicle, he can easily verify its statements by keeping sober next Christmas Eve, and patrolling the quiet streets until he meets the ghost. And if he doesn't see the specter, he will at least enjoy the singular sensation of going home sober Christmas Eve, a thing of much greater rarity and wonder to most of "the boys" than an interview with a Moneyed Ghost.

MIDDLERIB'S PICNIC.

"IT isn't age that makes people grow old," Mr. Middlerib remarked to his family as they were gathered at the breakfast table. "It is incessant application; it is unending, incessant work and worry. The mind, the body, all the faculties, mental and physical, are kept on the alert without rest or recreation, until outraged nature rises in rebellion against the slavery to which it is subjected, and deluded man, with all the aches and tremor of senility in his young joints, awakes to find that he has lived his three score years and ten in half his allotted number of days." And with this sage remark Mr. Middlerib leaned back in his chair and regarded his family with the air of a man who has just imparted a volume of information that would stagger the average comprehension.

"That's what ailed these spring chickens, I reckon," suggested Master Middlerib, struggling with a wing that was supplied with the latest improved fish-plate joints; "wore themselves out trying to lay ten years' eggs in five."

Mr. Middlerib gazed at the boy in a meaning manner, and the young gentleman immediately elevated one of his elbows until it was as high as his head, and held his guard up while he warily regarded his parent's disengaged hand. But the usual consequences did not follow, and Mr. Middlerib proceeded to announce that he would shake off the sordid cares of business, and free

MIDDLERIB'S PICNIC.

himself from the shackles of commercial servitude, and enjoy a picnic with his family and a few chosen friends. And immediately upon this, the family loosed their tongues and talked all together, and as loud and fast as possible for twenty-five minutes. Then, Mr. Middlerib, smiling benignly upon the scene of pleasure which his announcement had created, went off to his office. When he returned, Miss Middlerib had a list made out of the people they would invite. It embraced one hundred and fifteen names, not including alternates, and Mr. Middlerib's jaw fell as he gazed at the catalogue.

"Daughter, dear," he remarked, as soon as he could command his feelings, "do you take me for Calvary Mission Sunday-school, that you have included the census of this city in our picnic?"

Then explanations were demanded, and it appeared that Mr. Middlerib's idea had been to take a couple of big wagons, furnished with temporary seats, and have a decidedly rustic, old-fashioned picnic, of an exclusively family nature. And Miss Middlerib sat down and blotted out an even hundred names with tears, after which Mr. Middlerib gazed upon the revised and corrected list, expunged edition, and pronounced it good. Then they fixed upon the day, which was settled after much wrangling and profound discussion. Mr. M. went out and looked at the sky, and noted the direction of the wind, and watched the movements of the chimney swallows with a critical and scientific eye, and came in and announced that it would not rain for five days, and they would have the picnic just two days before the rain. And from the hour of that announcement the Middlerib family and their invited relations did nothing but bake, and roast, and stew, and iron clothes, and declare they were tired to death and would be glad when it was all over and done with. It is a somewhat remarkable fact that all people who make up their minds to go to a picnic, always do say that they will be glad when it is over, and act as though they were going merely as an act of self-denial and a mortification of the flesh.

But when the day finally rolled around, as days will roll, the excitement was at its height. The sun struggled to his place at the usual hour, as soon as he was called, and his broad, red face had a terribly wild and dissipated look as he glared through the bank of clouds that curtained his getting up place, as though he had been tearing around all night, and had never had his boots off, and had only got up to collar the water pitcher. No wonder the whole party lost confidence in such a sun the moment they looked at him. He looked too much like a prodigal sun, just before he got starved into reform, rather than a smiling, cheery picnic sun. And the Middleribs took turns going out singly and in small groups to look at him, and revile his unpromising appearance, and after each observation they would return to the house and ask each other in tones somewhat tinged with a tender melancholy, "Well, what do you think of it?" And the questioned one would stifle a sigh and reply "I don't know, do you?"

There is no scene in all this wide world of pathos more pathetic than a group of anxious mortals, on the morn of a picnic, trying to delude each other into the belief that when the sky is covered with heavy black clouds, 800 feet thick, and a damp scud is driving through the air, and the sun is only half visible occasionally through a thin cloud that is waiting to be patched up to the standard thickness and density, it is going to be a very fine day indeed. So the Middleribs looked at the coppery old sun, and the dismal clouds, and tried to look cheerful, and said encouragingly that "Oh, it never rained when the clouds came up that way;" and, "See, it is all clear over in the east;" and, "It often rains very heavily in town when there doesn't a drop of water fall at Prospect Hill." And thus, with many encouraging remarks of similar import, they awaited the gathering of the party, and the human beings finally climbed into one wagon, put the baskets and the boys in the other, and drove away, giggling and howling with well dissembled glee.

The happy party, although they well knew that it would not rain, had taken the precaution nevertheless to take a large assortment of shawls and umbrellas. They were a quarter of a mile from town when it began to thunder some, but as it didn't thunder in the direction of Prospect Hill, distant some three miles, they went on, confident that it wasn't raining, and wouldn't, and couldn't rain at Prospect Hill. They were half a mile from town when the cloud that all the rest of the clouds had been waiting for came up and remorselessly sat down on the last, solitary lingering patch of blue that broke the monotony of the leaden sky, but the party pressed on, confident that they would find blue sky when they got to Prospect Hill. They were a mile from town when old Aquarius pulled the bottom out of the rain wagon and began the entertainment. It was a grand success. The curtain hadn't been up ten minutes before all the standing room in the house was taken up and the box office was closed. The Middlerib party having gone early, and secured front seats, were able to see everything. They expressed their pleasure by loud shrieks, and howls, and wails. They tore umbrellas, that had been furtively placed in the wagon, out of their lurking places, and shot them up with such abruptness that the hats in the wagon were knocked out into the road. Then the wagon stopped and people crawled out and waded around after hats, and came piling back into the wagon, with their feet loaded with mud. The umbrellas got into each other's way, and from the points of the ribs streams of dirty water trickled down shuddering backs, and stained immaculate dresses, and took the independence out of glossy shirt fronts. And the picnic party turned homeward, but still the Middleribs did not lose heart. They smiled through their tears, and Miss Middlerib, beautiful in her grief, still advocated going on and having the picnic in a barn, and wept when they refused her. It rained harder every rod of the way back. Then when they got everybody and every thing into the house, the heart-rending discovery was made that the boys had taken the rubber blanket which was to have covered the baskets in case of rain, and spread it over themselves when the moisture gathered, and consequently the edibles were in a state of dampness.

Then the clouds broke, and the sun came out, and smiling nature stood around looking as pleasant as though it had never played a mean trick on a happy picnic party in its life; and the Middleribs hung themselves out in the sun to dry, and tried to play croquet in the wet grass, and kept up their spirits as well as they knew how, and were not cross if they did get wet. If smiling nature had only given them a show, or even half a chance, they would have got along all right. They were bound to have the picnic party anyhow, so they kept all the relations at the house, and when dinner time came, the grass was dry and they set the table out under the trees and made it look as picnicky as possible. It clouded up a little when they were setting the table, but nobody thought it looked very threatening. The soaked things had been dried as carefully as possible.

and the table looked beautiful when they gathered around it. And just about the time they got their plates filled and declared that they were glad they came back, and that this was ever so much better than Prospect Hill, a forty acre cloud came and stood right over the table, and then and there went all to pieces.

That was what spoiled the picnic.

The pleasure-seekers grabbed whatever they could reach and broke for the house, uttering wild shrieks of dismay. They crowded into the hall, which wasn't half big enough, and there they stood on each other's trains, and trod on each other's corns, and poured coffee down each other's backs, and jabbed forks into one another's arms. When one frantic looking woman would rush in and set a plate of cake down on the floor while she dived out into the rain with a woman's anxiety to recover some more provisions from the dripping wreck, a forlorn looking man would immediately step on that plate of cake, and stand there gazing wonderingly and apprehensively at the shrieking crowd around him, pointing their forks and fingers at him and at his feet, and yelling, in a deafening chorus, something as utterly unintelligible as " shouting proverbs." And when the man, in a vain effort to do something in compliance with the shrieking which was evidently intended for him, stepped off the cake and stood in a huge dish of baked beans for a change, the wail of consternation that went up from the congregation fairly rent the bending skies. And when Uncle Steve, who had found Aunt Carrie's baby out under the deserted table, maintaining an unequal struggle with half of a huckleberry pie and a whole thunder-storm, came tearing in with the hapless infant, and, dashing through the crowd, deposited it on top of a pile of hard-boiled eggs, Miss Middlerib fainted, and the youngest gentleman cousin was driven into a spasm of jealousy because he couldn't walk over a row of cold meats and lobster salad to get to her, and had to endure the misery of seeing the oldest and ugliest bachelor uncle carry her drooping form to a sofa, and lay her down tenderly, with her classic head in a nest of cream tarts and her dainty feet on Sadie's Jenny Lind cake. And when Mrs. Middlerib looked out of the window, and saw the dog Heedle with his fore paws in the lemonade bucket, growling at Cousin John, who was trying to drive him out of it, she expressed a willingness to die right there. And when they were startled by some unearthly sounds and muffled shrieks, that even rose above the human babel in the hall, and found that the cat had got its poor head jammed tighter than wax in the mouth of the jar that contained the cream, everybody just sat on the plate of things nearest him, and gasped, "What next?" while Cousin David lifted cat and jar by the tail of the former, and carried them out to be broken apart. And when old Mr. Rubelkins lost his teeth in the coffee pot, half the people in the hall began to lose heart, and one discouraged young cousin said he half wished that they had put the picnic off a day. And finally, when the uproar was at its height, the door-bell rang, and the aunt nearest the door opened it, and there stood the Hon. Mrs. J. C. P. R. Le Von Blatheringford and her daughter, the richest and most stylish people in the neighborhood, arrayed like fashion-plates, making their first formal call. While they stood gazing in mute bewilderment at the scene of ruin and devastation and chaos before them, Mrs. Middlerib just got behind the door and pounded her head against the wall; while Miss Middlerib, springing from her sofa, ran to her room, leaving a trail of Jenny Lind cake and cream tarts behind her, as the fragments dropped from her back hair and heels. And the rest of the company, staring at the guests with their mouths full of assorted provisions, and their hearts full of bitter disappointment, mumbled, in hospitable chorus, "Wup pin," which, had their mouths been empty, would have been rendered, "Walk in."

This blow settled the picnic. Gloom hung over the house the rest of the day. Mr. Middlerib decided, after the company had departed, that the easiest and cheapest way to clean the hall would be to turn the river through it. And that night, when they were assembled at a comfortless tea table—Master Middlerib having been sent to bed so sick that they didn't think his toe-nails would be able to hold down till morning—Mr. Middlerib said:

"It isn't the steady, honest, ambitious devotion to business that makes men old. Labor is a law of our nature. We are happiest and most content when we are busiest. It is the healthful labor of the day that brings the sweet, refreshing repose of the night. Pleasure flies us when we seek her; she comes to us when we least regard her calls. Remember what I have always said, and find your pleasure in your daily work—in the regular routine of daily life, and its duties and useful avocations —and age will only come upon you slowly, and youth will linger in your hearts and on your faces long years after the allotted days of youth are past. The next time you want to have a picnic, remember how often I have warned you against them."

MASTER BILDERBACK'S POULTRY YARD.

IF there was anything she abominated more than one thing, Mrs. Bilderback used to say with some warmth, it was another, and that was chickens. And she resolutely protested against keeping any of them about the place. She wanted to keep a few flowers this year, and she wasn't going to be mortified again as she was last Summer, by having every woman who called at that house smile at the forest of bare stalks and scraggy branches that stood for the collection of house plants that she and her daughter tried to raise for ornaments to the place, but which were really of no use except to fill the crops of a lot of long-legged, hungry chickens. And for a long time the good lady held out stoutly against the chicken proposition, but was at last over-argued and over-persuaded and gave her unwilling consent for Master Bilderback to keep three dozen chickens, the party of the second part binding himself to keep the table supplied with fresh eggs and spring chickens, and to keep all hens, roosters, and all young chickens of unknown sex, but of sufficient physical development to scratch, out of the front yard and away from the flower beds. This contract Master Bilderback placed himself under heavy bonds to carry out, by saying, "honest injun," "pon nonnor," and "'cross my heart," and having solemnly repeated this awful and impressive formula, he went sedately out of the room and immediately threw himself down on a verbena bed, where he pounded the ground with his heels in the ecstasy of his joy. In due time the new hen-house was completed, and Mr. Bilderback, breathing maledictions on the wretches who pulled the picke's off his front fence for kindling wood, had that important boundary repaired before he noticed that the apertures in the fence corresponded to certain neat looking improvements on the hennery. The house was stocked rather slowly, for it was part of the contract which Mrs. Bilderback had drawn that the party of the second' part should purchase his own stock. It was noticeable that Master Bilderback's taste ran greatly toward gamey looking roosters, and as the perches in the hennery became more and more populated, the outlook for fresh eggs and spring chickens became very discouraging indeed. The first fowl the poulterer brought home was a gaunt Hamburg with one eye and a game leg, but beautifully spangled, which interesting bird, Master Bilderback informed his sister, was the worst pill in the box and had lost his eye while fighting a cow. The next day he traded a pocketful of marbles for a little bantam that crowed twenty-four hours a day, could slip through a season crack in a warped board, and could dig a hole in the middle of a flower bed that you could bury a calf in. There wasn't a moment's silence about the house after the bantam's arrival, for when he was not fighting the Hamburg, which was only when that valiant but prudent bird got up on top of the house and hid behind a chimney, he was wandering through the house trying his voice in the different rooms, or standing on the front porch issuing proclamations of defiance to all roosters to whom these presents might come, greeting. A day or two after the bantam's arrival Master Bilderback traded his knife for a Black Spanish rooster with a broken wing. The Spaniard when put in the coop proceeded at once to clean out the disheartened Hamburg, who fought on the tactics which had so often proved of so great value to him, and amazed his furious antagonist by the briskness with which he got out of the coop, up on to the barn, and perched himself on the restless and uncertain weather-cock. The Spaniard and the bantam then had it until neither of them could stand, when the pacific Hamburg improved the opportunity to come down and partake of the first square meal he had eaten since the new boarders had come to the house. Two days later, Master Bilderback brought home a vile looking white rooster with no tail feathers, his comb shaved off close to the head, and spurs as long as your thumb, a vile plebeian of a rooster without a line of pedigree, of no particular strain, except a strain that made his very eyes turn red when he growled, which he had bought for an old base ball club. But the nameless stranger amazed the proprietor of the hennery by waltzing into the establishment with a terrific rooster oath, and following it up by kicking the bantam clear out of his mind, jerking the wattles off the Spaniard, and chasing the persecuted Hamburg half way up the side of the house. This was the last addition made to the happy family for some time, Mr. Bilderback declaring that he was not going to have his premises turned into a cock-pit, and Master Bilderback was sternly forbidden to arrange any more meetings in the alley, with other boys and their birds. But a few days afterward, when Master Bilderback came home from school, it was evident that he had made a trade. He had some other boy's shabby old hat on his head, and there wasn't a lead pencil, piece of string, pistol cartridge, top, fish-hook, chalk line, marble, dime novel, or street car ticket in his pockets, and he had a new rooster, the crowning glory of the vast collection of fowls that were to furnish forth his mother's table with fresh eggs and spring chickens. It was a Shanghai; young one, Master Bilderback said, as he prepared to untie its legs and wings and introduce it to its new home; hadn't got his growth yet, but he was "a buster." And Mrs. Bilderback thought he was. When he was untied he stood up and flapped one of his wings in his proprietor's face, until that young gentleman was ready to "cross his heart," that somebody had hit him with a clapboard. And before he had recovered from the effects of this blow the noble bird kicked him under the chin and darted off toward the front yard, with prodigious strides. He uttered a most awful croak as he neared Mrs. Bilderback, who was trying to get out of his way, and in a vain attempt to fly over her, he struck her on the head, just abaft her ear with his heel, gently dropping her; "grassed the old lady," Master Bilderback afterward explained to his sister, "like a shot." The wretched bird paused as he passed the sitting-room window, which was just about on a level with his head when he stooped, to look in and make some unintelligible remark in a guttural tone of language, and snatching up a new tidy that Miss Bilderback was at work upon, swallowed it and passed on. Wherever he trod, he smashed a house plant, and whenever he croaked, he threw somebody into a fit. He met Mr. Bilderback as he suddenly turned the corner of the house, ran against the old gentleman with a wild kind of a crow that sounded like a steamboat whistle with a bad cold, and as he trampled over that good man's prostrate form, he plucked off his neck-tie and swallowed it. Then the "buster" wheeled around and straddled into the sitting-room window, and before they could head him out of the house he swallowed two spools of cotton, a tack hammer, a set of false teeth belonging to Mrs. Bilderback, a cake of toilet soap, a shoe buttoner, a ball of yarn, an arctic overshoe, and finally choked on a photograph album which flew open when it was about half way down. The bird when last heard from was still at large roaming around South Hill, but Master Bilderback's hennery is empty and lonesome, because his parents are, from some unaccountable reason, bitterly prejudiced against keeping chickens.

A SUNDAY IDYL.

YOU see, the tenor had got kind of abstracted, or restless, or something during the long prayer, and was thinking about the European war, or the wheat corner last week, or something, and so when the minister gave out hymn 231, on page 67, and the chorister whispered them to sing the music on page 117, it all came in on the tenor like a volley, and as he had only the playing of the symphony in which to make the necessary combination of time, hymn and page, he came to the front just a little bit disorganized, and his fingers sticking between every leaf in the book. And the choir hadn't faced the footlights half a minute before the congregation more than half suspected something was wrong. For you see, the soprano, in attempting to answer the frenzied whisper of the tenor in regard to the page, lost the first two or three words of the opening line herself, and that left the alto to start off alone, for the basso was so profoundly engaged in watching the tenor and wondering what ailed him, that he forgot to sing. The music wasn't written for an alto solo, and consequently there wasn't very much variety to that part, and after singing nearly through the first line alone, and receiving neither applause nor bouquets for one of the finest contralto efforts a Burlington or any other audience ever listened to, the alto stopped and looked reproachfully at the soprano, who had just plunged the tenor's soul into a gulf of dark despair by leaving him to find his way out of the labyrinth of tunes and pages and hymns into which his own heedlessness had led him, by giving him a frantic shake of her head, which unsettled the new spring bonnet (just the sweetest duck of a Normandy), to that extent that every woman in the congregation noticed it. All this time the organist was doing nobly, and the alto, recovering her spirits, sang another bar, which, for sweetness and tenacious adherence to the same note, all the way through, couldn't be beat in America. By this time the bass had risen to the emergency and sang two deep guttural notes, with profound expression, but as those of the congregation sitting nearest the choir could distinctly hear him sing "Ho, ho!" to the proper music, it was painfully evident that the basso had the correct tune, but was running wild on the words. At this point the soprano got her time and started off with a couple of confident notes, high and clear as a bird song, and the congregation, inspired with an overready confidence, broke out on the last word of the verse with a discordant roar that rattled the globes on the big chandelier, and as the verse closed with this triumphant outbreak, an expression of calm, restful satisfaction was observed to steal over the top of the pastor's head, which was all that could be seen of him, as he bowed himself behind the pulpit.

The organist played an intricate and beautiful interlude without a tremor or a false note; not an uncertain touch to indicate that there was a particle of excitement in the choir, or that anything had gone wrong.

The choir didn't exactly appear to catch the organist's reassuring steadiness, for the basso led off the second verse by himself, and his deep-toned "Ho, ho!" was so perceptible throughout the sanctuary that several people started, and looked down under the seats for a man, and one irreverent sinner, near the door, thrust a felt hat into his mouth and slid out. The soprano got orders and started out only three or four words behind time, but she hadn't reached the first siding before she collided with a woman in the audience, running wild and trying to carry a new tune to the old words. And then, to make it worse, the soprano handed her book to the tenor, and pointed him to the tune on page 117 and the words on page 67, and if that unhappy man didn't get his orders mixed, and struck out on schedule time, with the tune on page 67 and the words on page 117, and in less than ten words ditched himself so badly that he was laid out for the rest of the verse, and then he lost his place, handed the book back to the soprano, took the one she had, and held it upside down, and no living man could tell from his face what he was thinking of or trying to say. Meanwhile the soprano, when the books were so abruptly changed on her, did just what might have been expected, and telescoped two tunes and sets of words into each other with disastrous effect. The alto was running smoothly along, passenger time, for the several wrecks gave her the track, so far as it was clear, all to herself. The basso, who had slipped an eccentric and was only working one side, was rumbling cautiously along, clear off his own time, flagging himself every mile of the way, and asking for orders every time he got a chance. The pastor's head was observed to tremble with emotion, and the people sitting nearest the pulpit say they could indistinctly hear sounds from behind it that resembled the syllables "Te, he!" As the organist pulled and crowded and encouraged them along toward the closing line, it looked as though public confidence might soon be restored and the panic abated, but alas, as even the demoralized tenor rallied, and came in with the full quartette on the last line, a misguided man in the audience suddenly thought he recognized in the distracted tune an old, familiar acquaintance, and broke out in a joyous howl on something entirely different that inspired every singing man and woman in the congregation with the same idea, and the hymn was finished in a terrific discord of sixty-nine different tunes, and the rent and mangled melody flapped and fluttered around the sacred edifice like a new kind of delirium tremens, and all the wrecking cars on the line were started for the scene at once.

The pastor deserves more praise than can be crowded into these pages for pronouncing the benediction in clear, even tones, without even the ghost of a smile on his placid countenance.

RUPERTINO'S PANORAMA.

OUR first view is leaving New York harbor. This is a beautiful picture. See the mighty vessel, spreading her snowy wings to the gale, glide through the water like a thing of life. There is nothing to hinder her, and nothing in that fact to make a fuss about. But if the water was to glide through her, it would be time for reflection on the brevity of one's life insurance policy. The noble ship is freighted with precious human souls, bright hopes, happy anticipations, hides, salt meat and highwines.

This is a view of the Bourse in Paris, a twin institution to the Burlington Board of Trade. The man in the background, trying to hang himself on a lamp-post, is a member of the Bourse. He has just been Boursted. He has been operating in corn. If you will hold a bottle or small tumbler to your mouth and look steadily at this picture, you will see how they usually operate in corn at the Exchanges.

This is a view in Egypt. The great city of Cairo. It is named after Cairo, Illinois. Cairo is on the river Nile. Cairo never struck ile that we know of, but we do know that Cairo seen Nile. We do not know, history does not tell us, what there was so important in this event, but we know it is commemorated by monuments erected all over America. You can't go into a cemetery in the United States without seeing one or more monuments erected to the memory of Cairo C. Nile. He was probably the inventor of a cooking-stove, as some reference is usually made to the kitchen fire.

This is a view of the Seine. This is the favorite place for the Parisians to shuffle off their mortal coil. The volatile Frenchman gets himself full of elan (you know what that is) and jumps off one of these arched bridges, the Pont Noof or the Pont de Jena, down by the Shong de Mar. The zhong darmay, which is French for river police, fishes the victim out; the coroner pronounces him incurably inseine, his property is confiscated, and his insurance policy declared void, so as to spoil his wife's chances of marrying again. Such is the grasp of an iron despotism upon the wretched slaves of down-trodden Europe. (Applause.)

Here is a view in London of the old Bucking'em palace. This is an exterior view. Inside there are several keno banks, some chuckaluck tables and a faro bank, and the nobility are in there bucking the tiger. King Richard came out of that palace once, cleaned out, after a run of bad luck. He remarked to a friend, "So much for bucking 'em." The quotation has passed into history.

A panoramic view of Scotland. The gentleman in the peculiar position in the foreground is scratching his back against a mile post and remarking, "God bless the gude Duke of Argyle." The children in Scotland are taught that the Duke of Argyle made the world. This is an error.

We stand among the antiquities of Rome—Rome that stood on her seven hills, like James Robinson in his famous eight-horse bareback act. This is Trajan's Column—his spinal column. This is the Arch of Titus. When he put up that arch he was Titus a brick. This is the place where the Roman mobs used to collect and the police went Forum. Here is the Coliseum. There is the bloody sand of the arena; there is the spot where "the dying gladiator" lied. "I see before me the dying gladiator lie." Some calm and temperate Roman ought to have cast the scoundrel's lies in his teeth. The Romans were very depraved, wicked people, and the entire civilized world yet suffers from the effects of their malicious iniquity. They invented the Latin grammar, Nepos, Cicero and Virgil, and hurled upon the boys of succeeding ages a language containing ten rules to every word, and twenty exceptions to every rule. This is a statue of a noble Roman, Julius Cæsar. He was named after the Fourth of July and President Grant.

We stand in Greece. "The isles of Greece! The isles of Greece!" Probably the poet referred to goose grease. The Greeks were an ancient people. They wrote their letters in cipher, and schoolboys of to-day sigh for hours over their letters. Here are the ruins of the temple of Jupiter O'Lympus, erected to him by the ancient Greeks, thus proving that the Irish nation sprang from these ancient heroes. Here is an ancient theater. It is closed now for repairs; has been closed for a few thousand years, and the actors have gone off to their Summer resort, at Hades on the Styx.

Behold buried Pompeii. The city was entombed in an eruption that hadn't been equaled since Job got well. The gentleman in a military position at the gate, dressed in a full suit of bones, is not only a charming specimen of anatomy, but was a brave sentinel, who was covered up with ashes before he could run. He would have been 1,795 years old to-morrow if he had run and kept on living. It appears, however, that he is dead. The fact is not substantiated by any direct evidence, as no witnesses can be found who saw him die, and his will, therefore, has not been probated. But it is generally believed that he is dead. Weep not for him, friends.

He was a heathen, and has gone to a place where he is probably used to volcanoes by this time.

This building, the venerable pile that rises before you, is 27,000 years old. It originally cost $850, and took ten men nearly all Summer to build it. It was whitewashed nearly 4,000 years ago, but received no later repairs. The room on the right as you enter the hall on the first floor, is the Torture Room. It is called the County Treasurer's office, and is where people go and mortgage their farms and homes for taxes. The room opposite is the County Insane Asylum. The juries are confined there while on duty, and the local debating societies also meet there. This court-house was built many ages before Burlington was settled. The massive walls are engraved with the names of eminent men who have served on the juries. A grim and imposing antiquity frowns upon us as we enter the Judgment Hall up stairs. The benches and desks are made of wood taken from the decks of the ark. The tobacco quids in the corners were piled there so long ago that people had not begun to remember anything. The wood-box is a pre-Adamic creation. It is modeled after the megatherium. The only man living who knows anything about the early history of the court-house is dead.

MIDDLERIB'S DOG.

MR. MIDDLERIB used to be a devoted dog fancier. About three years ago he owned a beautiful hound pup about five months old. It was considered an ornament to the neighborhood. A hound pup at that age is an object of surprising beauty, under any circumstances; but when you consider that Mr. Middlerib had raised his pup on scientific principles (boiled beef and rice), you can readily imagine what a canine divinity it was. Gaunt legs, longer than your grandfather's stories, and the hind ones so crooked that the dog sticks his foot into everything in the yard every time he tries to scratch his ear; sides look as though he had swallowed an old hoopskirt, and the springs showed through; more ribs under his hide than there are spots on it; tail as long as the dog, and two inches across the big end and tapering down like a marlinspike, so lean you can count every joint in it, and so hard that you couldn't scratch it with a diamond—has every appearance of having been made ten years before the dog was, and then hung out to bleach in the rain and dry in the sun until the dog came along; ears soft as a kid glove, and about the size and appearance of a blacksmith's apron—bear every evidence of being considered by all other dogs in the precinct as dreadful nice things to chew. Beautiful eyes; open twenty-three hours and fifty-nine minutes of the day; scare every woman into fits that looks into the back yard after dark. Sweet mouth, opens on a hinge at the back of his head, and is never shut unless there is something in it. That's the best picture of a growing hound, one of this kind with liver colored spots, that we can draw, and Mr. Middlerib's was just like that, only more so. His principal characteristic was a tendency to lunch. He was fond of nibbling little things around the house. Split his face one Sunday while the folks were at church, and shut it down over a whole ham. Liked to peck at odd bones and scraps, and one Monday morning he ate two tablecloths, a flannel shirt, a big roller towel, half a dozen clothes pins and thirteen linear yards of clothes line, before the washing had been hung out half an hour. Fond of eggs, too, and knows every hen by sight in the neighborhood, and sets off on a friendly call every time he hears a cackle. Mrs. M. wants to sell him, but Middlerib says gold couldn't buy him. So he stays, and eggs are as scarce in that ward as ever.

Well, one night, Mrs. M. had made something by pulverizing a lot of very hot potatoes. We believe it was yeast. Any how, it was necessary that it should cool very presently, and after some misgivings relative to the dog and his weakness, which were dispelled by Middlerib's indignant defense of that sagacious animal, the dish containing the fiery compound was placed on the outer edge of a window sill, to cool in the night air.

Then the family resumed their occupation of hearing Middlerib explain the causes that led to the recent revolution in politics.

Such a weird, unearthly, piercing wail hadn't been heard since Dresseldorf learned to play the clarionet. It seemed to come out of the ground, out of the sky, out of the air around them, and for an instant the frightened Middleribs gazed at each other with white, terror-blanched faces. Then they rushed to the door and looked out. A gaunt, ghostly form, with liver colored spots and a mouth full of red hot potato yeast thrashed wildly up and down the yard, splitting the darkness with terrific yells at every jump. It was Middlerib's dog, and it was apparently feeling uneasy. It dashed madly around in short circles and screamed "Police," and scraped its jaws with its paws, and wept and rubbed its chops along the cold ground, and swore and howled for water, and pawed the earth and sang psalms, and in several ways expressed its disapprobation of potato yeast as a diet. Finally, the dog wedged himself in between the fence and the ash-barrel, and told all about it, how it happened and what it felt like, and how he liked it as far as he'd got. He never slept a wink that night. He was too anxious to get his narrative completed and see the proofs of it. Neither did anybody in the neighborhood sleep, either. And every time a water pitcher would crash down into the yard, or a boot-jack bang against the fence or an andiron plunge madly into the ash-barrel, the dog would laugh in mocking tones, and go on with his testimony. About midnight a vigilance committee waited on Mr. Middlerib, but he wouldn't come out, and they couldn't stand the noise long enough to break in the door. The dog finished his statement about sunrise, when the committee rose. The family ate baker's bread the next day, and Middlerib so far yielded to Mrs. M.'s entreaties as to say that if any man will make a fair offer, he might sell an undivided third of the dog.

A BOY'S DAY AT HOME.

MASTER BILDERBACK had been home all day, confined to the house and barn by the rain, and excited by the prospect of unlimited fun during the long vacation. He was a blessing to his mother and sister, and his affectionate parent caught her death of cold by running around after him in one stocking foot, searching out the tender places in his nature and anatomy with a four and a half slipper. He tied one end of his sister's ball of crochet cotton to the fly-wheel of the sewing-machine and the other around the tail of the cat, and by the time his mother had sewed half way down one of the long seams in Mr. Bilderback's new shirt, all but a few yards of that cotton was a chaotic mass about that fly-wheel and shaft, and the cat was waltzing in and out of the kitchen, sprawling along backward, tail straight as a poker, fur up and eyes aflame, snowling, and spitting, and swearing like mad, and Mrs. Bilderback and her daughter climbed upon the table and shrieked till the windows rattled, while Master Bilderback, hid behind the clothes-horse in the kitchen, lay down on his back and laughed a wicked gurgling kind of a laugh. Then he went out and jammed a potato into the nose of the chain pump and the hired girl went out and pumped till her arms ached clear down to her heels, and then told Mrs. Bilderback the cistern had sprung a leak and was dry as a bone. And then Mrs. Bilderback, declaring she knew better, went out and turned the wheel till her head swam and she gave up, and Miss Bilderback went out and turned till she cried, and then Master Bilderback, rather than go to the neighbor's for water, went out and fixed the pump and came in to be praised, and was duly praised with the slipper, for he had been watched. He put an old last year's fire-cracker in the kitchen stove; he insured a steady run of strange visitors for about two hours, to the great amazement of his mother and sister, by pinning a placard on the porch step, plainly seen from the street, but invisible from the front door, "Man wanted to drive carriage; $35.00 a month and board." Mrs. Bilderback drew a sigh of relief when she heard Mr. B.'s step in the hall, and informed her son that as soon as his father came in he should be duly informed of all that had been going on. A most impressive silence followed this remark, and the trio in the sitting-room listened to Mr. Bilderback's heavy breathing as he divested himself of his wet boots, and prepared to assume his slippers. Master Bilderback's face wore an expression of the deepest concern.

Suddenly the silence was broken by a shout of astonishment and terror, followed by a howl of intense agony, and there was a clattering as of a runaway crockery wagon in the hall. The affrighted family rushed to the door, and beheld Mr. Bilderback cleaving the shadows with wild gestures and frantic gyrations. "Take it off," he shouted, and made a grab at his own foot, but, missing it, went on with his war-dance. "Water!" he shrieked, and started up stairs, three at a step, and turning, came back in a single stride, "Oh, I'm stabbed!" he cried, and sank to the floor and held his right leg high above his head; then he rose to his feet with a bound and screamed for the boot-jack, and held his foot out toward his terrified family. "Oh, bring me the arnica!" he yelled, and with one despairing effort he reached his

A BOY'S DAY AT HOME.

slipper and got it off, and with a groan as deep as a well and hollow as a drum, sank into a chair and clasped his foot in both hands. " Look out for the scorpion," he whispered hoarsely, " I'm a dead man."

Master Bilderback was by this time out in the woodshed, rolling in the kindling in an ecstasy of glee, and pausing from time to time to explain to the son of a neighbor, who had dropped in to see if there was any innocent sport going on in which he could share, " Oh, Bill, Bill," he said, " you wouldn't believe; some time to-day, some how or other, a big blue wasp got into the old man's slipper, and when he come home and put it on —oh, Bill, you don't know!"

WHY MR. BOSTWICK MOVED.

YOUNG Mr. Bostwick has moved. He liked the house he has been living in well enough, and Mrs. Bostwick fairly cried her eyes out when they left it, because it had a bay window and blinds with slats that you could turn so that you could see anybody in the street and nobody could see you. But old Mr. Glasford, the landlord, was very deaf, and it was on account of this infirmity that his tenant left the house. Mrs. Bostwick said she couldn't see what Mr. Glasford's deafness had to do with the house, but her husband only looked worried and said it made a good deal of difference with a man's peace of mind, when he had something he wanted to whisper, and had to whisper it to a man who couldn't hear anything if he went into a boiler factory. Mrs.

Bostwick didn't understand what difference it made anyhow, but then she wasn't down town that terrible Wednesday, when old Mr. Glasford went into the store where her husband was selling a lovely young divinity from Denmark a dress pattern off a piece of Centennial percale. Mr. Bostwick saw the old gentleman coming and felt very nervous. Eager to anticipate the demand which he knew the old man was going to make, he dashed toward him with an abruptness that astonished the fair customer who had just lost herself in admiration of Bostwick's diamond pin, and the fact, just confidentially imparted to her, that he was not a clerk but the silent partner, holding about $475,000 worth of stock in the concern, and that he just worked from pure love of employment. Mr. Bostwick checked the old gentleman about ten feet away from his customer, and leaning over the counter so as to get as close range on his ear as possible, whispered hoarsely that "it wouldn't be convenient to pay that rent to-day."

"Hey?" shouted the old man, looking at Bostwick's agitated face in some alarm, "why, why, wha's the matter? 'S happened?"

Mr. Bostwick made a futile effort to catch hold of the old man's ear, intending to pour his explanation into it as one pours water into a funnel, but his landlord briskly dodged and waved Bostwick away with an expression of considerable apprehension. Mr. Bostwick groaned and endeavored to explain to the old gentleman in a manner that would convey to the pretty customer and the others in the store the idea that he was refusing to give the old party credit, and at the same time let old Glasford know that he was bankrupt.

"Can't do it!" he shouted.

"Can't do what?" inquired the mystified old gentleman in those stentorian tones so popular with deaf people.

"Can't help you!" shouted Bostwick, in tones the sternness of which contrasted ludicrously with the sheepish expression of his countenance. "Can't do anything for you!"

The old man looked at Bostwick in helpless wonder and then at the door, with his mind half made up to run away, under the impression that the young man was crazy. He finally stared at him in open-mouthed amazement and speechless bewilderment.

"Oh, Moses," thought Bostwick, "he's mad as a hornet, he'll break out in a minute; I know he will." Then he tried him again, in a voice like a steam whistle.

"I can't do anything for you!"

The old man's mouth opened still wider, and his eyes stood around on his cheek bones in their amazement.

"Who asked ye to do anything for me?" he finally gasped. "What is it ye can't do?"

Bostwick groaned, and in a fit of desperation he broke down, and gave it up.

"I can't pay that rent to-day!" he shrieked, and the pretty customer was so shocked that she dropped her parasol, fan and paper of gum drops.

"What went to-day?" asked the old man, waving Bostwick off with his stick.

Here the proprietor officiously interposed to cover Bostwick's confusion, speaking in the highest key he could assume.

"Rent! Rent! House rent, you know! He says he can't pay his house rent to-day!"

"Rent day?" echoed old Glasford, "yes, oh yes, that's past, two weeks ago; first of the month."

"Yes," shrieked Mr. Bostwick, while the store full of

customers and his fellow clerks stood around and smiled, "I know it, but I can't pay it to-day; haven't got a cent!"

"Oh!" exclaimed the old man, with a gleam of intelligence passing over his face, "I don't care about that; that isn't what I come for. I come to tell you if your wife wanted that front room down stairs papered, to go ahead and have it done, and I'd allow it."

The pretty customer wouldn't have a word to say to the discomfited Mr. Bostwick when he went back, and the old man told the proprietor as he went out of the door that he believed that young man was just about half crazy, and the clerks were all so pleasant that Bostwick nearly went mad every time he was reminded of his unfortunate precipitancy, and that is the way he became convinced that it was altogether lighter than vanity to rent of a deaf man.

SPECIAL PROVIDENCES.

THERE was wailing and woe in Burlingtown,
    For every other day
The humid showers came tumbling down,
    As they had come to stay.

There was water enough in the land to spare;
    And men who were wont to pray,
When they looked in the cellar each morn would swear
    And wrathfully turn away.

All out on South Hill they pumped and pumped
    From morn till dewy eve,
But their every effort the storm king trumped,
    And laughed him in his sleeve,

Till the South Hill man his spirit was broke,
    And he sate him down on his hill.
"Though I pump till my back cries out," he spoke,
    "My cellar still keeps its fill."

"Now lithe and listen, good pump of mine,
    If ever I touch thee more,
May never again the bright sun shine
    As it shone in the days of yore."

Then he took his pump and he hung it up
    Where it might not taunt his sight,
And he drowned his grief in the poisonous cup
    Which "moveth itself aright."

And he vowed him that if the immortal gods
  Would hold up their rain for a while,
He'd build him a cellar and take the odds —
  On top of his domicile.

"For what was the use," he grimly said,
  "Of a cellar in the ground,
Into the which, if you went for bread,
  You were pretty sure to be drowned?"

"I hate the cellar; oh winds of the south,
  Thy rains, as hard as I can;
I wish I could strike them both with a drouth,"
  Exclaimed the South Hill man.

He lifted his eyes to the city road
  A coming figure to scan,
And a wild fierce light in his optics glowed
  When they fell on the hated gas man.

He carried his book and his railway lamp,
  And wore a sinister frown;
And he sought out the meter in cellars damp,
  And he noted the figures down.

And whether a man burned much or small,
  Or how often the gas man came,
Or whether they turned on the gas at all,
  The meter just counted the same.

So the man of South Hill, when he saw him come,
  Supposing that he had come th—
Rough ignorance, said, in tones full glum,
  "You cut off my gas last month."

The gas man he winked, and eke as he wunk,
　　He shook his head knowinglee,
And, as though he something suspiciously thunk,
　　"We'll look at the meter," said he.

Then he opened the door of the cellar so damp,
　　And he stepped where the pump log had been,
And he went out of sight, with his book and his lamp,
　　As the water he tumbled in.

"Oh, help!" loud he shrieked as his noddle came up,
　　"Hubbulubbulup!" as his noddle went down,
While the man of South Hill on the cellar door sill,
　　Was the happiest man in the town.

Splash! Splash! Blubbulup! in the cellar he heard,
　　And he hugged himself close in his glee;
And whenever the gas man would sputter a word,
　　"Oh, catch hold of the meter!" cried he.

And he shut down the doors, and he locked them up tight,
　　And into the well threw the key,
And, " Providence always and ever is right :
　　Rains and cellars are useful," said he.

MR. BARINGER'S HOUSE-CLEANING.

YOU see, Mr. Baringer has only been keeping house about a year, and they took the carpets up this Spring for their first general house-cleaning. Mrs. Baringer's mother was there, because she said Olivia was a mere child at such things, and she didn't believe that Aristarchus was much better, and it was better to have some one around who could manage. The young people, however, felt very confident that they had, by numerous consultations and many well-laid plans, reduced house-cleaning to a perfect science, a system that had never yet been attained by any other housekeepers, and they were all impatient to get at work and clean the whole house, from garret to cellar, and have all the pictures back on the walls and carpets nailed down again before dark. They were disgusted at the way other people cleaned house, and Olivia thought it was perfectly wonderful how Aristarchus could have such beautifully lucid and systematic ideas on matters of which most men, and she would say most women as well, were so deplorably stupid and ignorant.

The stirring notes of the alarm clock dragged Mr. Baringer out of bed at 3:15 A. M., and he thought he felt intolerably sleepy for five o'clock, but he didn't look at the clock until he was dressed, and then he was too mad to swear. He merely woke Mrs. Baringer up to tell her that he'd bet a thousand dollars some stupid had changed the alarm after he set it and then he flopped down on a lounge to sleep till daylight. He awoke at half-past seven o'clock, the hour at which, by their prearranged system and calculations, the two up-stairs bedroom carpets were to have been beaten and ready to put down as soon as the floors were dry. Then the kitchen fire went out twice, and they finally sat down to breakfast at half-past eight o'clock, Mrs. Baringer's mother beguiling the time during that matin meal by asking Olivia if she minded how she used to be half through her house-cleaning by nine o'clock in the morning. But Mr. Baringer bore up very well under it, and immediately after breakfast, he took up the bed-room carpets. It was slow work, jerking the tacks out one at a time. Some times they flew up into his face; some times he pulled the head off and left the tack in the floor; and when they got to be rather thickly scattered around the room he put his knee down on one occasionally and talked in a fragmentary manner about certain mill privileges in connection with house-keeping which Mrs. Baringer couldn't understand. At last he noticed that by lifting up the edge of the carpet, a gentle pull would bring up half a dozen tacks in rapid succession. Happy thought. He rose to his feet, grasped the bound edge of the carpet in both hands, gave a mighty lift and a tremendous pull — k-r-r-r-r-r-t! and when the dust settled a little, Mrs. Baringer and her mother were discovered standing in the door, looking in speechless horror at Mr. Baringer, who stood like an image of despair, holding a carpet with a fringe in one hand, and a long line of carpet binding in the other.

"How *did* you do it?" shrieked Mrs. Baringer.

"How *ever* did you do it?" echoed Mrs. Baringer's mother.

Then they both said something about the general incapacity of a man, and Mr. Baringer endeavored to explain that in going across the room for the tack hammer he had caught his foot in the edge of the carpet, with the result as above. And at the conclusion of his explanation, Mrs. Baringer's mother gave a sniff that blew dust out of the carpet, and there was a general expression of incredulity on the faces of the congregation.

It was a long time before they got the carpets down in the yard, and on the line. Then Mr. Baringer approached and smote the first carpet with a long stick, and the next instant he was feeling his way out of a dense cloud of dust, coughing, sneezing and snorting, and wildly gasping for air. He went around on the other side, and as he aimed a terrific swipe at the carpet, he struck the clothes prop, and his nerveless arm stung and tingled to his neck, while his wail was heard down to the city building. Then he got at it again, and found that his stick was too light, and he took another one. A few strokes sufficed to convince him that it was too heavy, and he took a lath. That broke in two at the first blow, and he tried an apple switch, but it was too limber. He finally gave up the idea of beating any more, and called to Mrs. Baringer that the carpet was ready to be shaken. Mrs. Baringer, with her head in an apron, came out. They gathered the carpet, and Mr. Baringer got the start of her and shook a roll clear down to her hands, exploding in a loud snap and a volcano of dust in her face. Then she dropped the carpet and sneezed and protested.

"You shook too quick, deary," she said.

"But you said you were ready, sweety," replied Mr. Baringer.

"But you shouldn't be so rough, lovey," she protested.

"Well, I have to shake hard to get the dust out, ducky," he insisted.

"Well, you needn't be so cross about it, deary," she said.

"Oh well," he said, "you must expect hard work house-cleaning days, and you mustn't lose your temper, sweety."

"It isn't me that gets cross and jerks people around, lovey," she said, "it's you."

"I never jerked you around," he retorted.

"Why, Aristarchus Baringer!" exclaimed his wife, making very large eyes at him and speaking in tones of the greatest amazement, "and maybe you didn't tear the carpet up stairs, either."

"I wish your old carpet was in Halifax," he said, savagely. "Pick up that end; let's get through with it. This is sweet work for a dry goods salesman, anyhow! Ready?"

"No," she snapped, "I ain't ready. Now wait. There. Hold on now; don't be in such a hurry. Now!"

And the next instant the carpet was snapped out of her hands, and it did seem as though her fingers had gone with it, while Mr. Baringer, pretending not to know that it had fallen from her fingers, kept on shaking violently at his end, filling the air with dust and grit. At this juncture Mrs. Baringer's mother, who had been a quiet spectator of the carpet shaking scene, approached and called him to desist. Then she gathered up the vacant end of the carpet.

"Aristarchus," she said kindly but firmly, "Olivia is not strong enough for such work."

Then she added:

"Have you got a good hold, Aristarchus?"

And Mr. Baringer said he had.

"Don't let go then, Aristarchus. Ready."

They lifted their arms high in the air and Mr. Baringer is undecided yet which part of him started first. He walked up the whole length of that carpet on his hands and then he fell over the edge and banged along the walk on his hands and knees until he reached the front fence, through which he plunged his head, and would have gone on through but for his shoulder catching against the gate post. The carpets did not go down that day, and a big Irishman was engaged to come and welt the fuzz off them, Mr. Baringer having privately and with some asperity informed his wife that he would rather live, sleep, and eat in dirt up to his eyes, than ever again to sweep, beat, or shake the lightest carpet ever trodden by the foot of man.

AN AUTUMNAL REVERIE.

"OH dreamy haze: veiling the murmuring river that stretches away like a silver thread under a mosquito bar, winding in wooded nooks and creeping through low lying islands where the balmy breeze is redolent with the odor of dead leaves and dead fish. Oh lovely haze; what dreams of soulful tenderness its name recalls. Oh, musty hays in the street car; oh, hays that used to be full of bumble bees; oh, hazel nuts on another man's farm with a big dog hid in the patch. Away; these memories are too painful.

"Afar, the hillsides glitter in gold and scarlet, and the sumach bushes, climbing the slope with their nodding plumes, look like a new express wagon coming down Division Street. The mellow air brings into the city the rustle of fallen leaves piled deep on winding cow-paths, threading through quiet dells and winding along the side of purling brooks. It brings an odor of something old. Because it blows over the cheese factory.

"How faint and far off every sound. The ghosts of the dead Summer flowers sigh in every breeze, and the phantom of the cow that butted the freight train tinkles her drowsy bell afar. And in muffled tenderness, as a falling star might drop on a feather bed, we hear the teamster's cheery call, 'G'up! ye lop-eared spavin, 'r I'll lam the hair off ye with a dray pin.' And the muffled creak of the wood wagon falls plaintively on the ear. Eight dollars a cord, and only cut three feet long at that, and piled so loosely that when you go to measure it you can throw a felt hat through the pile any place and never touch a stick.

"List to the plaintive piping of the quail in the stubble. Ah, quail on toast, and the plaintive piping of the anxious waiter for seventy-five cents. Avaunt, dull dotard, take thy black shadow from the fairy scene. (This remark was addressed to the waiter, and not to the quail on toast.)

"Why, in these dreamy dark autumnal days — we don't know what kind of a day a dark day is, but we wanted another word that begins with d and could only think of dark and another one, and the other one wouldn't do at all; these kind of days then, bring with them a sad — a sad — sad something, we knew what it was when we started out, but stopping to explain about that dark knocked it clear out of our head; sad — it isn't saddle, nor Sadducee, nor — ah yes, now we have it. These dreamy days, that come like a tender poem, veiled in the delicate drapery that hangs over the distant landscape, bring with them——"

At this critical juncture a man with a business-like look in his eye burst into the sanctum, slapped his hat down on the paste cup, banged a sample case on the ink stand, and proceeded to remark in one long unpunctuated sentence, "Good morning not a word my dear fellow I know the value of an editor's time I wish you just to glance at this prospectus of the most valuable work that has ever been issued from the American press it is the American Centennial Portrait Gallery and you will observe contains exquisite steel engravings full page of all the Presidents with the autograph of each one appended and complete biographical sketches. Observe that engraving of Washington through this glass if you please bank note engraving not more perfect not a single line crosses or becomes merged into another one what expression what fidelity to nature what marvelous portraiture what minute attention to detail Notice the folds in the cloak and the exquisitely penciled pattern of the ruffles at the wrists. And so with Adams and Jefferson and Madison and Monroe and Jackson and all the rest of them with biographical sketches compiled from the best authorities with facts incidents and reminiscences never before published — a book that no American of intelligence should be without a book without a rival in its field of patriotic biographical excellence. In different styles of binding — $3.00, $3.50 and $4.25. Now, sir, shall I have your name right here?"

We felt all around the room before we could catch our breath, and when we regained it we told him we didn't believe we could put $4.25 worth of signature anywhere that morning, and, after a struggle of fifteen or twenty minutes with him, we got him close enough to the stairway to push him over the railing and heard him reach the ground floor and disappear into the street and around the corner with the long introductory sentence of his prospectus trailing after him like the dribbling shower of a runaway street sprinkler. And we went on with the dreamy, sad, sweet reverie:

"The tender song of a day whose wordless beauties haunt the mystic scene; the dreamy, vague, imperfect memories that bring——"

A man with a black coat and a high hat came softly into the sanctum, and after he laid a flat oil cloth case on the table, he lifted his hat off with both hands and said, speaking in soft and distressingly deliberate tones, and articulating with awful distinctness and precision:

"Ah — is the editor in?"

We imparted the desired information, and the deliberate man went on,

"I have taken the liberty to call on a matter of some importance to yourself, as well as to the great masses of the American people. I have here the artist's proof of a new ker-romo entitled 'Columbia.' It is a centennial allegory, and is designed by Mr. Alfred Reynolds Vincenzo Fitzdaub, one of the most eminent artists of America, at immense outlay of time, labor and money. The tube colors used on the original painting alone cost seven dollars and a half, while the can-vas, when prepared and stretched for the pict-ewer, was worth nearly doubbel that sum. Here you see, we have in the foreground Columbia, her sandaled feet resting upon the broking canning to signify that war is no more. At her right hand sits the American eagil, ger-rasping the olive ber-ranch of peace in his talents, and lifting his wings as though pluming himself for fe-light. Here on the left we have the artisin in working-dress, the statesman, the teacher, the farmer, the sai-leure, repperesenting the various callings, and here rushes a train of cars, while in the background an old-fashioned stage coach is disappearing, illustrative of the perrogeress of the past hundred years. The original painting is yalued at $2,500, but these ker-romos we supply for $18 a piece, mounted ready for framing. No man of culture or artistic taste can afford to be without this ker-romo. The eye of a connoisseur can not distinguish it ferrom an oil painting. Observe the transparency of the atmosphere; notice the soft natural blending of the high light and middle tint into the hazy shadows of the backger-round, and the bold effects of the heavy cul-louds that overshadow the past, where the dim edges are silvered with the sunlight that ber-reaks ferrom the veil of the few-chewer. And here, you observe, is a blank tablet at the right of the figewer of Columbia, for a family record. Only eighteen dollars. They will be ready for delivery about the first of Jewen, and if I may have the pleasure of seeing your signature in this book, just here, it will cost you but the trifling sum of eighteen dollars, and establish more fully the reputation you have already acquired as a man of culture and refined taste."

We got rid of him after a heated session of about half an hour, and he went away, mourning over the depravity of a man who had acquired a reputation for culture and refined taste under false pretenses. Then we resumed:

" Over the distant hills, hushed in the misty haze that hangs like a veil of peace over the motionless landscape, the fleecy clouds, like drifting air-ships on the broad expanse of melting blue, bring the sweet ——"

A man with a mahogany box came in and sat down, and talked as he opened it, and displayed a variety of phials and boxes.

" The profession of literature, my dear sir," he said, " is of all others under the ban of the fell destroyer, dyspepsia, and it is especially in the Spring of the year that literary workers suffer most keenly from its dreadful effects. An ounce of prevention, etc.— you know the old saying. Now I can see by your heavy eyes that you are at this moment suffering from headache. This "Centennial Cordial and American Indian Aboriginal Invigorator" is one of the latest and most valuable discoveries in the world of medical science, and has positively no equal for the cure of jaundice and all manner of liver disorders, headache, indigestion, want of appetite, dyspepsia, bilious, remittent and intermittent fevers, ague, giddiness of the head, rheumatic affections, poverty or impurity of the blood, salt rheum, teething, cholera morbus, croup, ophthalmia, asthma, hay fever, sea-sickness, diphtheria, catarrh, toothache, sleeplessness, gray hair, pimples, tan and freckles, kleptomania, emotional insanity, growing pains, stone bruise, rattlesnake bites, jimjams, katzenjammer, tight boots, bad breath, warts, soft corns, old clothes, tailor's bills, spring fever and all other ills to which human flesh is heir. Compounded purely of herbs and the finest cologne spirits, and selling at the ridiculously low price of $1.75 per bottle. Now sir, let me ——"

And we let him out of the door and he went away, after marking us for the tomb in a few short weeks. And then we tried to get back to our reverie.

"The sweet days come and go, in hallowed rythmic cadences, like the half forgotten chords of some tender, sobbing nocturne, while they bring the——"

"No, sir, this is not the tobacco factory; it's the next building up the street.—Thank heaven, he's gone."

"—— bring the sad yearning of a restless heart, that reaches out amid the hectic flushes of the dying year, as it would clasp the ——"

"No ma'am, we don't want to buy 'The Centennial Gift Book for Young Ladies;' no, we have no young lady friends; we have no friends of any kind; we have no sisters, or brothers, or relations, we have no money, we have no literary taste, we have no desire to read anything; we can't read, and we don't know anybody who can."

"—— amid the hectic flushes of the dying year, as it would clasp ——"

" Have no use for a fly trap, sir; don't keep house; ain't married; don't expect to be; haven't seen a fly in Iowa for a thousand years."

"——the hectic flushes of the dying year, as though——"

"No, no, no! this is not the barber-shop. No, we don't know where the barber-shop is; there is none in this block; there are no barbers in Burlington; the nearest barber-shop is at the North Pole. No, sir, you needn't apologize, we are *not* annoyed. *Good* afternoon, sir."

"—— amid the dying flushes of the hectic year whose pulses throb so faintly that——"

"No, we don't want any 'Wonderful Saponifier and Dirt Eradicator for the Toilet and Laundry.' No, we have no family, and we never wash; never heard of such a thing as a bath; don't want to be clean; never shave, never clean our nails, and have on the same shirt we wore the day we were born. No, sir. Yes, sir. *Good* afternoon."

"——amid the flying dushes of the pulsing year whose hectics faint so throbly that——"

"Yes, sir, this is *The Hawkeye* office. No, sir, we do not buy sand; no, we have no old clothes to exchange for tin ware; no, we don't want any superior stove blacking. *Good* afternoon, sir."

"—— amid the dusting fishes of the throbling hectics whose painted ear is throoming in the gulch, so faintly fleam the glib and——"

[Note by the editor. We entered the office at this point and found the writer of the above in convulsions.

From the ravings of his delirium we gathered that he was trying to write something nice, and was tormented by innumerable interruptions. Medical assistants were summoned, and we were told to keep the young man's head cool and he would get well. So we cut it off and had it packed in ice. It weighed two and a half ounces. The young man is doing finely, and will not need it again this year.]

INFANTILE SCINTILLATIONS.

AH yes, we do love children. We fairly dote on them, and enjoy and admire their sweet, innocent ways, from the dear little cloudy-faced, bare-legged cherubs that swear and throw stones at you as you go past Happy Hollow, to the sweet-faced but pampered angel that sits in the golden lap of luxury and breaks the mirrors and your head with pa's cane. It was purely our love for the little innocents that induced us to comply with the urgent request of many parents, and open a department in *The Hawkeye* for the smart sayings of precocious children.

Mrs. H—y B—k, of North Hill, has a sweet little rosebud, of four bright Summers, who came into the house and lisped, " Ma, Ith tho theepy."

" What makes you sleepy?" asked Rosebud's mother.

" I don't know," murmured the child.

Strange yearning after the incomprehensible in an infant heart. Could any of the children of an older growth have made a better answer?

Then there is little Freddy L——, out on West Hill.

Although he is but three years old, he put his father's watch in the shaving mug, filled the mug out of a kerosene lamp, and set the mixture in the oven to dry, where it presently dried—soon after the hired girl made up the breakfast fire—with such abruptness that three of the stoveplates haven't been found since. After the excitement had subsided, his mother took him on her lap and said:

"Freddy, did you put papa's watch and the mug full of oil in the oven?"

And the dear child, opening wide his innocent eyes, and smiling in tender confidence in her face, said placidly:

"No, ma'am, 'deed I didn't."

Sweet, cautious instinct of an untried heart. Could any of us get out of it any better than that? Who can tell what vague, uncertain dreams of congressional honors float through that busy little mind?

Johnnie K—— is a charming little cherub of four bright Springs. One day he poured the ink into the globe where the gold-fish were, submerging them instantaneously in total eclipse; then he put the Bible in the fire, threw a bronze paper-weight through the looking-glass, broke four eggs in his sister's new hat, and wound up his artless sport by throwing the cat down the cistern. His mother, discovering all this mischief, suspected who was the author, and sought her son.

"Johnnie," she said, sadly, "Why did you act so naughty?"

"I didn't," he persisted. "Deed, muzzy, it was ze cat!"

Sweet child! Does it need the prescience of a prophet to see that he will some day make an excellent witness in a great scandal case?

Then there is another sweet little tid-toddler out on

Seventh Street. The other day one of his parents, the female one, put him to sleep and laid him in his little crib, and then she ran over the street to ask Mrs. Muldoon how she washed flannels, and got to talking about the last funeral, and the mission circle, and the new preacher, and forgot all about the baby, and when she went home there that dear little blessed was, flat on his back, with his little crib lying on top of him, and he yelling like a scalded pig.

Ah, the wild, weird, ventures and dreams of child life. Try it, gray-haired man; see if you can fall out of bed and flop your bedstead, slats, springs, mattress and all, on top of you as you land on the floor. You can not do it, but the tid-toddler of three sweet Summers—ah, well, who shall say how their untried instinct shames the lore and knowledge of our elder years.

SETTLING UNDER DIFFICULTIES.

STRANGERS visiting the beautiful city of Burlington have not failed to notice that one of the handsomest young men they meet is very bald, and they fall into the usual error of attributing this premature baldness to dissipation. But such is not the case. This young man, one of the most exemplary Bible-class scholars in the city, went to a Baptist sociable out on West Hill one night about two years ago. He escorted three charming girls, with angelic countenances and human appetites, out to the refreshment table, let them eat all they wanted, and then found he had left his pocket-book at home, and a deaf man that he had never seen before at the cashier's desk. The young man, with his face aflame, bent down and said softly,

"I am ashamed to say I have no change with —— "

"Hey?" shouted the cashier.

"I regret to say," the young man repeated on a little louder key, "that I have unfortunately come away without any change to —— "

"Change two?" chirped the old man, "Oh, yes, I can change five if you want it."

"No," the young man explained in a terrible, penetrating whisper, for half a dozen people were crowding up behind him, impatient to pay their bills and get away, "I don't want any change, because —— "

"Oh, don't want no change?" the deaf man cried, gleefully. "'Bleeged to ye, 'bleeged to ye. 'Taint often we get such generous donations. Pass over your bill."

"No, no," the young man explained, "I have no funds —— "

"Oh, yes, plenty of fun," the deaf man replied, growing tired of the conversation and noticing the long line of people waiting with money in their hands, "but I haven't got time to talk about it now. Settle and move on."

"But," the young man gasped out, "I have no money —— "

"Go Monday?" queried tne deaf cashier. "I don't care when you go; you must pay and let these other people come up."

"I have no money!" the mortified young man shouted, ready to sink into the earth, while the people all around him, and especially the three girls he had treated, were giggling and chuckling audibly.

"Owe money?" the cashier said, "of course you do; $2.75."

"I can't pay!" the youth screamed, and by turning his pocket inside out and yelling his poverty to the heavens, he finally made the deaf man understand. And then he had to shriek his full name three times, while his ears fairly rang with the half-stifled laughter that was breaking out all around him; and he had to scream out where he worked, and roar when he would pay, and he couldn't get the deaf man to understand him until some of the church members came up to see what the uproar was, and recognizing their young friend, made it all right with the cashier. And the young man went out into the night and clubbed himself, and shred his locks away until he was bald as an egg.

HAWK-EYETEMS.

SOMEBODY told Billinger that stamps were not required on notes, and Billinger, overjoyed, asked the crowd to drink, and said he pitied old Gunnybags who had been trying for six months to get the stamps on a note he holds against Billinger. Billinger says he knew he would get the law on the old gouge if he held on long enough.

"PULL out, Bill!" shrieked an engineer's son to one of his playmates, a brakeman's boy, who was in imminent danger of getting smashed by his mother, who was coming after him, "Git on the main line and give her steam! Here comes the switch engine!" But before the juvenile could get in motion, she had him by the ear, and he was laid up with a hot box.

A NORTH HILL man refused to give his boy thirty-five cents to go to the minstrels, because the entertainment was demoralizing and vulgar in its nature. He then bought a quarter's worth of chewing tobacco, went home and read the *Weekly Moral Guide and Guardian*, and spit all over the front of the stove, and made the parlor smell so much like a stale bar-room that the baby had three whisky fits before ten o'clock.

A YOUNG editor out in Floyd County, gushing over his first, asks, "Did you ever watch a dear little baby waking from its morning nap?" N-not exactly; but we have watched a dear little baby's fond pa gliding up and down the fireless room, trying to induce the dear little baby to take a morning nap, at 2:15 A. M.—pressing offers but no takers—which was about as much fun as it can be to see the baby wake.

A MAN out on Summer Street has eight daughters, and when they cleaned house last Spring, the woman raked 9,724 quids of chewing gum down from the window casings, chair backs, door panels and sofa backs, the accumulation of the past Winter. And this does not include the wads which the man, at various times sat down on and carried away on the tails of his coat, for which no accurate returns have been made.

OLD Middlerib came home one night and ordered a light lunch before going to bed. "Just a mouthful of tea and a bit of bread," he explained. "Do you want just plain bread?" asked Mrs. M., with reference to the presence or absence of butter. And the old reprobate said he would take one piece plain, and the other with a looped overskirt, shirred down the gores with the same, and held in place with knife pleatings of grape jelly. He got the heel of the loaf.

EVERYBODY thought it was a match, and so did he, and so did she. One evening at a croquet party she hit her pet corn a whack with the mallet that sounded like a torpedo, and he—he laughed. "We meet as strangers," she wrote on her cuff and showed it to him. "Think of me as no more," he whispered huskily, and when the game was ended he rushed down to the Mississippi* and drowned†.

"I WOULDN'T be such a Christian as you are, John," said his wife, as she stood in the doorway, dressed for

---

* Saloon.   † Sorrow.

church. "You could go with me very well, if you wanted to." "How can I?" he half sobbed. "There's the wood to be split, and the coal to be shoveled over to the other side of the cellar, the baby to be dressed, and no dishes washed for dinner yet." "Ah, I didn't think of that," she murmured thoughtfully, and, giving her new cloak a fresh hitch aft, sailed out alone.

ONE night last Summer a tired, discouraged man out on North Hill went home and flung himself down on a lounge, and said "he wished he were dead, dead, dead." In two hours he was writhing in a premature and unseasonable attack of cholera morbus, and howled, and prayed, and sweat, and had four doctors in the house, and drank a quart of medicine, and had mustard plasters smeared all over him, and wept, and said he wasn't half tended to, and he believed they would like to see him die.

"ARE the children safe?" asks the *Christian Union*. Quite safe, we assure you. They are up in the garret, playing hotel fire. Jimmie is the clerk, and is trying to slide down the water pipe to the ground, Willie is a guest, hanging to the window sill and waiting for the flames to reach his hands before he tries to drop to the shed roof, two stories below, and Tom is a heroic fireman, and has tied his fishing line around the baby's body, and is letting it down to the ground. Oh, yes, the children are all right: just finish your call and don't fret about the children.

"RENTS," said Mr. Middlerib, with a sigh of not unmixed satisfaction, "are coming down. Yesterday morning I tore the back of my coat on the wood-shed door, last night I snagged the foundation of my trousers on a nail in a store box, and this morning I fell down on the frozen sidewalk and split the knee of the same trousers clear across. Rents are certainly getting lower." "Yes," responded Mrs. Middlerib, looking across toward the busy figure at the sewing machine, "and seamstresses are getting hire." Mr. Middlerib looked up at his quiet spouse in vague astonishment, as if for explanation, but she looked sublimely unconscious, and the good man went off down town with his napkin tucked under his chin, wondering all the way to the office if she meant it or if it was only his interpretation.

"A MERCIFUL man," tenderly remarked a Ninth Street man one bitter cold January morning, " is merciful to his beast," and he called the dog in out of the snow, gave him his breakfast in a soup plate, and laid a piece of carpet down behind the kitchen stove for him to snooze on. Then the man went down town, and the neighbors watched his wife shovel snow-paths to the woodshed, cistern, stable, and front gate, and then do an hour's work cleaning off the sidewalk.

WHO does not love a faithful, honest dog, man's faithful friend? And yet who is there, stretching out in the shade for a quiet afternoon nap, who has had man's faithful friend come panting up, and, in an excess of honest affection, lay a great broad, hot tongue over one's cheek, from chin to eyebrow, that does not get up and seize man's faithful friend by the tail and one ear and try to throw him across a prairie fifteen miles wide?

THE New York *Herald* says: "Bake your ripe pear in a tart, and eat it with brandy and cream." We'll do it. Here, Alvaretto, bake us that ripe pear in a tart and dress it with brandy and cream. What! the pear eaten? Well then, the tart crust and the trimmings. The tart gone! Is it possible? Then the brandy and cream.

Amazement! no cream? Ah, well then, we must not neglect good advice. Bring what is left of the recipe.

A MONKEY that can say "papa" and "mamma" and "Brazil" is going to the Paris exposition. America can send a donkey that can say, "Haw—yaas, dweadful baw; somebody wing faw the pwopwietah."

THEY have just found the skin of another Dane nailed to the oaken door of an old, old church in England. The skin isn't entire, only scraps of it remaining under the broad flat heads of the nails. It was a pleasant way the Danes had of destroying the beauty of their criminals—they skinned them and then nailed the skin to a church door. History does not tell us how the unfortunate victim employed himself during the operation, but it is quite likely that, having nothing else to do, he was into some deviltry.

OLD Mr. Troph went into the parlor the other night at the witching hour of 11.45 and found the room unlighted and his daughter and a dear friend, one of the dual form of garmenture variety, occupying the tete-a-tete in the corner. "Evangeline," the old man said sternly, "this is scandalous." "Yes, papa," she answered sweetly, "it is candleless because times are so hard and lights cost so much that Ferdinand and I said we would try and get along with the starlight." And the old gentleman turned about in speechless amazement and tried to walk out of the room through a panel in the wall paper.

A WOMAN out on North Hill, being counted out the other morning, after a debate on the question, "Who shall arise and build the fire?" got up and split her husband's wooden leg into kindling wood, and broiled his steak with it. It made him so mad that he got hold of her false teeth and bit the dog with them. She cried until she had a fit of hysterics, and then flipped out his glass eye and climbed upon the bed post and waxed the glaring eye to the ceiling with a quid of chewing gum. Then he took her wisp of false hair and tied it to a stick, and began whitewashing the kitchen with it. Then she started off to obtain a divorce, but Judge Newman decided that he couldn't grant a divorce unless there were two parties to the suit, and there was hardly enough left of them to make one.

"You don't look at all well," a venerable gobbler out in a North Hill poultry yard remarked to a melancholy-looking young rooster, a short time before Thanksgiving day. "No," was the reply, "I have reason to look solemn: I expect to die necks tweak." The gobbler smiled grimly and pondered over the uncertainty of poultric life as he slowly swallowed a two-inch bolt head.

MRS. MIDDLERIB paused to take a final survey of the table before she called the ladies out to tea. She started as her eyes fell upon the plate of lemon tarts. There were five where there had been nine. She sought her only son and put him in the witness box. He objected to her putting her own construction upon his answers, and was subjected to the usual punishment for contumaciousness. And the next "composition day" at school, Master Middlerib amazed his teacher by reading, as the title of his essay, "The Lost Tarts, and why They can Never be Recovered."

SWEET, gushing, artless girl! She came home just before the Christmas holidays. She went away from Burlington one September; went to England first; spent the Winter in Italy; sauntered through Germany in the

Spring, came back to America and trifled away the Summer at Saratoga, Long Branch and the White Mountains; previous to this trip she had been away to school five years, and when she jumped out of the palace car into her father's arms, she said, impulsively, " Oh, Paw, Paw, deah, deah Paw, thay's no place like home!" And Paw's face was a study as he replied, "Well, no; no; reckon not; must be quite a novelty to ye."

THE worst thing we have seen about Oliver Wendell Holmes, and the only stain on an otherwise irreproachable character, is that he is the inventor of that parlor aggravation known as the hand stereoscope; a vexatious contrivance for which the pictures are always too large to be crammed into the springs or too small to stay in them, of which the slide is always shoved off the end of the stick in the vain efforts of the observer to find a focus, and of which the glasses always make you see the picture so double that it gives you the headache and finally compels you to peep over the top in order to gain the information necessary to make some intelligent remark about the jumble you have been staring at.

A YOUNG man out on North Hill bought a parrot some months ago, and in anticipation of the fact that he was going to be married and go to the Centennial, he secretly taught the parrot to say, " Welcome, thrice welcome home," every time anybody opened the front door, thinking what a delightful surprise it would be to his young wife to be thus cheerfully welcomed home on their return. But while they were on their tour, the nervous woman who was left in charge of the house taught the parrot a new remark, as a protection against burglars; and when the young people came home on the night train and let themselves in at the hall door with a latch key, they were shocked and appalled by a terrific shout of "Thieves! thieves! Police! police! Here Bull! here Bull! Scatter, ye son of a thief, or I'll tear your heart out!" Next day the parrot died, and the young wife now says she wouldn't stay alone in that house, not for a divorce.

A BURLINGTON naturalist last Sunday, while investigating the causes and effects of the poison of a wasp sting, nobly determined to make of himself a martyr to science, and accordingly handed his thumb to an impatient insect he had caged in a bottle. The wasp entered into the martyr business with a great deal of spirit, and backed up to the thumb with an abruptness which took the scientist by surprise. He was so deeply absorbed in the study of remedies that he forgot to make any notes of the other points in connection with stings, but his wife wrote a paragraph in his note-book, for the benefit of science, to the effect that the primary effect of a wasp sting is abrupt, blasphemous and terrific profanity, followed by an intense desire, fairly amounting to a mania, for ammonia, camphor and raw brandy.

ONE day, just after King Solomon had written a column of solid nonpareil wise and moral proverbs, he took his eldest son by the elbow, led him down the back stairs of the palace, through the back yard, past the woodshed, out into the alley, backed him up behind Ahithophel's wood-pile, looked warily around to see that no one was listening, and whispered into the young man's ear, " My son, a little office in a spread-eagle life insurance company is better than a cart-load of preferred stock in the Ophir mines." And then the monarch threw his head on one side, drew in his chin, shut one eye, and gazed at his offspring in silence. Three years afterward, when the Great Hebraic Consolidated Stormy Jordan Life

Assurance Company, of which that intelligent young prince was president, went into bankruptcy, the young man was able to let his father, who was a little short at the time, have 275,000 shekels for ninety days, on his simple note of hand.

THEY were very pretty, and there was apparently five or six years difference in their ages. As the train pulled up at Bussey, the younger girl blushed, flattened her nose nervously against the window, and drew back in joyous smiles as a young man came dashing into the car, shook hands tenderly and cordially, insisted on carrying her valise, magazine, little paper bundle, and would probably have carried herself had she permitted him. The passengers smiled as she left the car, and the murmur went rippling through the coach, " They're engaged." The other girl sat looking nervously out of the window, and once or twice gathered her parcels together as though she would leave the car, yet seemed to be expecting some one. At last he came. He bulged in at the door like a house on fire, looked along the seats until his manly gaze fell on her upturned, expectant face, roared, " Come on! I've been waiting for you on the platform for fifteen minutes!" grabbed her basket, and strode out of the car, while she followed with a little valise, a band-box, a paper bag full of lunch, a bird-cage, a glass jar of jelly, and an extra shawl. And a crusty-looking old bachelor, in the farther end of the car, croaked out, in unison with the indignant looks of the passengers, " They're married!"

MR. and Mrs. Bilderback were walking slowly home from church one Sunday, when they met a young lady of singular beauty and sweetness of countenance, who was quite lame. And Mrs. Bilderback turning to her husband, said, " Did you ever notice what a sweet, uncomplaining look of resignation rests like a halo on the faces of young girls who are so sadly afflicted as the lady who just passed us?" And old Bilderback said that indeed he had, and he begged his wife to observe him very closely, and notice what a sweet, uncomplaining expression of peaceful and holy resignation spread itself over his face, like a halo, or like a lump of butter on a hot buckwheat cake, at such times as his corns tried him unusually bad. And she only remarked casually that when they got home she would hang a halo around his irreverent head that would make what little hair there was left on it think the millennium was a million years farther away than ever.

"They had a rather odd race out at the old Acme ball grounds yesterday," Trotters remarked to Ponsonby when they met yesterday morning. "Jones rode his little calico pony around the block, and Brown rolled an empty flour barrel the same distance, even start, for $10." "Jones beat him, of course?" said Ponsonby. "Brown was a fool to make such a match." "Don't be too sure," rejoined Trotters, "when they reached the outcome, the barrel head; blowed if it didn't." Ponsonby stared, then slowly smiled, giggled, and finally guffawed. "Good enough," he said. "I'll get that off to Mrs. Ponsonby." So when he went home he told her all about it. "Well," said she, "that's just about as much sense as I supposed that precious Brown of yours has. I'm glad he lost his money." "Go slow," yelled the delighted Ponsonby, who doesn't often have a chance to sell his wife, "go slow! By George, Samantha, Brown beat!" And Mrs. Ponsonby stared and said he must think she was as big a fool as Brown. "No," said he, hastily correcting himself, "no, that wasn't just the way of it, the barrel beat, that's it! The barrel beat; Brown led, did, for a fact, by Jove." And Mrs. Ponsonby scornfully told him to go out to the woodshed and see if he could find any sticks that would go into the kitchen stove — she couldn't. And Ponsonby confidentially told the gentleman who saws his wood an inch and a half too long for every stove in the house that you might as well tell a joke to a sawbuck as to his wife, for she hadn't as much conception of genuine humor as a cow.

ONE bright May morning, when the building season was at its busiest, a careless mason dropped a half brick from the second story of a building out on Jefferson Street, on which he was at work. Leaning over the wall and glancing downward, he discovered a respectable citizen with his silk hat scrunched over his eyes and ears, rising from a recumbent posture. The mason, in tones of some apprehension, asked: "Did that brick hit any one down there?" The citizen, with great difficulty extricating himself from the glove-fitting extinguisher, replied, with considerable wrath: "Yes, sir, it did; it hit me." "That's right," exclaimed the mason, in tones of undisguised admiration. "Noble man! I would rather have wasted a thousand bricks than had you tell me a lie about it."

THE papers in this country are quite generally publishing the following *mot* of Talleyrand's, which is read with the greatest enjoyment by all classes of newspaper readers:

It is said that the notorious M. De Manbreuil, whose name of Marquis d'Orvault came so scandalously before the public a few years past, proposed to have Napoleon assassinated, and that the Abbe de Prade was in favor of the scheme, and discussed its execution with Talleyrand, and that the following words passed:

"Combien vous faut-il?"

"Dix millions."

"Dix millions?" said Talleyrand, "mais ce n'est rein pour debarrasser la France d'un el fileau."

This is pretty good, but it reminds us of a much better one, though it may be somewhat old, which was related to us by Rev. Jasper C. Romilly, formerly of this city, about himself. Mr. Romilly, whose distinguishing personal characteristic was an immense black beard, was for some years a missionary at Ugobogo, in Farther India, and on one occasion he dined with the Bugaboo of that province. When the wine and walnuts were brought in the Bugaboo said:

"Marcharikai hoi-to-po ke-tee nomkidom?"

"Jabbero pompety doodle de wonk klonk kobberee jam," replied Mr. Romilly.

"Yowk?" exclaimed the potentate, "chickero boobery hong dong choi-ke-ree yang ste' boi."

This was, indeed, too good to keep.

WOMAN is a natural traveler. It is a study to see her start off on a trip by herself. She comes down to the depot in an express wagon three hours before train time. She insists on sitting on her trunk, out on the platform, to keep it from being stolen. She picks up her reticule, fan, parasol, lunch basket, small pot with a house plant in it, shawl, paper bag of candy, bouquet (she never travels without one), small tumbler and extra veil, and chases hysterically after every switch-engine that goes by, under the impression that it is her train. Her voice trembles as she presents herself at the restaurant and tries to buy a ticket, and she knocks with the handle of her parasol on the door of the old disused tool-house in vain hopes that the baggage man will come out and check her trunk. She asks every body in the depot and on the platform when her train will start, and where it will stand, and, looking straight at the great clock, asks:

"What time is it now?" She sees, with terror, the baggage man shy her trunk into a car where two men are smoking, instead of locking it up by itself in a large strong, brown car with "Bad order, shops," chalked on the side, which she has long ago determined to be the baggage car as the only safe one in sight. Although the first at the depot, she is the last to get her ticket; and once on the cars, she sits, to the end of her journey, in an agony of apprehension that she has got on the wrong train and will be landed at some strange station, put in a close carriage, drugged, and murdered, and to every last male passenger who walks down the aisle she stands up and presents her ticket, which she invariably carries in her hand. She finally recognizes her waiting friends on the platform, leaves the car in a burst of gratitude, and the train is ten miles away before she remembers that her reticule, fan, parasol, lunch basket, verbena, shawl, candy, tumbler, veil and bouquet, are on the car seat where she left them, or at the depot in Peoria, for the life of her she can't tell which.

How often a little careless action, a thoughtless word, a restless gesture, brings a flood of thoughts surging into the soul, that almost tear away the veil of mystery that hangs between to-day and to-morrow, and give us vague and hasty glimpses into the dark uncertain future. When you see a man come out of a drug store, for instance, with a "prescription carefully compounded," in his hand, and dash away at break-neck speed, and then see the pharmacist come to the door carrying an uncorked bottle, and smell at it earnestly with one nostril, gaze anxiously down the street after the man, smell at it long and intensely with the other nostril, stare wildly up the street after the man, and then sniff at it once or twice with both nostrils, read the prescription over, and retire into the medicine shop with a gloomy brow and sad shakes of the head, how many things you begin to think about then, as it might be.

"My son," said a pious father out on South Hill to his hopeful son, "you did not saw any wood for the kitchen stove yesterday, as I told you to, you left the back gate open and let the cow get out, you cut off eighteen feet from the clothes line to make a lasso, you stoned Mr. Robinson's pet. dog and lamed it, you put a hard-shell turtle in the hired girl's bed, you tied a strange dog to Mr. Jacobson's door bell, you painted red and green stripes on the legs of old Mrs. Polaby's white pony, and hung your sister's bustle out in the front window. Now, what am I — what can I do to you for such conduct?" "Are all the counties heard from?" asked the candidate. The father replied sternly, "No trifling, sir; no, I have yet several reports to receive from others of the neighbors." "Then," replied the boy, "you will not be justified in proceeding to extreme measures until the official count is in." Shortly afterward the election was thrown into the house, and before half the votes were canvassed, it was evident, from the peculiar intonation of the applause, that the boy was badly beaten.

Passing by one of the city schools one day we listened to the scholars singing, "Oh how I love my teacher dear." There was one boy, with a voice like a tornado, who was so enthusiastic that he emphasized every other word and roared, "Oh *how* I *love* my *teach*-er *dear*," with a vim that left no possible doubt of his affection. Ten minutes afterward that boy had been stood up on the floor for putting shoemaker's wax on his teacher's chair, got three demerit marks for drawing a picture of her with red chalk on the back of an atlas, been well shaken for putting a bent pin in another boy's chair, scolded for whistling out loud, sentenced to stay after school for drawing ink mustaches on his face and blacking the end of another boy's nose, and soundly whipped for slapping three hundred and thirty-nine spit balls up against the ceiling, and throwing one big one into a girl's ear. You can't believe half a boy says when he sings.

"Who dem, Cassius?" a visiting freedman from Keokuk asked a friend the other day, as a Masonic lodge, in funeral procession, passed by.

"Dey's de Free and Expected Masons."

"'Mazin' what?"

"Why, mason nuffin, jest on'y Masons."

"Sho! How long dey bin free?"

"Oh, gory, long time. Spects ever since de mancipation proclamation, anyhow. Some on 'em was free before den."

"Dat so? Went off to Canada, mos' likely?"

"Spect so."

"Who's done expectin' of 'em?"

"Nobody; jest expectin' demselves. Dey's on'y jest Free and Expected Masons, dat's all."

"Sho! Well, I'd jest like to know what dar is 'mazin' about 'em an' I'd done be satisfied."

Oh, the artless prattle of an innocent childhood! How the sweet music of their hearts and voices calms the wild yearnings of the sorrow-crowned years of maturity. At a happy home in Burlington the other evening, where the family was gathered around the tea-table entertaining unexpected guests, the fond mother said to the youngest darling, "Weedie, darling; be careful; you mustn't spill the berries on the table-cloth." "'Taint a table-cloth," promptly responded darling, "it's a sheet." And late at night, when the company had gone away, and that sweet child was standing with its head nearly where its feet ought to be, catching with its tear-blinded eyes occasional glimpses of a fleeting slipper that fluttered in the air in eccentric gyrations, one could see how early in the stormy years of this brief life, one may begin to suffer for the truth.

WHEN you see a young man sitting in a parlor, with the ugliest six year old boy that ever frightened himself in the mirror clambering over his knees, jerking his white tie out of knot, mussing his white vest, kicking his shins, feeling in all his pockets for nickles, bombarding him from time to time with various bits of light furniture and *bijouterie*, calling him names at the top of his fiendish lungs and yelling incessantly for him to come out in the yard and play, while the unresisting victim smiles all the time like the cover of a comic almanac, you may safely bet — although there isn't a sign of a girl apparent in a radius of 10,000 miles — you can bet your bottom dollar that howling boy has a sister who is primping in a room not twenty feet away, and that the young man doesn't come there just for the fun of playing with her brother.

IT was at the sociable. Young Mr. Sophthed, who reads poetry oh, *so* divinely, and is oh, *so* nice, stepped on her dress as she was hurrying across the room. K-r-r-rt! R'p! R'p! how it tore and jerked, and how Mr. Sophthed looked as though he would die. "Oh, dear, no, Mr. Sophthed," she sweetly said, smiling till she looked like a seraph who had got down here by mistake, "it's of no consequence, I assure you, it doesn't make a particle of difference, at all." Just twenty-five minutes later, her husband, helping her into the street car, mussed her ruffle. "Goodness gracious me!" she snapped out, "go way and let me alone; you'll tear me to pieces if you keep on." And she flopped down on the seat so hard that every thing rattled, and the frightened driver, ejaculating, "There goes that brake chain again," crawled under the car with his lantern to see how badly it had given way.

ART has its votaries even amid the untaught children of the wilderness. A few days ago a savage Indian painted his own face, went into an emigrant wagon that was sketched, by himself, out on the prairie after dark, and drew a woman from under the canvas and sculptor.

MRS. J. C. MCWHELTER, who lives out on Ninth Street, worked three weeks building a rookery out of cracked geodes, and threw the whole pile away in fifteen minutes yesterday afternoon, bombarding a neighbor who said her baby's hair was red enough to heat its catnip tea on.

AN enraptured Burlington lover, hearing his sweetheart sigh dejectedly the other evening, rapturously administered a quartette of kisses and exclaimed, "You're mine, now, in spite of fate!" "And why?" she asked. "Because," he said, "four of a kind beats ace high." But she believes to this day that he played a cold deck on her.

"ALL flesh is grass," as the reaping machine said when it chawed up the harvest hand.

A MAN may carry a load of guilt concealed in his tortured soul for years, and hide it with a veneering of hollow, heartless, deceitful smiles, but it doesn't take five minutes for the thoughtless world to observe and understand the one-shouldered gait of a man whose larboard suspender button has parted.

THE other day a public reader, while entertaining an audience with a masterly rendition of an extract from "Macbeth," dropped his false teeth out, but he went right on with the soliloquy, " Ig gish a daggag ash I see befog me? Cug, leg me glug ghee!" And then the audience got up and howled and threw all the chairs out of the window and sent out for somebody to come in and hold them while they hollered.

A SOUTH HILL man complained to old Dibbs, the other day, that his house was infested with chimney swallows, but old Dibbs says he is ready to bet fifty dollars that the man swallows twice as much as the chimney does.

A YOUNG native poet, who is writing a "song of olden Rome," asks us to give him a rhyme for Romulus. A dozen, if he wants them :
" If o'er that wall you leap, oh dunce,
 The lightning stroke would harm you less "
But Remus laughed and leaped ; at once
 His head was punched by Romulus.

A FELLOW never appreciates the tender beauty of a sister's love half so much as when he makes her get out of the big rocking-chair, and let him have the morning paper, while she goes off and leans up against the end of the bureau and feeds her starving intellect on the household receipts at the back of Jayne's family almanac. A brother's love is like pure gold. It's dreadfully hard to find, and when you find it, it's very apt to be pyrites.

"DID you never," asked a transcendental young lady just three weeks from Vassar, of the West Hill young man, "Did you never feel a vague, unrestful yearning after the beyond? a wild, strange, impulsive longing and reaching out after the unattainable?" And the West

Hill man said he often had, last Summer, at such times as he was trying to scratch a square inch full of hives, right between his shoulder blades, and just out of reach of any thing.

A BENEVOLENT clergyman recently helped a profane Burlington inebriate out of the gutter, and gently rebuking him reminded him that the "wages of sin is death." "I know 't," replied the erring one, "but I've worked so much over time, and the shop is so far in arrears to me that I'll never get half that's comin' to me any how." And he went off to work right along on the same old job.

THE tramp has his revenge on society after all. If they refuse his request for a square meal at any house, he lurks around the vicinity with threatening glances until nightfall, when he skulks rapidly away with the cheering, comforting knowledge that while he is snoring all the hours of that long Summer night away under a haystack, every being in that house will sit bolt upright in bed all night, frightened by the wind, terrified by the rustling of the leaves, scared into fits when even the dog barks, and fairly bounced out of bed every time the clock strikes, while a nightmare of burglarious tramps fills every drowsy moment with awakening terrors. No wonder that tramps always look happy and contented.

OLD Mr. Balbriggan is very much pleased with a gentleman whom he has engaged to saw wood. "When he piles the wood," said old Balbriggan to his friend, "if one stick projects beyond the others, he pounds it in with the ax." "He's a slouch," replied Bifelstone, "you should see my wood sawyer. When he gets the wood all piled he takes off the rough projecting ends with a hand saw." "He couldn't pile wood for me," broke in old Mr. Pilkinghorn, "my sawyer piles the wood carefully, then goes over the ends with a jack plane, sand-papers them down and puts on a coat of varnish before he ever thinks of asking for his pay." And then they all went in after a big drink before Throckmorton could tell how his wood sawyer silver-plated all the ends of the wood and nailed a handle on every stick to pick it up by. Because, you see, Throckmorton is such a liar, and they all know it.

A WEST HILL minister picked up a frozen wasp on the sidewalk, and with a view to advancing the interests of science, he carried it in the house and held it by the tail while he warmed its ears over a lamp chimney. His object was to see if wasps froze to death, or merely lay dormant during the Winter. He is of the opinion that they merely lie dormant, and the dormantest kind at that, and when they revive, he says, the tail thaws out first, for while this one's head, right over the lamp, was so stiff and cold it could not wink, its probe worked with such inconceivable rapidity that the minister couldn't gasp fast enough to keep up with it. He threw the vicious thing down the lamp chimney, and said he didn't want to have any more truck with a dormant wasp, at which his wife burst into tears and asked how he, a minister of the gospel, could use such language, right before the children, too.

WHEN a man accustoms himself to owning a dog, and turning around at every corner to look up and down street for him, and whistle him out of stairways, or yell at him to stop his fooling with other dogs and come along, or make dashes into a crowd of earnest and excited dogs who are holding a caucus and have each other by the ear, and especially his dog—that man is a slave to a habit that he will never break. It will cling to him, we believe, after he gets to heaven, for most men who love dogs are pretty sure of going to heaven. We once saw an old settler standing at the Barrett House corner, peering up and down street, and stooping down to look under the hacks, and "wondering where he could be," and whistling and growing impatient, and scolding and calling, "Hyuh, Turk! yuh! yuh! yuh!" until every dog in Burlington was sitting around the Barrett House corner, patiently pounding the snow with his tail and mentally resolving to lay for Turk if he ever came. Presently a young man came along and, greeting the anxious dog hunter as his "Father," asked what he was waiting there for? The old settler said he had lost Turk somewhere right around there, and couldn't see hide nor hair of him, and couldn't imagine where he had gone to. "Turk!" roared his dutiful son, "Turk! Suffering Moses! And him dead eight years ago!" And he hustled the old man away before he could begin to whistle up any more ghosts.

THE balmy breath of Spring is so entwined with the fragrance of new onions that a man has to grip his nose with a spring clothes pin every time he stoops to pluck a violet.

A GIFTED contributor sends us a poem beginning "Open the doors to the children." You'd better, if you don't want all the paint kicked off the panels.

THERE is nothing that tends to destroy popular sympathy for the working classes so much as the habit a bricklayer has of dropping bits of mortar from the top of a five-story wall into the eye of the wondering man who stands under the lofty scaffolding and looks up.

A PORCELAIN-LINED kettle in a berry-stricken neighborhood is the nearest approach to perpetual motion that has yet been realized. Its incessant motion is only rivaled by the slow, steady growth of the sugar bill.

ONE of the discoveries made by the latest arctic explorers is that the length of the polar night is one hundred and forty-two days. What a heavenly place that would be in which to tell a man with a bill to call around day after to-morrow and get his money.

A FASHION journal says "white velvet dresses give a roundness to the figure." They give an awful lankness to the figures on a hundred dollar bill.

Multum in parvo: Iowa tramp, to lady of the house: "Please, missus, won't you give me something to drink? I'm so hungry I don't know where I'll stay to-night."

AN eminent New York jurist, who has retired from the bench, always shakes hands with his friends by turning around and passing his right hand behind his back. It is supposed the peculiar habit was contracted during his active professional life.

CARDS of invitation in Utah, issued by a young lady and her mother, always present the compliments of "Miss Smith and the Mrs. Smiths."

WE are told by a Russian traveler that the summit of Mt. Hood is a single sharp peak of lava. White or Balaclava?

A SCIENTIFIC gentleman sends us an elaborate treatise on "the healthiness of lemons." They may be dreadfully healthy, but they are terribly soured in their dispositions.

A RISING young tenor of Burlington has a neck eight inches long, and it gives him an immense power over his voice; enables him to throat a long ways. (Tra, la, la!)

The whale is the sulkiest of all fishes. He is the worst pouter in the business.

About the oldest little game of draw we know of was played when Joshua razed Jericho, and the fellows of the city wished they hadn't stayed in.

Your landlord is probably the finest example of filial affection and duty you ever met. He is unremitting in his attention to and care of his pay rents.

"Was it her brother?" is the title of a new novel. We think not. It is our impression that the large gentlemen in a plaid coat, who was kicking him down stairs and calling for the dog, was her brother.

George Washington's strongest hold upon the American people is the fact that he never wore a box coat and a plug hat.

History says, "Cæsar had his Brutus." But somehow or other we always had the impression that Brutus rather had Cæsar.

By some wicked and unpardonable error, the case of the photographs of editors on exhibition at the Centennial got misplaced, and was exhibited in a frame labeled "Native woods of the United States."

Nature's effort to maintain equilibrium is never better set forth than in the instinctive struggles of a man with one suspender to carry both shoulders even.

On account of the Turco-Russian war and the failure of the American cabbage crop last year, nearly all the genuine imported Turkish tobacco used in this country this Summer will have to be made out of plaintain weed.

The day after Christmas, father and mother no longer come sneaking in at the back door with mysterious looking bundles. No, indeedy. Mother is gliding around with the expression of a Christian martyr with the toothache, because she didn't get what she expected, and father is sitting around, holding his breath till the bills come in.

You can utilize your cake of maple sugar, if you find there is too much sand in it to make molasses of, by putting it in a neat frame of card-board, or some kind of fancy work, in bright colors, and hanging it up against the wall to light matches on. It never wears out.

FLIES are made for some good and useful purpose after all. If it wasn't for the busy flies, men with their never dying souls to save and lots of work to do, would lie down after dinner and sleep till six o'clock every day.

A NASHVILLE bank robber burrowed under a street for five days, and at length came up in the coal vault of a beer saloon, three doors away from the bank, and bit himself in eleven places with the most uncompromising dog he ever tried to conciliate. The next time he attempts any mining operations he will take a practical engineer along.

IT was intensely hot in Salt Lake City last Summer, and one night about 1,820 linear feet of prickly heat broke out on the infant backs in Brigham Young's nursery. The eruption hasn't been equaled since Mt. Vesuvius cooled off.

IT is in the merry month of Spring that a tree peddler comes around and talks you to death, and sells you a plum tree that bears fruit so bitter that it poisons every curculio that tastes it, and some cherry trees that send up one hundred and fifty sprouts to the square inch and will lift the house off its foundations in two years' growth, and some apple trees that neither sprout, blossom, nor bear fruit, and some blackberry bushes that spread all over a ten-acre lot the first season, and some gooseberry bushes that have thorns on a foot long, and never have anything else, and some peach trees that break out in bloom from the ground to the tip of the topmost branch five days after they are put in the ground and die as dead as a flint the sixth day, and a climbing rose tree that turns out to be wild ivy and poisons every soul about the house before the Summer is over.

WHEN the late Governor of the Persian province of Fars retired from office, the Government officials put him in the stocks and pounded the soles of his feet until he disgorged $300,000 of crooked salary. If the Government of the United States would adopt that system, five hundred million pairs of crutches would carry the population of the republic to and from its daily labor. And if we knew where we could get hold of a man who would give down like the late worthy Governor of Fars, we would gather him by the ankles, stand him on his head, and welt the soles of his feet until his backbone went through the top of his head and stuck nine inches in the ground.

THERE is a junior in the Burlington high school who, when his father cuffs his scholastic ears for leaving the wheelbarrow standing athwart the front gate, can go out to the woodshed and swear in French, grumble in German, threaten to run away and be a pirate in good classic Greek, and blubber in honest United States.

ONE day last Winter a young lady broke through the ice of a deep skating pond near Toronto, and a young man rescued her at the risk of his own life. As the half drowned girl was recovering consciousness, her agonized father arrived on the spot. Taking one of her cold, white hands in one of his own, he reached out the other for the hand of her rescuer, but the young man, realizing his danger, with one frightened glance broke for the woods, and was soon lost to view. He has not been heard of since, and it is supposed that he is traveling in the United States under the false and hollow name of Smith.

WE haven't given the subject enough study to speak very confidently upon it, but we rather believe, when the end of the world comes, and the last trump calls all mankind together, that the man who died with rheumatism will lie still a long time, and will feel the small of his back, and rub his knees slowly and thoughtfully a great many times, before he finally groans and makes up his mind to get up. And, as like as not, by the time he gets on his feet everybody else will be gone.

MAN—What power of nature has he not subdued? What climate has he not trodden under foot? What arctic rigor and tropical heat, what polar snows and equatorial sunstrokes has he not laughed to scorn? He has tamed the elements, he has made the ocean his highway, he has made fire and water, earth and air, his servants, and bent beneath his all-subduing yoke even the wild lightnings to be his messenger. And yet he can not, arching himself upon the back of his head and on his heels, scoop with his eager palm, cracker crumbs from the irritating sheet with a sufficient degree of success to insure himself a good night's sleep. He can not, he can not— oh, might of the giant, it kaint be did!

A WOMAN will take the smallest drawer in a bureau for her own private use, and will pack away in it bright bits of boxes, of all shades and sizes, dainty fragments of ribbon, and scraps of lace, foamy ruffles, velvet things for the neck, bundles of old love-letters, pieces of jewelry, handkerchiefs, fans, things that no man knows the name of, all sorts of fresh-looking, bright little traps that you couldn't catalogue in a column, and any hour of the day or night she can go to that drawer and pick up any article she wants without disturbing any thing else. Whereas a man, having the biggest, deepest and widest drawer assigned to him, will chuck into it three socks, a collar-box, an old necktie, two handkerchiefs, a pipe and a pair of suspenders, and to save his soul he can't shut that drawer without leaving more ends of things sticking out than there are things in it, and it always looks as though it had been packed with a hydraulic press.

ONE day a young man of respectable appearance attracted considerable attention on Third Street, while crossing over to the Barrett House. He stopped in the middle of the street and yelled, and danced up and down on one leg, while he held the other out and kicked, like the can-can lady on the bulletin boards. The bystanders thought he was crazy, and threw stones and mud at him, and knocked him down and choked him, and held him still, while he never ceased to shriek, "Snake up my leg! Snake up my leg!" Then they reached up and pulled a small roll of bills out of his trousers leg, and let him up, when he raised his hands to heaven and swore he would never carry money in a hip pocket again, hole or no hole.

IT was on a bright April morning that Mr. Alanson Bodley, who lives out on Summer Street, stepped out of the house in a tender frame of mind, singing softly to himself, "Oh had I the wings of a dove, I'd fly, Away from——" Just then the hired girl threw the bed-room carpet out of the window, and as its dusty folds enveloped Mr. Bodley, and threw his struggling form down stairs, he was heard to exclaim in muffled tones, "If I get out of this, if I don't cut the raw heart out of the bloody-minded assassin that slung that carpet, strike me dead!" Thus, too often, the tenderer influences that bring into life and being our higher and noble emotions and transcendental longings, are warped and distorted by the stern realities of life, like a wet boot behind the kitchen stove.

THEY had the awfulest time up at Jerome Cavendish's house, on West Hill, one evening, and Mrs. Cavendish went into hysterics, and Miss Cavendish fainted, and young George Cavendish grabbed his hat and ran out of the house, and old Cavendish raved and ramped around like a crazy man, all just because they had waffles for tea, and Miss Cavendish found a—"oh! *ow! ow!!* oo-oo-oo!!! EE-E-E-E!!!" hard-baked beetle in a waffle. Oh, it was terrible! It was awful! It was too awful! Too awful! Two waffle!

ONE day last Spring a sweet-faced woman, with a smile like an angel and a voice softer and sweeter than the sound of flutes upon the water, was walking up Fifth Street. She was walking very slowly, enjoying the cool, soft air, and the delicious shade of those maple trees just below Division Street. Her languid motions were the perfection of grace, and she was the admiration of every pair of eyes on the street, when suddenly she threw her parasol over the steeple of the church, screamed till she rattled the windows in the parsonage, jumped up as high as the fence three times, and whooped and shrieked, and wailed, and howled, and kicked until everybody thought she had suddenly become insane. But when they ran up and caught hold of her and poured water on her head and $15 bonnet, and shook her until she quit screaming and began to talk, they found that one of those green worms, about an inch long, had dropped from the maple leaves and slid down her back. And they didn't wonder that she yelled and made a fuss about it.

SOME years ago a public-spirited citizen of Burlington died, and left, by his will, $175,000 to found an orphan asylum; and his sons and daughters, and nieces and nephews, and cousins, and brothers and sisters, and all his wife's relations, contested the will, and fought and wrangled and called each other names, and told hard stories about each other, and proved up wonderful claims, and hired lawyers by the acre, and kept the fight up manfully until quite lately, when it transpired that the man only had $35 in the whole wide world when he died, and owed that to his grocer, and was in debt about $300 beside, and that the coffin he was buried in hadn't been paid for yet. And it was sad to see those claimants standing around the streets with grip-sacks in their hands trying to get out of town, with a lawyer and a capias lurking behind every corner.

A PAIR of deaf mutes were married in Monroe, Georgia, three years ago, and now it is more fun than a circus to see them quarrel and make faces at each other with their fingers.

IT IS a remarkable coincidence, and shows the beneficent watchcare which a kind Providence exercises over mankind, that the advertisements of new and infallible cholera mixtures should appear in the city papers just about the time watermelons come in.

WHEN a man, coming down to breakfast half awake, with his uncertain feet shod in a pair of slip-shod slippers, steps on a spool on the first step, he is generally wide-awake enough by the time he tries to break the last step to have a very vivid and not entirely incorrect idea of the power and indestructible force generated by the Keely motor. But that isn't what he talks about when he goes into the breakfast room and the folks ask him what made such a noise in the hall?

At a charity ball in New York one lady wore diamonds valued at $85,000, and another belle wore a $23,000 dress, and so all the way down to the poor people, whose clothes didn't cost more than $1,800. The net proceeds of the ball, which were to be devoted to charitable purposes, amounted to $11.25, which the door-keeper and ticket-seller spent for hot drinks.

Two young ladies of Tama County, have finished a quilt containing 10,696 pieces, and the local paper proudly asks if anybody in Iowa can beat that? We haven't anything in Burlington like that in the quilt line, but Caspar Cruger, up on Eighth Street, fell down the plank walk steps leading down to Valley Street, one morning, and ran 10,697 pine slivers into his back and legs, and a Tama man than he was when he got up you never saw.

Another "wild boy" has made his startling and erratic appearance in Texas, but since the fact has become generally known that the first time a stranger takes a drink of Texas whisky he goes out on the prairie and looks for a clean place to have a fit, public confidence in Texas "wild boys" has been sadly shaken.

The Massachusetts papers are discussing the question, "May Cousins Marry?" We should hope so. We don't see why a cousin hasn't as good a right to marry as a brother or an uncle or a son or sister. They all get used to cousin' after they marry, anyhow.

Abdel Moulk Kahn, the eldest son of the Emir of Bokhara, has made a pilgrimage to Mecca, in accordance with the Mohammedan custom. In this country it is customary for the Moulk Kahns to Mecca pilgrimage to the nearest river just before milking time.

A Burlington man, who is a monomaniac on the subject of roller skates, and who spent ninety-two days in the rink during the past season, and got more falls than he has hairs on his head, and got himself stuck so full of slivers that he wears through his clothes like a nutmeg grater, calls himself a "hard rinker," and consequently he is haunted by traveling agents of temperance societies.

John Thompson, of Muscatine, ran away from home with a circus three years ago, and now he is posted on the bill boards of his native town as "Giovanni Tiompeonatti, the Inimitable and Unapproachable Grand Double Flying Trapeze and Philo Protean Prestiditateurean Athleto-Acrobat." Oh, why should the spirit of mortal be proud?

Steel ropes are being introduced into the British navy in place of the clumsy hemp hawsers. They had better enlist a few good government contractors from America. They'll steal ropes, swabs, tar buckets, marlin-spikes, capstan bars, or anything else that isn't nailed down and under guard.

The French know how to cook an egg three hundred and sixty-five different ways, and yet, if it is a little bilious to begin with, the strongest combination of all these ways won't make a very eggy egg of it.